The Risk
of Trading

The Risk
of Trading

*Mastering the Most Important
Element in Financial Speculation*

MICHAEL TOMA, CRM

WILEY

John Wiley & Sons, Inc.

Published by John Wiley & Sons, Inc., Hoboken, New Jersey.
Published simultaneously in Canada.

For general information on our other products and services or for technical support, please contact our Customer Care Department within the United States at (800) 762-2974, outside the United States at (317) 572-3993 or fax (317) 572-4002.

Wiley also publishes its books in a variety of electronic formats. Some content that appears in print may not be available in electronic books. For more information about Wiley products, visit our web site at www.wiley.com.

Library of Congress Cataloging-in-Publication Data:

Toma, Michael, 1966–
   The risk of trading : mastering the most important element in financial speculation / Michael Toma, CRM.
       pages cm. – (Wiley trading series)
   Includes bibliographical references and index.
   ISBN 978-1-118-10083-7 (hardback); IBSN 978-1-118-22376-5 (ebk);
       ISBN 978-1-118-26207-8 (ebk); ISBN 978-1-118-23710-6 (ebk)
   1. Speculation. 2. Risk management. I. Title.
   HG6015.T66 2012
   332.64'5–dc23

2011048577

Contents

Preface

From corporate offices to trading desk, the two words "risk management" together have long sparked curiosity, bewilderment, and even confusion. But recently, the profession has received more respect and recognition in our everyday business world and includes a much bigger scope than "those people in legal" or "that guy in charge of insurance policies."

The Risk of Trading takes a holistic, or enterprise-based, approach that encompasses not only risks on a trade, but also for the trader and ultimately the business of trading.

WHY USE A DATA-DRIVEN APPROACH?

Anyone in the trading jungle knows that a comparison is often made between trading and gambling. This book looks deeply into this analogy and discovers the statistical principles are, in fact, quite similar. When I first mention a risk-based approach to stock, futures, or options trading to the casual investor, the words "risky" and "gambling" often follow. Using a mechanical method to trading supported by a statistically strict data-driven approach often invites even more questions.

"You really don't care where the market is going?" "Don't you want to beat the market?" "Isn't that a bit boring?" "Is that what you do all day?" My response to these alleged market-predictors is, "I don't find winning boring at all. I execute my plan when I have an edge. All the rules are in my plan. What I do is execute my plan with precision just like a project manager building a house or a homeowner mowing the lawn. I'm not concerned about beating the market. I just focus on executing winning trades, and I only execute when I have a better chance of winning than losing."

There is a certain level of pride when so-called traders talk about their success in predicting market movements. Anyone can do it for a time without any charts, data, or trading experience. You have about a coin-flip chance of being right, and most just hype the few successful predictions over and over again. There's no pressure for them, of course, since most of the time there isn't any hard-earned capital at risk. Performing hours of analysis takes much more energy and certainly comes across as less sexy, if in fact data analysis can have such an alluring appeal. The casual investor tends to be resistant to any form of analytics, since the word itself is reflective of lots of work and analysis. When these methods are presented with simplicity, the better the chance that more will want to hear about them. Combining the conversation with success in trading the markets usually results in a captive audience.

Establishing a culture of trading analytics and metrics is about performing statistical analysis to shift the odds where one can be successful. There is a value proposition in using information and events that have occurred in the past to predict the probability of their occurring in the future under similar circumstances. Although sometimes associated with a geek dynamic, a data-driven approach is evident in many successful areas of business. Service industries currently use customer and vendor data to determine methods to improve quality of service. Internal risk control data generated from process improvement assessments can assist in improving product quality and efficiency. Data-driven decision making is even used to determine if a football quarterback should pass or hand off during certain situations. The book *Bringing Down the House* describes the MIT blackjack team's winning formula for beating the casinos using data-driven analytics. The book takes a microscopic approach to using data to manage risk and identify those opportunities that present an advantage. Simply put, past data and statistics that have provided positive results in your trading will tend to continue to do so in similar market conditions, thus providing you with the competitive advantage eagerly sought in trading. Combine this methodology with solid risk planning, and you now have access to one of the most powerful trading tools.

Mutual fund companies, hedge funds, and proprietary firms have used risk protocols for some time, but only recently has the average swing or day trader making a living from his or her basement computer had a risk component to trading. It is now commonplace to have a risk section appropriately titled in a trader's trading plan; or at least for those who in fact have created one.

The title of this book reflects the essential principles of the risk management concept required in trading stock, ETFs, futures, or other securities and derivatives. Any type of loss, financial, physical, and even loss of opportunity is a fact of life. If they were not, how we optimize the best use of the ways to minimize loss would be meaningless and unnecessary. One trader's work venue may be vastly different than another's in the same profession. One can perform his or her craft at a hedge fund, prop desk, or at the kitchen table. In this book, I take traders on an assessment journey of their trading business, regardless of venue. The principles of risk theory and the management and application of such ideologies are universal to all who place buy and sell orders for a living.

My personal objective is to build and transform your trading venture into a culture of analytics; simply put, using past performance and historical data to allow you to make decisions that over time will lead you to meeting your trading goals and objectives. While traditional risk management focuses on pure loss, enterprise risk management, or ERM, widens the scope to incorporate how a trader maximizes opportunity on the reward side. Your historical data are the key to gaining that edge required to be successful.

I often say, if you take away all my knowledge about the markets, I could probably be back on my feet in less than six months. Take away my data and I'm out of the business. For those concerned by being bombarded with information on variance, probability, statistical theory, and central tendency theorems, I understand your pain. Risk management conferences are filled with reinforcement of the driest of educational topics. Rather than put you through the pain and perhaps boredom of educating you on the latest and the greatest holy grail, these essential analytic principles are explained in a direct no-nonsense manner using examples that you can immediately use in your daily trading.

My first book, *Trading with Confluence*, focuses on data analytics where clusters of different data conclusions all lead to the same action. *The Risk of Trading* captures the essence of my first book and expands the confluence trading concept using data mining and trade data analysis. All this fun with data interwoven with the risk management process somehow has to be summarized in a format that can allow for new decisions to take root.

The objective of an enterprise risk management platform is to act as a repository for all direct and indirect exposures to losses associated with trading. While most focus on trade management and loss of a trade, a true risk manager is aware of all potential risks to his or her trading business, understands the potential impact of each, and has mitigation plans for those worthy of concern.

THERE WILL ALWAYS BE RISK

One of the most popular questions I receive is related to the relationship between risk management and stop-loss orders on a trade. The chapter on risk control deeply penetrates the stop-loss technique as a valid tool in one's risk management arsenal. My biggest concern, however, is the notion that the scope of risk management that protects one's trading account and livelihood, sadly, lies in the use of a simple bracket order feature provided free on a brokerage trading platform. My personal goal with this text is to widen the scope of this topic for traders who believe managing trade risk simply means using stops.

As long as we perform an activity, no matter how much we try to eliminate loss from anything we do, we face the fact that some form of loss could occur. Exposure can strike anyone or any business at any time. Businesses seeking a profit or a charitable organization seeking to provide services with a challenging budget both perform activities that are subject to loss. We perform activities that are subject to a form of loss every day in our lives, and it can interfere with our ability to achieve our desired objectives. As traders, we have ventured into a business where the chance of loss is one of the basic tenets of speculative activity, yet many ultimately find it impossible to accept.

Despite the vast opportunities and possibilities of loss that can occur, the risk management process exists to minimize the frequency and severity of such disruptions in a quest to reach our trading objectives. Being able to apply this process to your trading business is ultimately the goal of this text. Taking a risk management approach and applying the risk principles to trading decisions will allow you to effectively manage your trades and your business.

A BUILDING-BLOCK APPROACH

The goal of this book is to provide you with the fundamental and applicable knowledge required to implement risk management principles in your trading. Ultimately the objective is to see vast improvement in trading performance and management of your operation. In order to implement and apply a solid risk-based strategy, it is essential to have an advanced understanding of risk theory and to continuously apply the steps within the risk management process. The book is therefore structured in three parts that build upon one another.

Part I acts as a foundation course for the reader to understand how we define risk and to understand the risk management process. The book discusses this five-step process extensively, because it is essential to have a thorough understanding of the decision-making process before attempting to apply the principles to your trading. In addition, enterprise risk management models will also be introduced as an effective methodology to protect trade management as well as the entire pool of risks that can affect your trading business. Whether you are a sole-entity trader trying to make it big or a structured firm seeking to optimize operational efficiency, the use of ERM models in your trading plan can improve your key performance results in a relatively short period of time.

Once you have obtained a solid understanding of the risk management process, Part II advances toward the level of utilizing practical applications to manage and measure risk using data analytics. Here we go inside the mind of a risk manager as he or she tackles the upcoming trading day and learn how to leverage solid trading strategies within a culture of metrics. Chapter 4 allows the reader to learn specific strategies that provide an advantage and to execute them within a variety of applicable risk-to-reward scenarios. You have undoubtedly heard that you must keep track of your trades in a trade journal. Chapter 5 discusses what data to capture and how to convert your journal data into a profitable trading machine using key performance indicators. I'll take you by the hand during the reporting process to determine how best to marry results with key performance measures and benchmark them to a common standard. If you have experience in the information technology world, you may find the teachings on business intelligence quite familiar. Here we introduce our ERM framework using data analytics and allow it to breed new life within the vast assortment of business intelligence software once only available to large hedge funds.

Part III has a psychological overtone to it and discusses the human risk elements that challenge every trader. No matter how many trading plans or trade journals I have assessed in my work, greater than 90 percent of all risk deficiencies are connected to a psychological root cause. Comments such as "I changed my plan because . . ." or "I just felt that . . ." and "I didn't want to take the loss so I . . ." are quite popular comments in trade journals. I easily could have titled this section "Reality" due to the bold instruction of some of the not-so pleasant parts of the trading business. Managing losing streaks and drawdowns is one of many psychological topics covered. Chapter 6 discusses how to manage your psychological risk capital and teaches how to use the appropriate share size for each trade. The "graduation plan" structure takes away the emotional decision making regarding size and effectively allows you to build your trading empire. The effective risk control and developmental techniques discussed can be applied immediately after reading this book.

Chapter 7 provides the information on how to prepare for loss and how to position trade risk and reward models most effectively, allowing you to capture the most opportunity from each trade. Chapter 8 dives deeper into the most overlooked risks that affect nearly every trader at some point during his or her career. Computer systems go down, data get corrupted, organizational structures change, personal conflicts arise, and sometimes traders gets a call from the school nurse saying little Britney caught a cold

10 minutes before a major Fed decision. They all involve decisions that need to be implemented to minimize loss, and we review how personal conflicts can impact your trading. Also discussed is how one assesses business continuity risks and how to minimize critical and often costly downtime as a trader. Understanding brokerage firm risks and the use of other vendors is also brought into the light in understanding their role in your day-to-day business planning, a must-read for those serious about becoming successful over the long-term.

You are on your way to exploring the avenues that guide you to being a more consistent and profitable trader. Whether you are trading as an individual or part of a trading firm, incorporating risk principles into your trading will strengthen the inner core of your venture and potentially provide that missing link for those who have the hunger but need more to succeed. I wish you all the best in your risk journey . . . and it begins now.

Michael Toma, CRM
November 2011

Acknowledgments

One would think that a second book on trading would sail smoothly from draft to bookshelf. I've learned a lot about the writing and publishing business by taking the initial concepts and bringing them to life in print. This was not the case, however, with *The Risk of Trading*. This book is designed for a broad audience of new traders to the established trading firms. There was also a need to consider the international audience, who prefers a different writing style and content than their Western counterparts. In the end, the project was completed with the help and inspiration of many. Many thanks to the team at John Wiley & Sons for their expertise, commitment, creativity, and ability to continuously keep me razor focused on allowing the vision to become a reality. I am so honored to be a part of the Wiley family.

In the trading world, I am extremely grateful for the opportunity to work with the professionals at MoneyShow.com. Any individual with a different concept needs an audience to be heard. These online and tradeshow pros really know how to provide the best forum for an average person from New Jersey to have the opportunity to give back to the trading community; they provided me with the educational foundation to become the trader that I am today. The venues also provided me with the opportunity to develop my trader and corporate network that has led to other ventures in the trading and risk management arenas. Whether I'm writing articles, taping educational videos, or presenting at the national expos, I'll always have the team at MoneyShow.com to thank.

The opportunity to branch out into teaching risk management and trading needs more than just a stage. It requires a person who believes that you not only should be heard but can capture an audience that wants you to be heard. Tim Bourquin at Trader Interviews took a chance on me. The flywheel started turning, and it has never stopped since. From subsequent interviews to video interview segments at the expos, Tim has been not only the quintessential business leader but an ethical professional who was willing to give an unknown a chance well before becoming one of the "young guns" on the expo circuit. I promise I will pay it forward.

I've crossed paths with many traders in my career, but one that has stood out as a great colleague and teacher is market profile expert Rick Vinecki. He is a master of market profile, and the trading concept has allowed many a paid vacation ever since. He is the ultimate pro in a business that needs more of his ethical professionalism and trading talents he brings to his students each trading day.

All the paths that have led me to this point would not have been available without The National Alliance group, which founded and supports the Certified Risk Management program. I am honored to hold such a prestigious designation and am well aware that the opportunities that I have been blessed with would not have been possible without their assistance. I look forward to working with you and continued writing through the Research Academy program for years to come.

In order to fulfill such dreams of being a writer, speaker, and educator, I needed the core professional competencies and mind-set required to allow the ability to succeed. I thank John Oliveira for providing the encouragement to always be thinking outside the box and to expand the limits of my destiny. This wisdom and spirituality has not only allowed me to become a better-rounded professional, but also a better giving person. Thanks to you, my journey is measured only by the number of lives I can enrich.

My family certainly deserves many thanks for their kindness and support during the writing journey. There was always a fresh pot of coffee on whenever I called up and said I needed a break from the book. My parents may not completely understand the concepts of such "a very involved book," but their telling me they are proud is more than enough fuel to allow me to complete such a challenging project.

Finally, thanks most of all to my darling wife, Nancy. Her encouragement for me to accept such an opportunity during some very long trading weeks will always be appreciated. Her sacrifice of sitting home during some beautiful summer weekends in New Jersey or editing a chapter or two in Shanghai just so I can complete this book will never be forgotten. Having your encouragement makes me believe that I can accomplish anything. Thanks to your love and support, I can truly say I've only just begun.

About the Author

Michael Toma is a corporate risk manager and specialist in trading the equity index and futures markets in the United States. A Certified Risk Manager, Toma is a frequent speaker on the industry trading conference circuit. His first book, released in 2010, titled *Trading with Confluence* (Outskirts Press), provides a first-hand perspective of risk-based trading and the challenges that new traders are forced to overcome. In addition to managing his own international risk management consulting firm, he is an active member of several risk management organizations and research academies that promote corporate ethics and risk management educational programs.

PART I

Principles of Risk Management

Foundations of Risk Management

The golden age of corporate and accounting scandals during the Enron era placed risk management on the lips of the average corporate employee. In an attempt to mitigate future scandals, the U.S. government passed the Sarbanes-Oxley Act in 2002. The U.S. Senate called it "The Public Company Accounting Reform Act," and the House called it the "Corporate and Auditing Accountability and Responsibility Act." I'll refer to it by its simple hybrid name, SOX. This legislation is at the heart of risk management today, so it's vital to begin any discussion with a little history. The goal of Chapter 1 is to provide an introduction to risk principles, which you will use in your day-to-day trading activities.

A BRIEF HISTORY OF THE LEGISLATION

The SOX Act brought new regulation to corporate board member responsibilities, oversight of accounting practices, corporate governance, fraud, internal controls, and enhanced financial disclosure. While there are debates over the effectiveness of the actual bills, mostly from cash-strapped companies that find the cost of SOX compliance to be more expensive than paying the fines, the need for managing risk has bubbled to the surface as one of the must-do's on the corporate budget sheets. Many companies that are not required to comply with SOX attempt to be within compliance due to the best-practice models inherent in the act's bylaws. Other risk control standards, such as the SSAE 16 assessment championed by the CPA community, also adjusted their prize audit standards in an effort to put on a cleaner pair of SOX.

Since the meat of the act involved the proactive identification, assessment, control, financing, and monitoring of risks, what better individual to implement such a monster than your risk management professional. Since 2002, a more holistic form of risk management known as enterprise risk management (ERM) has grown in popularity. Rather than just identify problems, the ERM specialist can also be viewed as a process improvement and efficiency resource that can assist in improving the bottom line. Technology, database management, data analytics, and the use of data-driven decision making has also resulted in a greater acceptance of the ERM framework. Along with a never-ending surge in data technologies, business analytics, and the sudden urge to measure everything that's measurable, the two have brought risk management to the forefront of today's trading. Many of these ERM models continue to grow in popularity and have a nouveau-risk appeal. Quickly fading are the more traditional risk models that have stuffed the file cabinets of institutions that see risk management merely as insurance policy management.

Using math and numbers to make proper trading decisions should be simple and transparent in communicating the value proposition for using such methods. There has been a dramatic shift in focus over the most recent decades regarding the application of financial risk management. It is important to be clear that the risk principles and theories noted earlier are a critical requirement in your ability to be successful. During the same time, data-driven decision making has accelerated the thirst to incorporate risk management into trading decisions and now is a critical component of any institutional process. In other words, "what is the data telling us?" is equally as important in directing managers on what to do as relying solely on theoretical and strategic methodologies. Many of the texts focus on trading theory only, and I find myself being extremely critical of this information when used in a live environment. The common securities industry phrase "past performance is not indicative of future results" may have some merit (particularly from a firm's legal perspective), but data analytics is founded on the principle that patterns or behaviors tend to repeat when similar market elements are present.

The term *risk management* has been used in an ever-increasing fashion in recent years. Regulatory changes, the need for greater compliance-based operations, the increasing cost of loss, and evidence of its impact on the bottom line has fueled discussion points on the previously closed-door topic. This chapter introduces the elements of risk management and the steps used in the process. We will also review the benefits of infusing risk concepts into your trading plans and operation.

It's important to note that people see risk differently in their professional roles. Of course, we focus our discussion on risk within the scope of a trading environment. Those in the mortgage industry, particularly underwriters, may see risk as the potential default on a loan. Mortgage brokers may see an increase in the fixed rate as a risk to their business, knowing that an increase in mortgage rates would slow demand. At the same time, other brokers may like a spike in rates that create a demand to lock in low rates or opportunities to convert those with adjustable-rate mortgages to a fixed-rate plan. Still others in the industry may see the regulatory agencies as their biggest risk since the passing of stricter processes or disclosure may hinder their ability to generate revenue from specific market segments. This was exemplified during the aftermath of the 2008 mortgage crisis when mortgage brokers were required to stick to tighter regulatory processes as part of the lengthy Dodd-Frank bill. In a hospital operation, a surgeon may see the primary risk of a procedure not working or even the death of a patient, while upstairs in the administration department, the risk of rising medical equipment costs may be on the identified list. Down the corridor, the legal department's top monitored risk is the public relations plan gaps that may be exposed during a crisis. As we progress through the risk management process, it is important for readers to establish their operational trading goals before actually identifying potential trading risks. Let us first define risk, at least within the context of a trader, before we proceed to determine how to manage it.

DEFINING RISK AND RISK MANAGEMENT

Various definitions of risk management are used depending on the industry, source, and purpose. For example, corporations tend to use a definition to define the purpose of their department with the same name. Others use their department's mission statement as the foundation for how the term is defined. The basic theme for most definitions of risk management includes the decisions made to protect the entity's assets and minimize the adverse effects of activities we perform in order to attain company goals. In the trading world, the term *assets* can refer to many things. Logically, our trading capital is probably one of our most essential assets. Capital in trading is the ticket to the show. Simply put, if there is no capital, there is no business; hence the important link of risk management to capital. Later we will discuss the risk identification process in depth. It is critical to also define the logical classification of a trader's capital or related company assets before the risk management process takes place. If not, how can we protect an asset that we haven't identified as an asset?

If risk management is based on the premise of protecting assets, we need to understand the term *risk*, bypass the lip service often given to the term, and define it, at least within the scope of this text. Being a professional risk manager and trader for many years, I've come across several definitions of this simple yet complex word and would probably receive 10 different definitions of the word if I asked as many people. The best definition that reflects the purpose of pure risk management and maintains its simplicity for explanation purposes is simply the chance or uncertainty of loss.

Pure vs. Speculative Risk

The trading community is certainly aware of the chance of loss on any given trade or trading strategy. We accept risk not so we have the opportunity to engage in risky activity (although our business is a magnet for those who relish risk taking), but to reap the opportunity of rewards or capital gain. The scope of pure risk is limited to those activities and decisions undertaken to avoid loss without the rewards found in speculative risk taking.

The insurance industry is based on an individual or entity's need to reduce loss without any opportunity to benefit from an event or decision. The term used in insurance is *indemnification,* or "to make whole." If you review homeowner, auto, or similar policies, you may not have to search deep to find the words indemnity or indemnification. Many have it as the first word on the policy right on top of page one. The basis of indemnification is to bring the owner of the policy's asset or use standard to where it had been before the loss. A car gets repaired, a home gets rebuilt, or stolen property gets replaced. Even in life insurance, the value of the policy is considered indemnification to the beneficiary, at least for policy definitions, upon the demise of an individual.

Speculative risks include a chance of indemnification plus additional gain. The desire for this gain is offset by the potential loss that may occur. The gaming industry is a perfect example of speculative risk at work. Companies allow customers to partake in speculative ventures, described in their eyes as entertainment. Casinos and financial markets provide the forum for speculators to execute their speculative risk-taking activities. In an ironic twist, both industries would be nonexistent if the speculator did not benefit from time to time. While reducing player odds in a casino would greatly benefit the house in the short term, these companies know that there needs to be the potential for speculation to pay off, whether it be in winnings or entertainment value, to maintain solvency. Gaming companies are experts in statistical probability, valid sample sizing, and mathematical edge, the same formulas used by successful risk-based traders.

As you read through the book, it is important to remember that although traders are generally placed in the box of speculators, they are subject to both pure and speculative risks. We limit our loss on a trade with the intention of making a profit of the same or even greater amount. This is speculative risk in its simplest form. A trading platform crashing in the middle of a trade can only be defined in the pure risk category. It is this lack of inclusion of both pure and speculative risk types in the risk management process that is one of the biggest identified concerns in my auditing work.

Scope of Risks

When performing risk assessments in the trading community, I frequently widen the scope of the pure and speculative risk definitions noted above. It's normal for traders to be concerned about their performance and desire to continuously improve. After all, that is what puts bread on the table. In determining chance of loss or level of uncertainty, always incorporate an element of variance into the definition of risk. In other words, risk is also the possibility that any outcome may be different from an expected outcome. For example, a trader may be extremely satisfied with reaching his or her profit goals for a defined period. A risk manager will assess the variability in outcomes that had resulted in the profit goal. Perhaps the trader took on too much risk or violated trading rules to obtain the goal. Maybe the goals are too conservative for the trading instrument or share size is too large, thus allowing the trader to easily reach the goal and allow psychological comfort for that period. As we walk through the risk management process, please be sure to consider the possibility of a variation of outcomes that may differ from the intended result.

CLASSES OF RISK

Although we will devote intensive study to risks directly impacting traders, such as trade risk or the potential for loss on a trade, it is common to find other classes of risks that typically impact traders' performance or overall business at least once during their careers. Here are some classes of risks that tend to be overlooked by the typical trader.

Industry Risks

Exposure to trends in the financial marketplace or financial structure often can impact traders' ability to meet their goals. Changes to instrument liquidity and bid/ask spreads can make a dramatic change to a trader's bottom line. Competitive product releases, particularly in the exchange-traded funds (ETF) community in recent years, while allowing a super-market of trading choices, have also have resulted in increased liquidity of some products. Traders who claim to be experts in one product expose themselves to a learning curve risk when forced to learn to trade new products.

Political, Legislative, and Juridical Risks

Legal changes and government interpretation of policies and laws can have an impact on the ability to trade and even directly to a trader's bottom line. A "trader tax" has been in discussion for many years now and has increased in the spotlight since the economic crisis of 2008 and the emergence of na-tional debt reduction ideas floating around in the legislature. One proposal called for a small tax on each trading transaction. Although it would be just a few pennies per trade, many traders who tend to scalp for pennies or ticks at a time could be exposed to a US$25,000+ impact. The "Let Wall Street Pay for the Wall St. Bailout Act" surely would be enough for some smaller accounts to close their trading doors. As a trading professional, it is always prudent to keep abreast of the latest discussions in the politi-cal arena that can impact your ability to trade and the potential effect on your bottom line. A good risk management plan would include a diversified strategy to seamlessly transition from one instrument such as stocks to fu-tures or forex or vice versa should political or regulatory risks emerge. The structural transition may only take one or two days in the form of opening a separate account or adding the trading feature to an existing platform. The true risk exists in the variation of results that may occur until reaching the level of trading precision with the new instrument.

Social Risks

Social risks include any impacts on your business from image-related changes, industry public relations challenges within the industry, or changes in social infrastructures and technology. During the 2008 eco-nomic crisis, it was common for pundits, news organizations, and the general public to blame Wall Street for the calamity in housing and the recession. The Wall Street versus Main Street bailout argument headlines on newspapers would lead anyone to say he or she was anything but a Wall Street trader. Any blip in oil prices is blamed not on demand, but the speculators in the trading pits in Chicago. Truth or conjecture, these social stigmas continue to exist in the world of finance and can place pressure on elected officials to make regulatory changes, which are inspired by social stigmas.

Technological Risks

Cultural change can also breed significant risks not only to trading performance but can affect an entire segment of the trading community. As day trading became more accessible to the home-based trader, floor trading in the Chicago futures pits started its decline. Many floor traders who excelled at their craft could not make the adjustment to the electronic platform. This failure to plan for technological risk was highlighted in the documentary *Floored*, in which director James Allen Smith focuses not only on the social transition from the pit to an electronic platform, but the lives that were changed due to the inability to prepare for the transition in the method in which one trades.

Physical Risks

These include any exposures caused by people or damage to property. Although one could argue that economic risks are a key area of focus for traders, it is physical risk that is commonly the root cause of trader loss. As a trader, one has the ability to control losses. Although economic conditions may have led to a trade reverting in the opposite direction than planned, it is the person behind the trade who often is at fault for the adverse result. Training, discipline, or ability to recognize favorable market conditions are critical components to master and allow for consistency in trading; all rely on the individual's ability to execute risk-control strategies. Many of the traders I have counseled often blame economic risks as the reason for their results rather than outcomes caused by their very own human decisions.

Included in the scope of physical risk is the loss of physical equipment, property, or tangible items. Have you ever considered the impact on your trading income if your place of business was unable to be used? If you work for a trading firm, do you know their plan to resume operations at a separate location? How long would it take you to recover if your computer system suddenly crashed or, even worse, if your data were lost? We will discuss risk management techniques used to minimize exposure to these and other low-frequency/high-severity events that can have devastating impacts on your business and career.

SUMMARY

Throughout the book, you will notice this holistic or "enterprise" approach toward managing risks as a trader. Historically, this practice focused on loss prevention, and still the term *risk management* to a trader often means "to lose the least" or "just use stop-loss orders." If there is one primary objective when reading this text, it is that we will use risk management in a much wider scope. It all starts with understanding the objectives of managing risk as a trader and attaining those objectives using the risk management process. This series of decisions allows all risks to be identified, assessed, controlled, measured, and monitored. Sounds like a handful at first, but in the rest of Part I, we will guide you through each step and allow the process to take immediate effect toward your trading results.

 REVIEW QUESTIONS

1. What concept is founded on the principle that patterns or behaviors tend to repeat when similar market elements are present?

2. Define the terms *risk management* and *enterprise risk management*.

3. Explain the difference between pure and speculative risk.

4. List and define three classes of risk.

5. Provide an example of how a trader can mitigate political, legislative, or juridical risk.

CHAPTER 2

Five Steps in the Risk Management Process

I f you ask what the primary objectives are for traders, it would be hard for the answer to be anything other than to generate profits through buying and selling. In fact, that may be the only objective. Reality is clear in that there is ultimately one performance metric, and that is profitable trading. Profitability, or more specifically, consistent profitability, is what separates the professionals from those seeking other work. The risk manager takes more of an internal approach to determine trading objectives. What are the conditions, actions, or behaviors that may prevent me from attaining my profit goals? How do I prevent emotions from hindering my execution accuracy? How do I stay disciplined? This chapter introduces you to the five-step risk management process and how it can be applied to your trading. We will refer to these steps continuously throughout the book to reinforce its purpose and effectiveness.

OVERVIEW

Before we dive into the five steps, it's important to get a better understanding of the primary purpose of following a risk-based approach. Is it only about profit and loss and making money? Not necessarily. Rather than be held to the continuous need to be profitable, risk managers focus on the following objectives or "risk tenets" to lead them to success in trading.

1. **Consistency in decision making**—The ability to make decisions in accordance with chart activity or similar events that historically have provided opportunities with a favorable outcome.

2. **Execution compliance**—To perform more like a project manager rather than a trader. The objective here is to implement a trading and business plan effectively. A risk manager's entire belief is that adhering to such a plan will allow the manager to reach his or her trading objectives.

3. **Focus on risk, not profits**—Understanding that any act of speculation will involve successful and unsuccessful trades. In an arena filled with randomness, the risk-based trader needs to focus on managing the potential loss on a trade and let the decision-making variables, such as setup edge, execution, and plan compliance, dominate.

4. **Mastery of variance**—Understanding that speculating in the financial markets is a virtual pool of randomness. The markets are a continuous basket of different players making different decisions for different reasons. The risk manager accepts this limited ability to determine market direction and focuses his or her efforts on having trading outcomes mirror an anticipated result given a large enough series of trades.

5. **Data-driven mind-set**—Trading decisions should rarely if ever be based solely on market intuition, bias, or gut feeling. The best traders often comment on their ability to read the market and "go with their gut." Risk managers are no different. In the end, however, we use historical data, chart patterns, or other activity that have been proven to have a historical edge of a valid series of occurrences as a major factor in our decision making. We measure practically everything to determine hints of an edge.

6. **Always aware of all potential risks**—Although losses on any trade are more frequent than any other types of trading business losses, risk managers tend to focus more on the low-frequency/high-severity potential losses. If I lose a trade or two, I often express it through laughter. Lose my data—my entire business structure is destroyed. We will discuss frequency and severity relationships and their importance in your overall planning in the next chapter.

7. **Focus on the big picture**—Survivability is king over all other objectives. A challenge for the newer traders is their immediate quest for profitability. Risk managers tend to focus on risk and ultimate losses. In trading, the ability to trade tomorrow is the ultimate objective. The most disheartening call received is one who finally "gets it" just after depleting his or her trading account—the perfect example of seeking profitability before survivability is attained.

8. **Don't risk more than one can afford to lose**—Heard over a million times but unfortunately overlooked by many and often intentionally. Trading is not a video game with a restart button in the bottom corner

of the screen. Risk management is in essence the art of managing the portion of capital at risk. A trader should not only consider the trading capital under this umbrella, but also the nontrading capital devoted to building his or her trading business.

9. **Don't risk a lot for a little**—Second only to stop-loss management, the most popular question I receive from traders is regarding risk and reward. Throughout the book we will discuss different ways to measure this popular ratio when considering a trade opportunity. We should be seeking the optimal gain for each unit of money we risk. The question, however, cannot be answered in a vacuum. Other variables such as individual or company risk tolerance are powerful components that one needs to consider. Risk analysis dives deeply into assessing risk-to-reward; however, we should avoid risking a lot of capital with the expectation of gaining a little.

10. **Consider the odds**—In addition to risk tolerance, a key component that risk managers are constantly obsessed with is the odds of success, or edge. Like an airport arrival screen that continuously updates plane gates and baggage carousels, we are always asking ourselves, "What is our edge?" Trading in live markets means that dynamics are always changing and the edge continuously requires updating. What does a risk manager do in the markets? The answer is simple. We continuously review for opportunities with odds that provide us with an edge and execute when it does.

Figure 2.1 shows the risk manager's trading pyramid. Notice how profitability is third from the bottom on the pyramid. The old adage "in order to make money, you first have to stop losing money" certainly applies here. Becoming profitable as a trader still does not mean you have reached your ultimate goals and objectives. I find many profitable traders have trouble increasing share or contract size even after consistency in generating trading profits. The best traders obtain success not by trading more but by trading the same plan with greater size. Many traders find this a challenging step and often consult with risk managers, coaches, and psychology experts to overcome this hurdle. Fortunately, all the above can be paid now that the profitability stage has been attained.

Fulfillment is a more subjective stage and has different components. One trader may consider achieving this stage after consistent growth in his or her trading business and in a state of happiness. Another may define it as achieving growth with the ability to reap the rewards of life and keeping family a priority. While one in the survivability or stability stage may have little sympathy for the yacht-owning trader who is not happy, many see this as the biggest stage to overcome.

FIGURE 2.1 The Risk Manager's Trading Pyramid

For many, trading can become monotonous and even boring at times. The lack of personal interaction in some venues and a need for a higher purpose can act as a brick wall at this fifth stage. I have known traders who actually found it too easy and reverted to professions with more fulfilling opportunities to make the world a so-called better place. Others have found the pyramid climb to be one of the most stressful ventures in their life. During this journey, family sometimes takes a back seat and often becomes a sounding board after a bad trading day. Others find other roles in the business such as mentoring or teaching as a way to obtain fulfillment and attempt to get that trading spark back. Many who can claim they have reached the pinnacle of trading often find that staying on top is much harder than the climb itself.

Expected events and those that are unexpected will be sure to occur if you trade long enough. Ask any trader who has been in this business a few years and they can fill a bar night with stories of the unthinkable, an occasional bad-beat, and a handful of trades where it ran to target only after getting stopped to the tick. The risk management process certainly is not designed to end the market cruelties that result as red entries in the journal, but it does play a critical role in setting the trade evaluation and decision process. As we discuss the five-step process, I urge you to utilize it for every business decision you are required to make as a trader. The risk framework standards are used in risk management roles across many industries, and the applications at the trading desk are no exception.

If you are a short-term trader, you may need to perform the steps rather quickly and with greater precision. Standard plan setup trades should be implemented with the process already performed prior to qualifying it as a valid setup in your plan. Other risks, such as business continuity or trade data integrity, should take a more formal and documented approach. Like any other task, the more you perform it, the more you will feel comfortable and confident. There are no guarantees in trading, but one thing is: If you do not identify a potential risk, you cannot manage it.

STEP ONE: RISK IDENTIFICATION

Considered the most important step in the risk management process, risk identification, or the process of identifying and examining potential exposures to loss in trading, is the first step. (See Figure 2.2.) Why so important? Simply put, if a risk is not identified, it cannot be assessed for impact, controlled, measured, or administered. What you don't know in trading can certainly hurt you. One of the skills required of a risk manager is to have an "anything can happen" mind-set and be prepared to run any potential exposures through the risk management process. Red audit flags go off on all trading plans that only include historical losses as worst-case scenarios, the reason being that the inevitable next bigger loss becomes the new worst-case scenario. No doubt the more visionary talent one possesses, the more capable one is of excelling at risk management. It's also advantageous to be a bit creative during the identification process. If you are an independent trader, no boss will chuckle at your silly scenario of asteroids

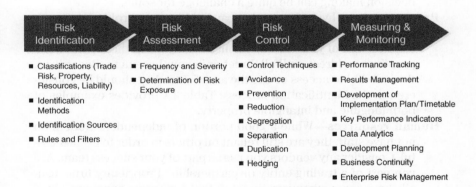

Risk Identification	Risk Assessment	Risk Control	Measuring & Monitoring
■ Classifications (Trade Risk, Property, Resources, Liability)	■ Frequency and Severity	■ Control Techniques	■ Performance Tracking
■ Identification Methods	■ Determination of Risk Exposure	■ Avoidance	■ Results Management
■ Identification Sources		■ Prevention	■ Development of Implementation Plan/Timetable
■ Rules and Filters		■ Reduction	■ Key Performance Indicators
		■ Segregation	■ Data Analytics
		■ Separation	■ Development Planning
		■ Duplication	■ Business Continuity
		■ Hedging	■ Enterprise Risk Management

FIGURE 2.2 Phases of the Risk Management Process

hitting your data server during a short trade with no stop. While working on an emergency evacuation plan for an operation on top of a steep hill, I was laughed at when the need for stored overnight supplies and blankets was identified should the primary access road be cut off from access for any reason. Although there had never been any exposure in the past, a large commercial development blocked an auxiliary exit with a smaller grade down the hill. Later that winter, four key employees were severely injured in their cars while trying to leave during a severe blizzard.

Risk Identification The process of identifying and examining potential exposures to loss.

Part of the identification process is to determine if the potential risk even needs to go through a thorough assessment. Perhaps a risk such as losing an hour of trading can be retained as part of the trading game. To the contrary, preventing devastating trading losses are an absolute identified risk and must be automatically put through the process. This qualifying methodology acts as a filter for all potential risks, which are ejected at any point where there is enough information to determine if the process should proceed to the next step or be deemed not necessary.

As we go through our initial attempt to identify trading risks, it is helpful to categorize them under the following classifications:

Trade risk—This involves the execution, management, and result of your trade activity. As traders, we accept this risk before we start our first day. Identifying risks within our trading plan and related decision making can be quite a challenge for some.

Property—Any physical asset that can be damaged, broken, stolen, or be unable to be used for a period of time. You should also consider the use of your trading facility. It may be on the top floor of a prominent address on Wall Street or in your basement. Regardless, the inability to access or use the area for trading should be considered in the identification process. Table 2.1 provides examples of both tangible and intangible property.

Human resources—While a good portion of independent traders do not have staff, they are still reliant on others in order to be successful. Consider any vendors you use as part of your success team. Are you part of a trading entity or partnership? Proprietary firms usually have some administrative staff that can create exposure. Once people start coming on the payroll, expect an increase in some form of risk. The red flag should rise as soon as paid staff enter

TABLE 2.1 Comparison of Tangible vs. Intangible Property

Tangible Property	Intangible Property
Office space	Data
Furniture	Records
Equipment	Documents
Data infrastructure	Licenses
Internet connectivity	Trade signals
Capital	Goodwill

the scene. Table 2.2 lists some common human resources you may encounter and their associated perils. A coach, trading room service, and accountant can be critical persons in your daily trading and should be considered in this process.

Liability—Individual traders tend not to have any liability exposures, but a review of any additional monies owed to others should be identified. Do you trade on margin? Are you trading other people's funds? Although liability is a nightmarish classification for most corporate risk managers, one should still use the risk identification process to identify any potential exposures. I once set up a trading plan and risk assessment for a trader that required the trader's spouse to be a key stakeholder in the venture. Her "blessing" for her husband to trade required weekly account statement reviews for me to sign off. The husband agreed to personally fund any losses to the account at the end of the month should there be any deficits. Is this a potential liability exposure to the trader? It sure is, at least from an identified risk perspective. The most prominent characteristic of liability risk is that it is difficult to measure the severity in advance of any exposure or event. Potential exposure amounts will depend on the circumstances, the severity of the matter, or even negligence in the case of a managed account platform.

TABLE 2.2 Human Resources and Their Common Perils

Types of Human Resources	Potential Perils
Business support team	Disability, retirement
Vendors	Noncompliance
Capital stakeholders	Redemption
Employees	Termination or theft
Trading partners	Negligence

Other exposures—The list of exposures for trading loss or loss or failure of your trading business are endless. This should not deter you since most can be controlled or eliminated in one form or another.

Contractual—Not meeting the obligations of a contractual trading agreement.

Negligence—Trading errors that result in financial loss for you or your stakeholders.

Noncompliance—Inability to follow the trading plan.

Performance management—Inability to trade consistently and effectively.

Tax related—Improper tax-related support documentation resulting in penalties.

Trading firms have extensive identification processes with particular focus on property, human resources, and liability. But it can be useful for independent traders to create a risk identification checklist for themselves (see sample checklist in the accompanying box).

The Independent Trader's Risk Identification Checklist

Utilize this template as a foundation for your risk identification process and customize it for your unique operation.

Not meeting a projected trade result
Missing entry on a valid trade setup
Not executing a stop-loss order to reduce risk
Losing essential support team members
Trade results negatively affected by market randomness
Need to produce financial results beyond market opportunities
Inability to identify change in market conditions
Inability to maintain discipline after losing trades
Market volatility greater than maximum risk plan
Trader's health
Loss of psychological capital
Frequency of overtrading
Fear of trading with larger size
Misinterpreting trade data
Technological platform failures
Trade execution inefficiency
Noncompliance with trading plan

Risk Identification Methods

Although the risk management process can be somewhat formal in its approach, I often suggest the identification process be as open and innovative as possible. There is no harm in throwing any ideas into the ID basket. The purpose is to create a potential list of decisions, processes, or actions that may result in a loss. Be reminded that these losses can come in many forms. Financial loss from trading is the obvious type we should be concerned with. Also consider how you allocate your time as a trader. Is there a trading instrument that you are required to devote more time to? Are the results over time meeting the return on time investment? Is your time watching one market taking away from your concentration from another during a peak time of the day?

We are merely looking to determine potential areas where losses outside our expectations can occur. Most of the risks identified here will never make it past the assessment phase of the risk management process. Here we determine if the risk is significant enough to warrant additional controls. For example, a long-term index options trader should assess implications of volatility or theoretical options pricing values rather than the precise entry price to the tick. Day traders should consider building your identification list based on trading costs or ability to consistently get filled at a desired price. A risk as simple as not getting filled at a target price can be costly for a scalp trader. Identifying such risk could result in assessing other brokers that have greater fill options or focusing developmental efforts on trade execution.

The following methods will help start the ID process.

Checklists and Self-Questionnaires   Sometimes the simple approach using pencil and paper works the best. Take a few minutes during your trading day to write down all the activities you perform as a trader. Ask yourself questions about what you are doing and why you are doing it. What is the objective of the task? What are the ultimate "worst-case scenario" risks? What could you lose? Account value? Time? Focus? Also take a look at your work environment. Traders rely greatly on their equipment and computer technology in order to do their work. Make a list of each piece of equipment and the potential chance of loss involved. You may find interesting differences regarding the risk of your printer crashing as opposed to your e-mail server shutting down. Of course, if you are the head trader of a proprietary firm and your agreement with your investors is to send daily e-mail summaries of your trading results, then your e-mail server's reliability is of great importance.

For the individual trader, a power outage may not seem to be a high priority on the risk identification list. When I first started trading, I would

TABLE 2.3 Common Risk Relationships in Trading

Relationship	Responsibility	Identified Risk
Broker	Trade execution	Slippage on fills
Trading room/advisor	Detecting trade opportunities	Cannot replicate room calls
Trading coach	Develop toward pro trader	Too many clients
Charting software	Detect valid setups	Charts freeze

just accept it as a business hazard and hope that I could reach my broker in time to flatten a position. As my trading business grew and had multiple stakeholders, an interruption of any significance could put a lot of funds at risk. Even without any open trades, a work stoppage clearly is an opportunity cost exposure, and as many traders regrettably know, the best trade setups occur during these times.

Table 2.3 shows an example of a typical self-employed trader and the direct relationships he or she may have in the trading business. Are some of them similar to your trading operation? As you walk through the identification process, seek to determine other possible scenarios that could occur and potentially place your funds or your ability to reach your trading goals at risk.

Your trading infrastructure and identified risks can be vastly different from the examples above. As part of your risk identification homework, take some time to think about your potential exposures to loss in your trading business and ask yourself the following questions: What could possibly go wrong? What more should I know about this particular task (person, item, etc.)?

One question to refrain from asking is any reference to the potential impact or severity on your ability to trade or risk to your trading capital. Impact analysis to identified risks will be assessed in the following step in the risk management process. Focus on the identification of potential risks for now, not their severity or impact.

Let's look back at the risk identification example in Figure 2.2. Notice that the individual trader can choose those most appropriate for that individual. Proprietary firms or hedge funds customarily have a risk management professional on their team and utilize assets and peril lists of a much greater scope that may include such events as embezzlement or even terrorism. It is common to have risk identification plans that include such events as landslides, earthquakes, and tidal waves, given their proximity to such exposures.

One can get extremely innovative during the identification process, but in the end it is realistic exposures and a practical approach that optimizes the balance between an effective risk plan and effective time management.

Consider that many of the identified risks will not make it past the assessment phase of the process, so you should not be intimidated over days of analysis and the fear of adding too many potential exposures.

Checklists are a great way to start your identification process. They are relatively easy and do not require expensive software or a mastery skill set or certification in risk management. They also can be standardized for an individual trader, proprietary trader, partnership, or any other entity form. Checklists and surveys, however, may have limitations in their ability to identify all potential risks. Those identified tend to be visually identifiable such as the failure of a setup or the lack of service from a broker. They are often the low-lying fruit of identified risks. Checklists also do not prioritize the items on the list and require manual decision making as to which ones are seen as the risks to move first through the assessment process. A coach or risk professional can assist in the prioritization process; however, the focal point of the risk identification process is in itself: Identify. You cannot assess, control, manage, and monitor an exposure if you first don't identify it.

Flowcharts and Other Process Maps Sometimes used as part of a trading plan or as a stand-alone, decision point charts are an effective tool for those who prefer a visual walkthrough to determine if a trade setup is valid. Many successful traders go without them, while for others they are a must-have desk item during the trading day. Some of the best traders have a decision process, but it is all in their head. They know what they are looking for in a chart pattern or setup and execute with near flawless precision. They still do have a process and an effective one. In order to take a closer look at identifying exposures or opportunities, you should attempt to create a written accounting of your decision process. Figure 2.3 shows an example of a simplified decision process chart to determine a valid setup on a trade.

During trade audits, I may come across a trade setup that may have one or two elements that are flawed. Perhaps the decision points show a method that is not compliant with one's trading plan. Maybe the steps in the process are accurate but virtually impossible to implement during fast-moving markets. By seeing the process visually, you or a team member can identify potential bottlenecks and critical decision paths more easily. You also can detect critical components often overlooked such as overall trends, news notifications, or other trading plan items. Many include these trade decision charts in their trading plan and consider a trade that does not follow these criteria a noncompliant trade. Without identifying the potential risk or assessing the exposure, a trader may put the setup on the back burner or do without it altogether, stating "That trade doesn't work, so I took it out of my plan." Yet, in fact, the setup was introduced to the

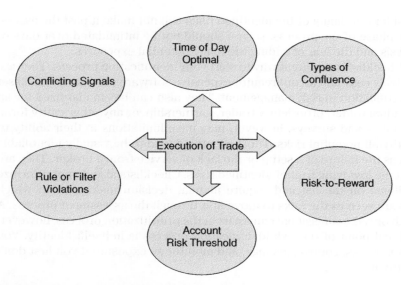

FIGURE 2.3 Example of a Trader's Decision Point Chart

trader with historically profitable or consistent results by a fellow trader. Placing the decision chart into the risk management process allows the assessment and subsequent processes to be performed.

Decision charts are more focused on plan compliance and will not detect frequency or severity, particularly of a minor flaw with big exposure potential. Like checklists, decision charts can be completed in the assessment phase of the risk management process. Some argue that this approach tends to be too process oriented, and their comments are valid in many cases. Documenting your decision process, however, will provide you with a solid and credible approach in the overall identification process. Again, keeping it simple and effective will allow exposures to come to the surface.

Audit Reviews A thorough compilation of items gathered during the checklist process and plan documents may only scratch the surface in the risk identification process. Some potential exposures are only detected during an internal cleansing of your processes. Exposure to loss exists in all facets of trading, such as in your decision making, ability to be consistent, plan deficiencies, and personal demons that are brought to the trading desk. External reviews can be best performed by a qualified coach, fellow trader, or risk manager. I have also witnessed success stories when traders are assessed by a psychologist, particularly when the issues at hand appear to be focused on emotional challenges, inconsistency in performance, and plan noncompliance. We sometimes bring many biases to the table when we perform self-assessments. We often focus on excelling in chart reading and execution and push aside the human side of trading. A common request I receive is to discuss setups that I use to trade the S&P futures and SPY index options. Many just want to know the setups. When my discussions turn toward building psychological capital or managing human capital risk, the audience participation fades in hopes of getting back to the chart setups.

Any good company will allow for independent reviews of their performance and processes. Granted, more often than not they are completed as part of a company's compliance or regulatory mandate program; however, the lack of requirements as a trader should not be the catalyst to invoke these beneficial reviews. Another value offering provided from an independent assessment is the advice that is included in the findings. An audit should not only identify risks in your operation but allow for suggestions that have resolved the issue with other traders who experienced a similar challenge.

Costs will vary based on the scope of the audit and the quality of the auditor or audit team. Perhaps in the early stages of your trading business you can use a coach or fellow trader, barter the same services to their trading business, and then graduate to a more formal independent assessment. In the end, there is good value offered when full-scale risk management assessments are performed by a professional with experience in trade auditing and the markets.

Use of Experts Business owners often find the biggest challenge is being able to focus on performing their job yet not letting the role of running a business get in the way. Bakers, for example, have to manage a store, employees, accounting, marketing, and yes, they have to bake well, too. Both elements of ownership are required for even a chance of success. Business owners including traders excel, or at least aspire to excel, in one or many essential tasks required for success. For a trader, the skill is obvious: Trade well. Similar to the baker, there are other roles that are required, which may lie outside the trader's comfort zone or expertise. I've always admired those who seek to tackle each and every challenge of being a self-employed trader. It is truly the epitome of the entrepreneurial spirit at work. For new traders, realization quickly sets in that this profession requires more than the pushing of buttons that allow $100 bills to be spitting out of their platform. They have to be excellent money managers, risk managers, IT specialists, bookkeepers, tax preparers, to name a few. Or do we? Ask any successful business owner; they credit their team as key components of their success. It is rare that a beginning trader has all the elements required to excel in trading. Fortunately, you don't need to have all of these skills. You just need the ability to recognize them and to have the experienced resources available to assist you regarding your areas of opportunity.

The motivation to write this book is to provide the risk management education required that will enable trading professionals to manage their decisions effectively. As professionals, we often need to have resources that excel in areas well beyond our capabilities. Perhaps you require an outside person to handle your taxes, which can be a daunting task for stock and options traders. Technology, or the ability to fix computer problems, may not be your strongest point. I hope by the end of this book that you have the basic education required to be a better risk manager and trader; however, your situation may require reaching out to such an expert. The use of outside experts also provides the most value-added service; it allows the trader the ability to focus on trading.

Experienced professionals can be found with a variety of expertise. You may have someone internally, such as a family member, fellow traders, or even a staff member if your business includes such resources. The trader who actively trades the markets may consider administrative support for his or her business. Pooling such talent with other traders is a great way to reduce administration at a reduced cost. Some resources may not be experts per se but certainly provide an avenue by which to outsource some duties. External experts come in many forms. Professional consultants, current and former traders, business owners, and even medical professionals are all potential resources to help you reach your trading goals. Risk management professionals are excellent resources to manage the identification process. Trader accountants and some in the legal services community may also add value.

The reality is that most beginning traders wish to use their entire capital base for trading. Why not? "The more money I have to trade, the more money I can make. I can trade bigger size and reach my goals quicker. I'm gonna be rich!" I have met hundreds of aspiring traders in my career; many have the talent required to be in the top echelon of the profession. Lack of capital is certainly a common reason for not investing in your trading business, but I have found that those who understand their strengths and needs and seek help from those who have succeeded tend to have better outcomes. Due diligence is certainly a prerequisite during the expert selection process and can sometimes be in itself a task for outsourcing, thus another reason why many go the do-it-yourself route. Price shopping is also a deterrent, especially for the small account/big dreams trader who soon realizes that the better the value, the bigger the cost.

How can experts help in the risk identification process? For starters, an outside and independent person tends to take an unbiased view during the process. When performing initial consultative meetings with traders, most of the areas of potential exposures discovered were linked to where the traders felt they did not have any reasons to be concerned. A good portion of them were not experienced in risk and data analytics. A red flag would always go off when I could not get a direct answer as to which trade setups or financial instruments were performing above and below expectancy. Evidence of bypassing valid trade setups was often overlooked during a trader's self-identification review. In summary, the consideration of which elements of your trading should be analyzed by external resources should be done before the first buy or sell order is placed. An a la carte service strategy focused on areas of need is a consideration and the use of such can be expanded as additional needs are identified.

Common Sources of Risk Identification

Those who keep a trade journal to track their trades have a tendency to also have a trading plan. Still, a majority of traders I have come across in my journey still do not operate under a set of rules. One of the first steps in starting any business is the need to have a plan. The plan includes not only the startup components of the business but also the rules that will govern how they operate. It is not just about profit goals. Most who fly by the seat of their pants in any business, especially trading, unfortunately have a poor outcome.

Trading Plan   Trading plans by nature are not stagnant and require continuous review and modification. As you develop toward the professional level, so does your plan. The trading plan must always be reflective of you as a trader and the level of skill you possess at any given time. I recommend review of your plan quarterly, upon significant changes to your business or trading style, or after specific events such as mentor reviews.

In regard to using the plan to identify potential problem areas, you should start with the foundation section of a trading plan. There is no perfect, right, or incorrect format for the best trading plan. Some of the better traders I have come across have inconsistent plans that are poorly formatted. Their core execution, objectives, and rules, however, are usually clearly stated and are able to be executed.

There are several elements of a solid trading plan that should be considered. Communicating the importance of having and adhering to a trading plan cannot be overstated. I have reviewed plans that can vary in length, content, scope, and expectation. All are valid if they support the core mission of the trader. All should address these minimum key components listed next and set the foundation of the traders' goals.

Business goals—These are your broad and qualitative ideas of what you are seeking to accomplish in your trading venture. Be as descriptive as possible. For example, "buy a new car and drive it to my new beach home where I will use the outdoor patio to conduct my morning trade activity." Perhaps you have family goals such as having the ability to spend more time with children or giving back in some capacity. These types of qualitative goals should come directly from the heart using emotion (and perhaps current frustration) as the catalyst. Do not overestimate the importance of creating qualitative goals for yourself.

Trading goals—These are generally quantitative and measurable achievements as a result of the trading decisions implemented as per the plan. Be as specific as possible. Read them to another person, preferably those outside the trading world. Do the goals make sense to them? Determine if they are able to comprehend them to a reasonable extent and be able to at least tie the goal to a measure.

When creating your goals, be sure they meet all of the following goal elements. These SMART goals (specific, measurable, attainable, realistic, timely) are commonly used in many enterprise risk management corporate operations and are equally as effective in setting your foundation in trading. In order for any SMART goal to be in compliance, it must be achievable under expected conditions.

Specific—A specific goal has a much greater chance of being accomplished than a general "wish list" goal. Ask yourself what you want to accomplish and why you want to accomplish it.

Example: Consistently achieve 1 percent profit on 70 percent of my trades and 10 points on any index futures contracts per week, which will enable me to fulfill my trading objectives.

Measurable—Establish criteria that enable you to determine progress toward the attainment of each goal you set. Ask yourself: How much? How many? How will I know when I have accomplished the goal?

Attainable and realistic—In the beginning, I recommend you set your goals within an easily attainable range and with reasonable effectiveness. This initial setting can be modified as you grow, improve, and reduce errors identified during the risk management process. Start with small and realistic goals. Building confidence is one of the most valuable assets you can own as a trader.

Timely—A trading goal should include an estimated time frame in which you expect to achieve the goal. Do not set timeliness standards that allow you to be in complete compliance yet do not provide valid information on your performance. Having a goal that is achievable in 25 years probably will not meet the standards required in trading. Another taboo often found in the audit process is having too many micro-goals in the plan, such as hourly or daily trading goals. Market randomness becomes more of a component in any timeliness metric when time frames are shortened.

Rules and Filters Rules are the controls that allow you to make the proper decisions that enable you to reach your trading goals. Rules generally are broadly based and should apply generically to your entire plan. If a rule is only valid for a particular portion of your plan, such as a unique trade setup, then you should specify such. They can tell you what to do and, equally as important, what not to do. Rules are risk controls to assure the trader migrates up the risk pyramid starting with overcoming survival. Rules should be targeted for specific trading objectives or for general business protection.

Rules are established not only to reduce risk, but also to keep one from making emotional decisions. Some trade opportunities will be valid at a time when the opportunity does not appear favorable. Or during a trade, it might be tempting to take profits early before the target. Remember, rules are established not only to prevent negative outcomes but also to play a role in the assurance that a trader will take specific actions when the appropriate market conditions exist. Lastly, remember that rule compliance and outcomes work independently. There will be many occasions when breaking a rule will work in your favor. It is designed to provide the framework for reaching your goals but not on every trade. In other words, rule violations that have a positive outcome are still considered a noncompliant activity.

Here are some examples of rules to consider when developing your trading plan:

1. Stop trading after reaching a specific target.
2. Do not risk more than 2 percent of trading capital on any one given trade.
3. Never add to a losing position.
4. Do not trade against a market with strong internal strength or weakness.
5. Do not trade the day after you reach your monthly target. Focus on development plan items.

6. All trade activity will be posted within 24 hours in my trade journal.

7. I will only trade standard-size setups during high-probability time frames.

8. I will not trade just prior to or during news events.

9. I will reduce my risk by 50 percent when a trade is 80 percent toward my target.

10. I will only trade the setups in my plan.

11. All trades must have a minimum of two forms of confluence as defined in the trading plan.

12. I will only trade minimum contract size on any valid setup against the trend.

13. Stochastic must be in favor of trade on pullbacks.

14. For a trade to be considered valid, I must have a minimum 58 percent historical winning edge on each setup.

Filters are designed to increase the probability of success by selecting criteria that have historically resulted in successful trading. The objective of filters is to keep your trading activity at an optimal edge to reach an expected positive outcome. Filters, however, will often keep you out of winning trades with less historical advantage. For traders, this can be frustrating at times. Success in trading is not trading every possible opportunity including a valid setup. It is taking the prime setups that meet your rules and filter criteria at the optimal entry and exit price. Compromising any of these three factors will result in minimal success if not failure.

Setups do not rest in your trading plan alone. They are accompanied by the rules and filters and cannot be traded without them. You will experience opportunities where you find multiple levels of support or "confluence" completely in compliance with your rules but with an unclear filter. Filters may also have some subjectivity in determining the validity of a trade. The nature of the markets, the continuous price movement, and the element of randomness allow this variability, particularly when technical analysis is being used. A filter that states to wait for certain volume thresholds to appear may not be valid during the holiday trading periods. Adjustments to filters are common and encouraged when realistically justified. Rules, however, are binary in nature and have little tolerance for subjectivity. They are also easier to assess for compliance. Simply put, the "never add to a losing position" rule clearly means under no circumstances. Rules are risk control mechanisms by nature and should never be broken even under abnormal market circumstances. Following the rules and filters established in your plan is designed to allow you the optimal opportunity to climb the trader success pyramid, maintain a minimum level of survival, and protect you from high-severity risk events.

Trade Activity and Trade Journals An important element of the risk identification process is related to the accuracy and consistency of trader documentation. The most valuable type of this information is that which is stored in your trade journal. Of course, it's difficult to use this method if you don't in fact use a trade journal to track your trades. To my surprise, I found many traders still do not do so, and a majority of those that do still do not use the information with any reliability of effectiveness. If you are one in this category, make it a top priority to start tracking your trade activity. Key performance metrics that missed the mark are an excellent source of areas where one can improve trading results. This information is generated primarily from your trade journal. Later in this book, we will go step-by-step on how to create a starter journal and the basic elements you should be tracking.

Using a trade journal for risk identification may be limited based on the credibility, accuracy, and consistency of the data. Some of the best journals were implemented using old versions of Excel. The important point here is that the data are tracked and able to be summarized. If you are new to trading, you may not have enough history to identify potential risks. Some of the data you track may become irrelevant over time. No time like the present to start the foundation of risk identification and analysis using your trade data. I have devoted an entire chapter of this book, Chapter 5, "Embracing a Culture of Analytics," to discussing how to use your trade data to optimize your ability to identify exposures.

Contracts and Agreements Key documents of the corporate risk profession are contracts and insurance policies. In the trading community, there is very little of each type, which adds to the uniqueness of risk management in trading. For the average individual at-home trader, you probably have signed a brokerage agreement that enables you to execute your trade orders. Included in that agreement were specific disclosures and language stating you understand all the risks you are getting into (as I'm sure we all do in fact understand). In nearly all cases, there is very little negotiation with most brokerage agreements. They are designed by brokers to protect brokers. While most would rather see ants build a house between the cracks of their front sidewalk, it is always good to glean through these agreements annually to see if anything in your business has changed that would warrant further investigation. Perhaps a beneficiary should be changed due to a marriage or other life event. How does your broker handle disputes on inaccurate price fills? I have found varying experiences in resolving disputes over trades that should have been filled and were not.

TABLE 2.4   Trader Document Risks

Trader Business Documents	Associated Risks
Brokerage account application	Dispute process/trader limitations
Options disclosure document	Understanding of options strategy risks
Trader education agreements	Refund policy
Partnership agreement	Liquidation rights and fees
Equipment service contracts	Replace or repair language
Office or home office rental agreements	Long-term lease requirements
Tax-related documents	Understanding trader tax status requirements

As a trader who religiously uses "bracket" orders to automatically place my stop-loss and target prices at the time of my order entry, this was very important to me. One broker simply quoted their data failure clause, which protects them from any error caused by exchange or platform orders, while another proactively credits any differential before the market close.

Table 2.4 lists examples of documents and potential identified risks to consider during your review. Each individual trader and the entities you contract with are different, but these examples should give you a nice start toward completing the process.

A complete gathering and review of your trading agreements is a part of the risk ID process and can be a great source of potential financial and business exposures. Are you using a third-party trading platform separate from your brokerage firm? Do you have a service agreement with your trading coach, trading room, or other educational vendor? The identification process is exponentially more valuable when you include outside persons in the process. Contracts and other agreements can help identify holes in your risk management plan, too. Because in many cases you are the second party in these agreements, you may have limited opportunities to improve your risk profile other than choosing service providers that cater to your needs.

Summarizing Risk Identification

We reviewed several different methods on how we can identify potential risks assumed by traders. It is common to have traders use only one or two risk identification methods. Often one method will reveal the greatest number of concerns anyway. It tends to navigate toward the risk manager's comfort choice or, in some trader operations, strict policy and procedure guidelines that dictate identification requirements. Regardless, risk is present and always will be in nearly any venture where there is a chance of gain or loss, and traders need to accept this. Unfortunately, the chance of loss or adverse outcome is not always self-evident. Since an unrecognized exposure cannot be managed, the identification process is often considered the most critical phase of the risk management process. Of course, risks cannot just be identified and placed in a desk drawer. They need to be prioritized and assessed for impact, and then you need to determine how they will be managed and controlled.

STEP TWO: RISK ASSESSMENT

Now that you have a comprehensive list and ideas of potential items that can go wrong in your trading activities, the next step is to determine if they in fact are an actual exposure and the extent of the issue. In this phase, you truly want to start getting your hands into the mix. Identifying these areas is of little value if they are not evaluated and resolved.

The risk assessment process is handled differently for risks identified from a qualitative analysis method and a quantitative analysis method. Qualitative assessment is the process of reviewing identified risks and exposures that cannot be measured by statistical or financial calculative methods. Generally they are challenging to quantify and thus overlooked in regard to their importance or even impact on one's performance.

Quantitative assessment lends more focus to using statistical analysis in determining impact on identified risks. "Quants" can also assist in predictive modeling such as the financial result of continuing a particular trade setup over a period of time. The power of data cannot be understated. The fast-moving business intelligence sector continues to provide significant value on performance and operational management. These quantitative methods are equally as powerful for the trader when performing risk assessments.

I'm trained to ignore short-term fluctuations.
—Jeffrey Ma, from *The House Advantage, Playing the Odds to Win Big in Business*

As technology has developed in the past decade in the areas of chip speed, programming, and data intelligence, the ability to perform risk analysis and business analytics has boomed. At times it feels as if qualitative risk management has stood still in comparison to its twin. Companies like IBM, SAP, Oracle, and smaller outfits have flooded the quantitative data scene, and the intelligence move does not appear to be slowing down anytime soon. A far cry from the days of Excel, qualitative assessment takes a hands-on or "feels" approach to assessing risk. A trader may not indicate it in a trading plan or even detect overall poor performance in trade data, however, for some reason, he or she may feel uncomfortable taking a specific setup. Perhaps it's a fade-type trade, and the trader is more prone to taking trend-based trades. I knew a trader who told me that he hated trading the Russell 2000 index. Calling it the "evil one," he would talk about how it had eyes for his stop orders and was convinced it had a devious personality. After reviewing his journal, I noticed his Russell results were on par with some of his other index results. It was evident that his stop outs were a bit more frequent, but his winning trades far exceeded those of other index setups. While you could argue that this assessment included a mix of qualitative and quantitative analysis, the core root of the assessment was qualitative. During a face-to-face meeting, I noticed his body language cringe at even the mention of the Russell. Qualitative analysis is more art than statistical science and a very important art to learn and understand when performing trade risk analysis.

The Relationship between Frequency and Severity

Certain identified risks dissected in the analysis phase may result in a financial exposure of some kind or in many cases have no impact financially. In fact, most of the trading risks identified will have some exposure to loss. In this profession, the nature of price randomness in itself can be the root cause of some risks. After all, we are performing in a venue where risk acceptance is a sign on the entry door. As risk managers, we have to consider how often we are exposed to such risk and the potential size of the loss during each occurrence. This concoction of frequency and severity is critical in the assessment phase of risk management.

For example, if every day you lost on a particular setup at least once, however, when you did, the financial exposure was $1, would you consider that a risk worth undertaking? Of course, you would need to factor in the potential reward. Continuing with the example, let's say the reward was $1 each time the trade was successful. Since these losses occurred daily, we can justify that the frequency of these losses was rather high, but the severity, at least in terms of financial risk, was minimal. In corporate risk management, it is the equivalent of missing a pencil or a postage stamp in a supply room once per year. These can be interesting assessments since they might shed light on a bigger problem, such as theft potential as in the case of the missing pencil, but from a financial exposure standpoint, there should be more of a need to focus on the risks that will hinder survivability, as noted in the trader growth pyramid discussion earlier in this chapter.

> **Frequency** The number of times a negative outcome occurs.
>
> **Severity** The impact that these negative events have on your trading account and continued ability to reach your goals.

When performing a trader audit, the risks that I spend most of my time identifying and assessing are the low-frequency/high-severity risks. Frequency represents the number of times a negative outcome occurs. Severity focuses on the impact of such negative events. In most cases, these are the exposures that have the greatest impact (severity); however, they do not occur with high frequency. In the business world, most risk managers do not lose sleep at night worrying about losing one customer on a list of one hundred. While all customers are important, the larger customers tend to have the biggest concern. Each company and their objectives are different, of course, and have their risk plans aligned with their goals, mission, and vision. Firms who rely on one customer for 85 percent of their business would have an entire risk plan devoted to renewal of that source of business given its level of severity risk. In a typical corporate operation where the risk management process is completed on many types of exposures, it is the low-frequency/high-severity risks that keep the risk manager up at night. The September 11 incident was the ultimate template for low-frequency/high-severity events. Many companies, regardless of risk planning depth, suffered greatly in all aspects of financial, property, and sadly, irreplaceable human capital.

For beginning traders, it is survivability, not profitability that should be the key objective in any risk management plan. More often than not, it is the low-frequency/high-severity exposures that result in a new and aspiring trading business going defunct. Let's look at some examples in trading using the severity/frequency paradigm.

The Frequency/Severity Quadrant

In Figure 2.4, you will notice the correlation and suggestive action required for each identified risk. Using this correlation, one can assume there are only four different actions for each frequency/severity correlation, discussed in the following paragraphs.

Low Frequency/Low Severity: RETAIN and ACCEPT Any activity that involves risk taking will include some form of frequency and severity. If you were to summarize the role of a risk manager in one sentence,

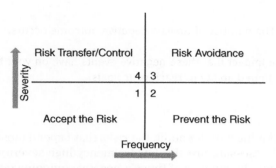

FIGURE 2.4 Frequency and Severity Quadrant

it would be: to perform the actions necessary to identify and to move all potential risks into this category. Is this realistic? It probably is not, depending on the level of risk in relation to your capital size in your daily trading. There tends to be an overall acceptance of small losses that do not occur often. Many of these risks that fall into this category may be a part of trading that simply cannot be eliminated. Often risks that were not initially identified in this category by the trader are picked up during an external risk audit. An example would be any profit opportunities lost from price reaching your target but unable to be filled at your preferred price. This loss of an extra tick in profits may not happen often and usually is not significant if the trader decides to close the trade at a slightly lower profit, realizing the price was not filled. As risk managers, there are simply bigger areas of concern, and it is considered poor enterprise risk management if too much priority is focused on activities that fall into this category. We still need to put an action plan in place to determine if any risk controls can be implemented to even further reduce future loss. For example, an infrequent power outage that forces you to flatten your order via phone may have an adverse effect on your profit and loss for any particular trade. We can impose certain risk controls to nearly eliminate any risks, but in general, we accept some small occurrences taking place the day we sign up to be traders.

High Frequency/Low Severity: PREVENT Negative outcomes that occur in this paradigm are in the quadrant where most identified risks tend to be placed. Rather easily identified through multiple identification techniques, they include any loss types that have not crippled a trader's survivability but yet still need to be addressed. These risks are also easily identified due to their frequent occurrence, thus they are fresh in the minds of traders when talking with other traders and mentors. Most questions I receive from traders commonly are of the high-frequency/low-severity genre. Here are a few examples of exposures that commonly fall into this category:

- Losses derived from improper use of your trading platform or equipment.
- Movement of stop-loss protection when not permitted as per trading plan.
- Decisions that are not in compliance with a trader's plan.
- General trading mistakes such as placing a long order when one was seeking to short.
- Inaccurate recording or assessment of trade data in trade journal.

These risks are a great source of potential learning and find their way rather easily into a trader's development plan. Fortunately, by category definition, they do not result in devastation to one's trading capital. It is critical, however, to address these risks, since if they are not rectified or controlled, they can act like termites in a house. Unlike the low-frequency/low-severity risks, here the frequency acts as the catalyst to take the necessary actions to migrate them into the "retain and accept" category. We will discuss specifically how to prevent these risks and how to manage your development plan in the chapters on risk control and reporting.

High Frequency/High Severity: AVOID This quadrant is the repository for identified risks that risk managers address with the highest urgency. As Figure 2.4 notes, the action is to avoid activities that subject traders to such risks. Most often, risks in this category are often associated with large share or contract size in relation to one's trading capital. There also is trading activity during periods of high volatility or just prior to a news event that could fall into this category for some traders. The potential for reward is usually the highest here as well as the risks, which is usually why traders tend to entertain activities and result in a quadrant 3 risk. Here are just a few examples:

- High quantity share volume trades during high market volatility or uncertainty
- Martingale or other money management systems that require doubling-down after a loss
- Using any trade size that is disproportional to their size of trading capital
- Trading using excessive margin or borrowed funds

- Traders who bring a gambling mentality to trading
- Traders who cannot accept loss

Often during assessments, I tend to find traders who have many category 3 exposures often require development with their psychological capital needs. You will notice that many of the examples above have a human psychological element to them. These traders are risk takers by nature and focus more on the rewards rather than risk; a sure sign of potential survivability failure down the road.

One of the simplest recommendations is to either avoid or reduce the frequency or severity or both regarding these exposures. Trading a high-risk event but with small share size greatly reduces the severity of any negative outcome. Selectivity of when to trade larger size, preferably with setups that historically produce a positive variance, will also assist in the movement of these risks into the less risky categories. Traders have heard it a million times, but sometimes not taking a trade is the best trade. Trading is a marathon and not a sprint, but the gambler sees the winner being the person with the most home runs. Most who expose too many risks in this category subject themselves to not making it past the survivability level.

Low Frequency/High Severity: CONTROL (or TRANSFER) The fourth quadrant is the most feared by the risk manager. Simply put, these expenses are difficult to identify, and some of the risks that are identifiable are a challenge to prevent, avoid, transfer, and certainly to retain. Included in this category are the unprecedented events that have no track record of managing. Some call it the "black swan" or the unthinkable. These risks can have devastating effects on one's ability to reach one's trading goals and even risk survivability. As risk professionals, we cannot just accept significant events as random and hope for the best. True experts in our business have a plan for everything . . . even the unthinkable. Quadrant 4 risks also tend to be discredited when identified and are considered a waste of time to address. The trader who continuously warrants the need for one more holy grail setup to add to his or her plan certainly isn't interested in a nuclear reactor leak shutting down your broker's office. For that matter, let's not think about your small Internet broker closing its doors. Experts in "quad-4" risk management require a great sense of imagination and the thinking that anything is possible.

Examples of Quadrant 4 Risks

Here are a few additional examples of quadrant 4 risks.

Loss of Ability to Trade and Perform Related Functions For some, this is one of the biggest exposures that an individual self-employed trader faces. There is a minimum requirement of physical and mental skills to perform the job as a trader. Any reduction in these abilities can cease the ability to generate trading income from the minute an incident occurs. Technology has helped reduce risks in this area, particularly with the availability of auto-trading systems; however, the ability for a trader to execute a discretionary trading plan may be forced to end. Contrary to the comfortable corner office job with medical, dental, retirement, and pension packages, most individual traders' professions are reliant on continuous health and accident-free living.

An Event That Causes a Trader to Leave the Business Many individual traders starting out with a relatively small size capital account understand this risk all too well. Regardless of their initial trading success, they still rely on spousal or other income to continue their dream of being a professional trader. A job layoff notice to the spouse or an unexpected family expense can be the ultimate low-frequency/high-severity event that forces the trader to change his or her career. Some had to go back to their prior professions because they were notified of a new addition coming into the family, clearly a sad and great moment happening at the same time. The most important element of new trader success is the spousal support for the venture. I have found that traders who have made it through the developmental stages of trading had some form of support team who not only allowed them to pursue their goal but truly encouraged them during this challenging process. Their role as a team allowed the trader to reach the level of self-sufficiency. To the contrary, being the spouse of a new trader can be quite challenging. Poor trading days, emotions brought home to the evening dinner table, and loss of family savings can put a dent in even the strongest and supportive of spouses. When that support dwindles, it can have the effect of a pillar cracking under a building and the added pressure to produce consistent income from a market filled with randomness. Of all the events that lead to traders closing their accounts, loss of spousal support is right up there as one of the most common.

Regulatory or Tax Changes That Affect Traders or Commission Schedules Since the 1980s, the regulatory environment for trading has generally been accommodating—anyone can open a brokerage account, fund it with capital, and start trading. As technology improved and the ability to work off an electronic trading platform became available, individuals had somewhat of a level playing field to trade like the pros. There were some setbacks in this environment, such as during the 1987 crash and recently during the 2008 banking collapse. Main Street's anger toward Wall

Street, including the casual trader working from home in his pajamas, gets the attention of regulators and House members. Short selling limitations and margin requirements were finagled in an attempt to keep the house in order. The trader tax regulation mentioned earlier still hovers over traders, and many consider it the ultimate "black swan" for the industry, or at least for those smaller traders who can never afford a transaction tax of significance. The modification of margin requirements for foreign exchange traders forced many small traders, who virtually ran their business on the excessive ability to "leverage-up" on margin money, to learn other financial instruments. The regulatory environment is rather difficult to assess and predict, but one thing for sure, there will always be changes. Many will provide opportunities for traders while others will close doors. The best of this profession are those who not only identify potential regulatory risks to their business but have a plan in place to adapt to an ever-changing environment.

Unexpected Industry or Technological Changes During your travels, ask any trader who has experience trading for several years, and most will tell you that their ability to change their trading style was a key to their long-term success. It can be a new product addition, such as exchange-traded funds, started an entire avenue for the average investor to transition to trading. A competitive marketplace and à la carte financial services have significantly dropped the cost of trading different instruments. Unfortunately, all these new products have their own logically classified risks. Even the venue in which one trades can change. One cannot find a better example than some floor traders who simply could not make the transition to the electronic marketplace. Many went from reaching the fulfillment apex in the trader pyramid to not surviving in this industry and the cultural change in how one trades electronic futures.

Significant Loss of "Borrowed" Funds As if risking your own capital in the markets did not include its share of risk exposure, the shock is magnified when the loss occurs when using borrowed funds. One of the lures to trading, particular in the futures and forex arenas, is the lucrative ability to trade on margin. Margin is simply cash borrowed from the brokerage firm in order to purchase additional shares of a stock or other securities. When trading on margin, the trader only has to put up a fraction of the actual purchase price of the security in his or her account to trade. The underlying security or other assets in the account act as collateral for the borrowed funds (the difference between the value of the asset less the amount of cash used from the trader's account). If at any time the amount of collateral in the account is not sufficient to cover the amount owed or falls below the minimum margin requirements, the account holder is required to place additional funds in their account or sell securities. It's not a pleasant feeling to get a margin call from your broker. It's the equivalent of having a date cancel just before the prom, plus owing money due the next morning. In summary, one of the highest exposures one can have as a trader is being subject to high-severity risks using borrowed funds.

There are endless high-frequency/low-severity events that the trader needs to consider during the risk identification phase. Nearly all or a portion can be controlled or managed in some fashion. As a general rule, survival is the optimal goal when addressing these exposures. Many will have impacts on your business capital or at a minimum prohibit your trading for a period of time. Minimizing risk so you can live to trade another day applies here.

It is important to note that a category 4 risk for some may only be a category 2 or 3 for others. For example, a $5,000 loss on a trade may be an average-size loss for one account while a similar loss in a smaller account may end a trader's dream. One who continuously backs up trading systems and has alternative office locations may consider an electrical fire causing evacuation a low-severity risk, while those unprepared may be rebuilding their trading desks for weeks into the future. Different trading infrastructures, capital amounts, risk tolerance, experience, risk management capabilities, and preparedness all can play a role in which category these risks are assessed and categorized in the frequency/severity matrix.

Summarizing Risk Assessment

The assessment step often is one of the most subjective components of risk management. The best corporate risk managers who are brilliant risk identifiers can be shown the door if their budgeted estimates to reflect impact fall short. As traders, do not limit your determination of impact strictly on monetary loss. Loss of time, productivity, discipline, and such abstract exposures such as levels of household stress can be incorporated into your assessment findings.

Now that you've identified your risks and assessed the level of impact that it may have on your trading, the next step is to attempt to mitigate or even eliminate the risks if possible. We now move to the third step where we discuss strategies to do just that.

STEP THREE: RISK CONTROL

A child goes out in the rain, and Mom tells the child to bring an umbrella. Reluctant to do so, he wanders outside without one (identification) and then comes home with an occasional sneeze. After finding he has a slightly elevated temperature and fever, she keeps him home from school the following day and brings him to the doctor, who determines he has a slight fever (assessment). The doctor's prescription for antibiotic medicine and fever reduction is the risk control used to mitigate the impact of the exposure. Notice how the mother's warning not to go outside with an umbrella and raincoat was a form of risk control, but the child, as many are, was noncompliant and subject to a loss of a school day. Of course, some kids may refer to that as speculative risk resulting in gain. Mom surely thinks otherwise, however, when she receives the bill for the doctor visit.

We now have reached the third step in the risk management process. After using the outlined methods on how to identify potential risks, we then assess these identified risks to determine frequency and severity or the potential impact on the portfolio or trading business as a whole. Until this phase, we have only identified risk and come to the conclusion that action is needed on the exposure. The level of exposure was determined during the assessment phase, and it was deemed worthwhile to put a control mechanism in place. Until now we have not addressed each risk issue or determined how to mitigate them.

Risk control includes any action designed to reduce the frequency or severity of a loss. The scope of risk control also includes the opportunity to reduce the probability and unpredictability of a loss occurring. During this process, the risk manager focuses on the solution to the problem. Unlike other corporate frameworks, traders do not have the option of transferring risk to protect them from trading loss. One of the primary functions of a corporate risk manager is to manage the company's insurance portfolio. Corporations customarily buy insurance to transfer many business risks. Traders need to determine alternative optimal solutions internally without having risk transfer as an option. The risk control process is designed to meet these objectives.

The documentation and data found in the risk identification source list plays an essential role in the control process. Trading plans, trade journals, and other sources are rarely standardized, thus not allowing for cookie-cutter risk control processes. Our attempt, however, is to teach a framework that allows each trader to conduct his or her risk control program with the opportunity to customize the process. Although the use of data in risk control is a focal point, risk control often involves a human process requiring decisions based on information obtained during the identification and assessment steps.

Primary Techniques

Earlier we introduced some risk control techniques during our frequency/severity discussion. Now we will take a further look at these control options that are best to consider within your trading program. More important than ever, our enterprise risk management definition of risk should be applied during our discussion on risk control. Risk is not only defined as a chance of loss, but also the chance of having an outcome that differs from the expected. These control methods are equally as powerful to optimize gains in trading and not just limited to reducing or eliminating loss.

> **Risk Avoidance**   The decision to entirely eliminate any possibility of loss.

Risk Avoidance   True risk avoidance is the elimination of any activity or exposure that may result in loss. Traders often overlook risk avoidance as a risk control technique, since avoidance translates to not trading. As a risk manager, it's a difficult sell when teaching traders about pure avoidance. Sure, it would be impossible to never have a trading loss. The randomness of markets alone prevents that from happening. The benefit of avoidance is better understood when discussed within the scope of a trading plan. For example, not trading during scheduled news events is a form of risk avoidance. How about during highly volatile markets defined by a rapidly rising stochastic indicator or expanded Bollinger band? Options expiration days were a personal favorite to exercise risk avoidance.

Risk avoidance is one of the easier techniques to administer. As simple as it was for Mom to tell her child not to go outside without rain gear, avoidance is more of a challenge for traders with temptation. It is self-sufficient in that as long as no trade or other action is warranted, risk avoidance is in practice. Traders practice risk avoidance every day in their trading, perhaps more than any other form of risk control, and a solid trading plan is the framework for such avoidance. Any environment or price activity that does not meet the minimum required statistical advantage on a trade should embrace risk avoidance–based techniques.

In other words, we only trade our plan setups when the setup components that provide trading edge exist. Everything else requires risk avoidance, or the trader is subject to breaching plan compliance. Perhaps you already refrain from some of the forms of risk avoidance listed below.

- Trading when preoccupied with personal matters
- Trading when complete daily preparation has not been completed
- Trading when tired, ill, or intoxicated
- Trading products that you have no experience with
- Trading during specific news events or expected high volatility

- Trading valid setups when there is no statistically proven historical edge
- Trading during high margin exposure or low liquidity such as overnight markets
- Trading on psychological "tilt"

Notice how some examples may be a primary cause for risk avoidance while some others may not apply to your trading style or plan. Some may not see any difference in results when trading without daily preparation. Other traders can be tired but can focus like a lion when their valid setup is forming on a chart. This is why risk identification is so important to the control process. It helps identify your specific exposures while the risk control process mitigates the exposure tailored to your personality, habits, and trading patterns.

Traders should seek to evaluate risk avoidance techniques whenever confronted with high frequency and moderate to high-severity risks (quadrants 3 and 4) discussed earlier. Attempting to avoid risks in an occupation that takes place in a virtual arena of risk can be quite futile. Any opportunity that cannot produce a loss also cannot produce any gain. Although avoidance is a valid risk control technique requiring little managing efforts by the trader, it has a very limited application to trading as a business. As with any other speculative ventures, risk avoidance is primarily managed in a trade selection scope or asset protection scope.

Loss Prevention   A method of risk control that seeks to reduce the frequency or the likelihood that a loss will occur.

Loss Prevention   Unlike avoidance, loss prevention techniques do not eliminate the chance of loss. Filters are a good example of loss prevention controls in a trading plan. Their role is not to avoid a trading opportunity but to attempt to reduce the amount of times the losing trade might occur. Following is a list of examples of loss prevention that one might include in a trading plan.

- Use of trading setups during times of day that have a historically high success rate
- Only using setups that work best under specific market conditions (i.e., trend, consolidation, etc.)
- Using multiple levels of indicators, or confluence, to support a valid trade
- Using trade "scale-out" exit strategies
- Developmental and continuing education

As we assess our identified exposures for potential loss prevention solutions, we should implement trade setups when optimal edge for trade success is present. The "LP" trading principle is simple: The lower your positive advantage on a trade outcome, the greater the frequency of a losing outcome. Since there is a close relationship between loss prevention and the cause of loss, it is important to determine what causes trading losses. There is much more to be discussed later in the book regarding the concept of edge, determining edge, and trade entry optimization using analytics. Often traders will overshoot or make their plan prevention techniques too "tight," resulting in missed opportunities. For now, understanding loss prevention is all about reducing trading activity that has an overall negative outcome.

> **Loss Reduction** Seeks to reduce the severity or impact of loss. Reduction does not eliminate the chance of loss itself.

Loss Reduction Loss reduction is the equivalent of having a fire extinguisher in a kitchen. The tool is used only once an event has occurred, and its intent is to reduce the impact of loss from the fire. The goal of loss reduction is to migrate quadrant 3 and 4 risks toward quadrant 1 and 2 risks.

The most common form of loss reduction is by the use of the stop-loss order. By placing an order to close a position at a price predetermined as the maximum risk for the trade, the trader limits the severity of the loss. Why traders use stop-loss orders is relatively simple to understand, but the "where" is one of the more common debates in trading rooms, educational videos, mentorships, and trader conferences. Some calculate their stop placement at a price that equals a particular percentage of loss on a trade or at a percentage of total account value. Scalp traders may only risk $0.25 on a stock trade or four ticks for a futures trader. Other long-term traders or options players may risk 50 percent or more on a trade. Others place the order where price would indicate the trade has lost its inherent edge and no longer contains the components of the valid setup at time of entry. Our discussion will continue about the art of stop placement when we attempt to take an analytical approach to determining optimal stop placement levels. In summary, loss reduction techniques are critical tools to maintain trader survivability. Here are some examples that you may already be using in your trading:

- Use of stop-loss orders
- "Tightening" stop-loss orders once the trade is in a profit area
- Exiting a trade once the initial trade parameters have been violated

- Trading with less share or contract size during periods of high volatility
- Ending the trading day after a set financial loss
- Techniques that include reducing trade size after a series of losses

Note: These are powerful risk control techniques that can and should be utilized from the first trade you ever place. I have been blessed with the opportunity to meet and speak with many traders in my risk management career spanning from several years' experience to the newbie seeking financial freedom. My conclusion is that traders tend to focus more on loss reduction techniques and not loss prevention. There are very few traders I have met that do not have some form of stop-loss reduction practice in their trading. How effective they are is a different story. A scaling-out strategy is one common prevention methodology. What I find lacking, however, is use of multiple loss prevention techniques such as the use of time-of-day filters, for example. I often see traders who use setups in their plan under any underlying market condition or price movement phase. The recent use of auto-trading has focused more on electronic controls commonly found in loss reduction rather than in prevention controls. Some may argue that controls are both preventive and reduce severity. No argument here. In summary, a solid trading plan will include a blend of both prevention and reduction controls that are both understandable and executable.

Segregation Seeks to reduce the severity or impact of loss by using multiple layers of persons, activities, or space. It is the technique most exemplified by "not putting all of your eggs in one basket."

Separation Involves dividing traders' assets or functions into two or more separate locations.

Duplication Concept of backup information or a process in case the original is not able to function or is not retrievable.

Segregation, Separation, and Duplication Segregation is a risk control method that is usually associated with designating a physical area or trading activities that will potentially contain high-risk exposures. A proprietary firm may have their trade execution data or servers in a secure, protected, and fire-resistant room with humidity control features. Some brokers allow you to store your charting features and displays directly on their servers, providing a simple way to segregate. A trading firm may segregate a specific account for higher-risk commodity futures transactions using multiple traders. Individuals trading from home may segregate a quiet area that allows for uninterrupted focus. Those who trade foreign accounts may allocate a portion of their entire trading capital to an overseas account that is subject to unique international risks.

Separation involves spreading assets and/or trading activities over multiple locations or entities. The objective with separation controls is to minimize the risk to any one single entity, location, or account. If one of them is exposed to a loss, the thinking is that the others will still function. Separation can also include having separate trading accounts with different brokers, clearing firms, traders, entities, risk profiles, or even different objectives. I have witnessed several incidents where a platform had shut down during an open position. Although a risk reduction method was in place via a stop-loss order, I suggest utilizing a separate account to take the opposite side of the trade. This strategy in essence flattens the position with zero trade risk exposure. This allows the trader to address the platform issue without being concerned about the ongoing trade. The objective of separation is so that one exposure incident doesn't severely impact the ability to continue implementing your trading plan or negatively impact your trading or business capital. Having an individual trading account and another via a partnership arrangement is another example. Separation controls are used in all facets of business or wherever exposure of multiple assets exists. The U.S. Navy adheres to a practice of never docking all warships in one location, a valuable lesson learned in risk management during the Pearl Harbor attacks.

Duplication, as the name implies, refers to backup controls. Traders can improve their risk profile by having backup platforms or computers should an unexpected event occur. Data is a common asset targeted for backup controls. It can be your trade journals, record keeping, tax data, and business documents. It's easy and inexpensive to do. Individuals and firms can combine both duplication and separation controls by storing backup data at an alternative location.

One key separation control individuals should consider is that of a backup trading location. Technology is a great thing...until it breaks down. If trading is your primary if not sole revenue source, having the inability to use a backup location can directly impact your revenue goals. It's the equivalent of a city restaurant shutting down on a peak dining night. Unlike a restaurant, we as traders can utilize a remote location to continue our operations.

Similar to risk prevention and reduction, the segregation, separation, and duplication controls do not attempt to avoid, prevent, or reduce the chance of loss. In fact, by spreading your risk, you may argue that you increase the potential of some form of disruptive loss. These control methods primarily address reducing the severity of risk, not its frequency.

Any of the control methods described will aid in reducing the chance of shutdown or potential financial loss. The best strategies often include a combination of control methods. Placing backup data at another location is a fine example. Backing up data using your broker's server is both duplication and separation. Coordinating a backup trading location with a fellow trader allows for multiple control functions and benefits both traders.

Hedging Transference of risk is a common control strategy used in any corporate risk structure. The purchase of insurance to protect an asset, individual, or entity is as common as going to the store for bread. Retail companies also use contractual risk transfer by requiring suppliers to absorb product returns or inventory risk, to name a few. Trading, however, is in the direct business of purchasing an instrument that continuously fluctuates in value. This unique characteristic allows a trader or firm to purchase another security to minimize or "hedge" the overall risk of both assets.

Farmers often use the futures market to transfer exposure to crop price fluctuations prior to harvest and delivery of their crops. Manufacturers perform similar transfer techniques to protect them from abnormal price fluctuations in raw materials needed to produce their product. A key decision point in an airline's bottom line is how they manage their hedging risks regarding fuel purchases. Individual traders may not be able to use hedging for risk transfer. Traders can, however, use hedging as a loss reduction technique. Hedging can limit the severity of loss by purchasing assets where price inversely correlates with the base security. Let's take a closer look on how this control option can be implemented in a trading environment.

For example, let's take a typical individual trader named Mark who is seeking to profit from moves in the U.S. equity market. He uses the highly liquid S&P 500 ETF known as the Spider ETF, or SPY. He anticipates a rise in price due to his plan indicators and valid setup pattern. The trader then executes the trade at a price of 1150.00 with an expectation target of 1190.00. He will risk 20.00 index points on the trade. Although he is aware that his trade is valid up to 20 points below the entry point, Mark is uncomfortable with risking the 20 index points on the trade. What are the different hedging options that allow Mark to reduce his loss (severity) on the trade?

An obvious option is for Mark to reduce the amount of shares purchased. By reducing the quantity of shares, he is reducing the potential severity of loss. Another way to hedge the trade is by purchasing the index at a lower price and risk missing out on a move in the intended direction. Notice how Mark is not practicing risk avoidance since his intention is to

TABLE 2.5 Examples of Hedging Techniques

Security Owned	Hedging Technique	Alternative Hedge
Individual stock	Put option on the security	Short single stock futures
Naked stock option	Naked put option	Short stock index futures
Stock index mutual fund	Index options puts	Commodities
10–30-year Treasury bond	Gold	Reduce average maturity
U.S. dollar	Non–dollar-denominated assets	Alternative currencies
Gold or oil	Bond call options	Short futures position

execute the trade. By waiting for a better price, Mark is reducing the severity of his loss, say, 15 points vs. his original 20 points, and still having the opportunity to participate in his intended move. Hedging in the traditional sense involves two separate transactions using separate instruments that historically tend to inversely correlate. In other words, when one instrument rises, the other tends to fall. In this scenario, the hedging instrument is used to offset any losses that may incur on the primary S&P 500 trade. In order to facilitate such hedging, we need to determine which financial instruments inversely correlate with Mark's core equity position. Table 2.5 lists some instruments that historically have provided traders with the ability to hedge.

Table 2.5 displays potential instruments that tend to inversely correlate with the core instrument. These relationships should only be used as a guide. The goal of introducing you to hedging is to consider it in your overall risk management plan. Hedging as a risk control method has its own risks. Are there risk control methods that have risks? Yes, and several of them.

Market randomness—Sometimes the hedging instrument does not trade in the intended direction, thus failing to perform the hedge. Randomness by definition incorporates an element of uncertainty. There is nothing more frustrating than having a hedged position on that does not provide the loss protection as needed. Price randomness, economic news events, or institutional trading programs are just some examples of why such hedging can fail. Hedging using foreign exchange instruments has its own list of country, political, and leverage risks that are well beyond the scope of this text but should be well anticipated in the forex arena.

Margin and capital requirements—Since the trader will be purchasing two instruments instead of one stand-alone instrument, hedging generally requires greater account liquidity. Liquidity and a general understanding of hedging are some of the predominant factors on why individual traders with smaller accounts refrain from this risk control technique.

Transaction costs—There is additional need for greater expense management when hedging since the risks associated with transaction costs and its effect on overall profitability are generally greater. Hedging does require more transactions resulting in greater commission and exchange costs that may erode your capital account over time.

Liquidity—Some instruments used in hedging may not have the liquidity, or the ability to enter and exit at a desired price, than other instruments. Generally, hedging is primarily used with highly liquid securities such as the S&P 500 index products and high-volume foreign exchange currency pairs, to name a few.

Having a successful hedging strategy may not be successful even if it correlates effectively. Having an instrument that increases in value when the core position decreases in value may act as the perfect protection hedge but will offset any gains of the core position when it is working in your favor. To have an effective strategy, you need to consider the ability to leverage your hedged position to assure limited downside risk. This is the reason why the use of options is a popular forum for this form of risk control.

Common Causes of Trader Loss

To understand the importance of the risk control process, we need to get a better understanding of the causes of trader losses. The most common response regarding this question is simply that the trade didn't work out. The obvious aside, the question really is seeking to learn *why* the trade didn't work out. There could be a million reasons why one can lose money on a trade. Determining which risk control method works best is better understood when we evaluate the root cause of loss. Let's take a closer look at other forms of loss to get a better understanding.

Why do people get into car accidents? Are they necessarily bad drivers? Is the driver who collided with the car a bad driver? Would your opinion change if this was the sixth accident in equally as many months or if the driver had little experience in driving? Most car accidents that suffer damage or another kind of loss stem primarily from two causes: unfavorable conditions or unfavorable decisions. It's no secret that more car accidents occur during inclement weather or adverse road conditions. Losses due to driver impairment have been in the spotlight for decades now. You can place teen or inexperienced driving on the same list. It is difficult to go one day without seeing careless driving, speeding, and other road violations. Traders often succumb to losses from performing outside the rules of the road and trading under less optimal conditions.

Trading is similar to driving, but the financial markets are truly a unique risk environment. At any given time, all the participants, activities, decisions, and conditions are different. Markets do not move the same way all the time, just as your favorite chart indicator doesn't work all the time. Unlike a road that is a fixed structure and angles a certain way, the markets are just a centralized mechanism that adheres to different players having different perceptions of the value of assets. Price moves in a random fashion in an effort to determine a fair value from a continuously different audience. This randomness of price movements and outcomes limits the ability for historically reliable charting indicators to always work or allow traders to continuously make accurate assessments on price movement. In essence, it is the element of unknown risk that hovers over trading plans across the globe.

So what can we do as traders to minimize loss? These three conditions require three different solutions:

1. **Unfavorable conditions**—Traders need to recognize market conditions that are the equivalent of an icy road or a heavy rain. Avoidance as a risk control technique would be recommended during unfavorable conditions. If the market is not providing us with a statistical edge, then we avoid trade activity.

2. **Unfavorable decisions**—While the markets can play demons with our heads at times, often there is no greater demon than traders themselves. Not complying with a valid trading plan is the root cause of many failed trading careers. Even the best traders at one time in their career are forced to leave the business due to a failure to properly execute a trading plan. Plan execution of valid setups and optimal risk management allows the trader to, at minimum, focus on staying clear of unfavorable conditions and managing randomness.

3. **Randomness**—One of the most difficult concepts to manage in trading is random price movement. Traders certainly should not ignore the randomness effect but surely need to accept the concept prior to making the choice of getting into trading as a business. Contrary to belief and trader folklore, the markets do not know where your stop-loss order is nor where your target price is. There are the days when price will just miss your target and then head in the other direction. Bad-beat trader stories usually will include a stop-loss price executed to the penny only to be followed by the anticipated rally that prompted

TABLE 2.6 Exposures and the Appropriate Uses of Risk Control

Exposure	Frequency/Severity	Technique
Extreme volatility	Risk avoidance	Platform shutdown
Multiple entry triggers	Risk prevention	Use of setup filters
Trade entry/exit risk	Risk reduction	Stop-loss order
Prop firm accounting risk	Separation	Trader does not have access to funds
Extreme loss on account	Segregation	Broker implements daily account loss limit
Data stored in one place	Duplication	Backup stored separately
Too much risk on long trade	Hedging	Use of put options

the trade in the first place. Top professionals accept this randomness as part of the business and do not allow any adverse result of any one trade to impact their ability to implement their trading plan with precision.

Summarizing Risk Control

As you embark on your risk-based journey into trading, you may be thinking that the risk management process and its integration into your trading business may be unachievable. The identification process alone can be quite cumbersome for many. How do I balance the implementation of risk principles with my other developmental and educational requirements? What is more important to my needs—frequency or severity? As you review Table 2.6 and read through the next steps on measuring and managing risk, the goal is for you to determine a balanced comfort zone where you have the opportunity to establish a core methodology of identifying, assessing, and controlling risk. Your program may be expanded or retraced as your trading needs and business grows. Once you witness the results from your efforts, the process will become a permanent fixture in your success.

STEP FOUR: MEASURING RISK

While sitting down with a fellow trader, I asked him how he was progressing in his trading. He had been receptive to including risk-based trading into his everyday trading the previous year, and so in our follow-up meeting we began to discuss his journey. I asked for his monthly summary assessments and trade journal. This was his response: "I just stopped tracking things.

My trades were doing fairly well and I just focused on the setups. I figured I was making money, so I got a bit careless. I also got a bit overconfident and started raising contract size based on feeling and started trading forex and other futures contracts such as grains and gold. One year ago I was so confident in what I was doing, but now I feel every day is like going to a casino. I'm still optimistic that things will turn around, but I have to get more consistent and back to basics. I know my setups work. I know it."

I was disappointed but not surprised. A lot of traders that break away from a supervised or mentored environment often will temporarily fall back to their unstructured ways of trading. Confidence and early positive results can have many negative effects on a trader. Some sleep in a bit longer and do not put in the premarket work needed. Others stop tracking their trades in thinking that the setup works and will always work in all markets under all conditions. Trading is no different from any other business. Those that commit themselves to dedication and excellence have an exponentially greater chance of success in such an unforgiving business like trading.

Once the framework identification, assessment, and control processes are in place, implementing a risk plan becomes a natural fabric in your work. The benefits alone of risk-based trading should be motivating enough to pursue it. In all risk work that I have experienced, whether in the corporate arena, compliance role, or in trading, I have found that traders as a whole tend to be more prone to deviation of plan compliance. Perhaps it's the continuous inundating of new products to help improve results, holy grail strategies that allegedly never fail, or automated trading strategies that allow one to leave the computer for a few hours and come back to haul in the $100 bills spitting out of the printer. Since many individual traders are self-supervised, there is little disciplinary oversight to assure one keeps to a successful strategy or continues to do the work required. Regardless of the reason, traders need to accept the risk management process as a continuous method of refining and improving results. It is not a task or a project, both of which have a beginning and an end. An important part of this continuous process is the measuring and monitoring of your trading and all other elements of your trading business.

The fourth step in the risk management process acts as the checks and balances for the plan in place. It also acts as your performance measuring tool to determine how well you are managing your business. This process has an auditing element to it, but its scope is far greater. The goal of measuring and monitoring is to not only bring risk exposures to the surface in one's trading but also to measure results and the trend of those results versus the expectations set in your business plan. Here are some of the key elements of the measuring and monitoring process.

Continuous Tracking

In order to determine if you are meeting your plan objectives, it will require stored trading information in a format that allows the ability to perform risk assessment. Trade data plays such a vital role in any quantification assessment and risk analytics. Without such tracking, how would we know which setups provide the greatest edge or the best market conditions to execute a specific strategy? There are endless tracking elements that can be tracked in a trading business. The dynamics of price, randomness, and psychology allow for an infinite list of data to be tracked. The objective is to track the information most pertinent to assist in the risk analysis step without hindering your ability to execute your business strategy.

Regular Evaluation of Results

If you have any experience in trading, you will know that trading is a profession that lives in the moment of now. Have you ever heard the phrase, "We are only as good as our last trade"? Some tend to lose confidence after a losing trade, while after a winning trade they get the belief that they are the best traders in the world, only to go back to self-doubt after the next stop-out. Traders need to train themselves to take steps back and see the forest since so much time each day is spent right up against a tree. This requires taking a step away from the charts and performing evaluations to determine plan compliance, key performance results, and to determine if they are progressing to assure your professional goals are being met.

Flexibility to Make Adjustments

The financial markets are a continuously evolving and changing environment. New products are launched while others change their parameters. Regulatory environments are also changing in the face of scrutiny in response to financial crises and government's attempt to create transparency, liquidity, and an equal playing field among market participants.

Gathering Internal and External Feedback

On the top of the list of biggest challenges to individual traders is their ability to obtain unbiased feedback and recognize areas of development. Traders with smaller accounts seek to devote as much capital as possible to their trading accounts and often do not invest in professionals to provide valuable feedback. In today's Internet and social networking world, those in this situation can have other traders act as an independent eye with the agreement of reciprocating the same work for the other. Feedback is one of the oldest tactics in the book purely because it is highly effective. Self-evaluation is much more challenging but can provide valuable information about you and your decision-making process. You'll need to check your ego at the door and be brutally honest about what your data are telling you. Ultimately, a combination of both self- and independent assessment will help you develop as a trader and help reach your trading business goals.

Summarizing Measuring Risk

After you have accumulated several months of trade data, there are hundreds of different ways and combinations in which to measure risk. Chapter 5 takes a closer look at these opportunities, specifically using performance management techniques. You will find there is no limitation as to what you can measure. The key is to gather the information you have obtained in the first four steps so you can properly monitor these risks; thus we come to our fifth and final step in the risk management process.

STEP FIVE: MONITORING YOUR RISK PROGRAM

At first the risk management process components discussed so far may seem overwhelming and confusing. You may be saying, "On top of all this, I have to trade too!" Like trying anything new, this process can be intimidating for some initially. Once the improvement in results and consistency starts to make its way into your P&L statements, motivation to continue using a risk-based approach is greatly enhanced. Identifying, assessing, controlling, and measuring risk are only beneficial, however, if the steps are done on a continuous basis. Risk management is a process and not a task. Some parts of your trading will be in the control phase while other risks will be newly identified and require starting from step one. It is this continuous flow of the five-step process and more importantly, the management of such that constitutes the risk management program. A common question I receive is, "I'm just an individual trader. Can I do this all by myself?" Individual traders certainly can do so, and in many cases, working directly with your own trading data forces you to take greater responsibility for your trading decisions. Individual traders commonly are their own boss and require the tools necessary to succeed in this challenging field. Individuals may not have the manpower or resources to rely on others to guide them toward growth. Coaches or mentors can add great value throughout the risk management process. Simply put, a second set of eyes that isn't positioned deep into the forest can be valuable in providing the advice and knowledge that allows one to be on the success path. I highly encourage an independent resource to assist you, particularly if your trading group has more than two persons or the financial resources to secure such talent. For many, reality limits them to steering the ship on their own, hence the purpose of completing this book.

What is the primary purpose of the monitoring process? We look to the monitoring step to determine if traders are properly identifying, assessing, and controlling the risks that would prevent them from achieving their trading and business goals. In essence, the monitoring step is performed to assure us that we are on the correct path toward success as defined in our business and trading plans. For example, monitoring our key performance indicators might trigger areas worthy of identifying possible barriers to our goals. New risks identified trigger the five-step process to start again. It is this cyclical process that, when mastered, allows trading professionals to reach their goals. I hope you can see that this process is not a project with a start and a finish. This continuous hunger for process improvement and development are the ingredients in the recipe for conquering the markets.

Should we monitor key performance indicators? Sure, that is a logical start. Unfortunately, most traders who do some form of monitoring limit their scope to performance metrics. It is a natural choice since continuous poor performance in trading will generally result in business failure. The monitoring function also serves as an opportunity to be valuable in the non–business performance aspects of your venture. These event-driven occurrences are worthy of review periodically as your business changes or develops. Often they are identified in your quadrant 4 low-frequency/high-severity risks. Here are a few examples to add to the monitoring process:

Business continuity—Perhaps you now trade in a different location or your backup trading location is no longer available? Maybe you are now trading solo after a brief stint with a partner that didn't work out. When was the last time you backed up your data or your platform charting preferences and programming language documents? Have you updated or reviewed your business continuity plan documents lately? It is surprising to notice how quickly your continuity plans become stale. Failure to review your plan on a regular basis is in itself a quad-4 risk.

Pyramid status—You have been trading for some time now and continue to make progress in your confidence and trading results. At what level do you now stand on the pyramid of success? Are you satisfied with your result? How does it compare with your plan goals? Are you ahead of or behind your expectations? As traders we tend to live our daily lives extremely close to the screens and need to be reminded about our larger scale purpose of why we have chosen this business for a living. The monitoring step acts as a reminder to continuously look at the big picture.

Development planning—The monitoring step is also a logical stop to review the actions you are taking to improve as a trader. Many developmental plans focus on improving results. Also consider the education and knowledge required to build your business. Perhaps it is learning about alternative trading products or understanding advanced platform features. Your first challenge on your development plan is to learn and master the risk management process. Fortunately, you have already taken the first step in this area. I have come across development plans that included pledges to improve in time management, discipline-related fears, and even improvements in health. All will make you a better professional and help you with your ultimate business goals. Development plans will be discussed at length in Chapter 8.

Figure 2.5 provides a sample monitoring schedule that provides suggestions on when to review the items in your monitoring process. The key to this task is to allow it to be manageable and understandable. Most importantly, it should allow the trader or coach to identify potential new or continuing risks to your business.

Figure 2.5 is merely an illustration of a monitoring schedule and its elements. As always, it is highly recommended to customize your schedule to meet your business needs. Also consider adjusting the frequency of a particular component or portion thereof, such as a key performance indicator

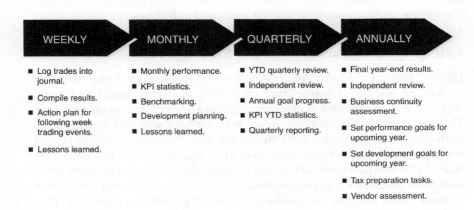

WEEKLY	MONTHLY	QUARTERLY	ANNUALLY
■ Log trades into journal.	■ Monthly performance.	■ YTD quarterly review.	■ Final year-end results.
■ Compile results.	■ KPI statistics.	■ Independent review.	■ Independent review.
■ Action plan for following week trading events.	■ Benchmarking.	■ Annual goal progress.	■ Business continuity assessment.
■ Lessons learned.	■ Development planning.	■ KPI YTD statistics.	■ Set performance goals for upcoming year.
	■ Lessons learned.	■ Quarterly reporting.	■ Set development goals for upcoming year.
			■ Tax preparation tasks.
			■ Vendor assessment.

FIGURE 2.5 Risk Monitoring Schedule for the Trader

should your results or recent activity warrant such. Perhaps you just created your first trading plan and have it set on an annual review schedule. It might be best to review the document quarterly in the first year of trading and then revert to an annual assessment thereafter. Specific events may also warrant adjustment. Consider review of all documents assessed after an independent audit is completed or after you make a major business decision such as taking on a coach, joining a trading room, or entering a partnership. There are no mandated rules regarding monitoring frequency. Practice and experimentation will lead you to the optimal balance of review frequency, allowing the ability to meet your trading goals without the cumbersome burden of frequent auditing.

What are your software options to help manage the program? Consider keeping it relatively simple in the beginning. If you are sophisticated in business analytics or intelligence software, you can consider several options with a wide variety of applications to choose from. In today's tech world, dashboard-based key performance indicators (KPI), project management, and performance management products are developed for businesses with 25,000+ employees or for the individual trading from his or her basement. Many entrepreneurial traders purchase the best in software tools too early in their trading careers. Each product has its own capabilities and constraints that tend to dictate the user's method of recording, reporting, and monitoring risk. A predominant aspect of risk-based trading is that of data analytics. Most of the core work can be done with the most up-to-date office software products. Trading partnerships, proprietary firms, or outfits with multiple traders and stakeholders tend to gravitate toward impressive business intelligence (BI) tools with fascinating reporting options. For the purposes of this discussion, you should focus more on the content of information rather than the format and its transparency or simplicity required to meet your trading goals and objectives.

Enterprise Risk Management and Risk Appetite

By now you should have the perspective that trading risk has really little to do with just the risk you place on a trade or overall stop-loss theory. The scope of trading risk is much broader and diverse than many perceive. This paradigm is the essence of the text. Historically, risk management in the corporate sector focused on risk transfer techniques. Insurance was the risk savior product that screamed, "You take the risk, I'll keep the reward." The first party transferred the risk and the insurance company had a customer. Insurance companies would determine the chance of loss, throw in some profit margins for themselves, and all parties were content. That is, until losses that exceeded expectations occurred. Insurance companies would adjust premium rates to reflect the new exposure. The premium consists of two parts: the cost of the loss and a portion of profit for the insurance company. The idea of transferring risk was and is still an effective form of risk control, and ultimately it is the insured that pays for their losses. Many companies now self-insure a portion of their risks. Whether they believe they could manage risks internally or attempt to keep the excess premiums that represented insurance company profit margin, most companies have a shared-risk structure with insurance companies handling low-frequency/high-severity risks or unforeseen risks. Similar to a deductible on car insurance, the car owner and insurance company share the risk with the car owner usually taking on the initial portion of exposure to a set dollar limit.

As risk management practices evolved, they became more than just a department that managed the company's insurance policies. Risk managers became more in tune to their individualistic corporate characteristics and strengths. During the 1990s, organizations started to take a finer look at these expense-only corporate support roles to determine their value within an organization. The definition of risk transformed from loss minimization toward risk optimization. Questions began to emerge such as, "How can the risk department impact our bottom line?" By the end of the 1990s, a penny saved truly was a penny earned, and quarterly profit–minded companies looked to previously expense-only departments to prove their value propositions toward the bottom line. Risk management was sought out by corporate leaders to play expanded enterprise roles in process improvement, efficiency, and similar roles that impacted profit and loss.

This risk-based approach to trading is no different from the corporate examples mentioned. Enterprise risk management takes this holistic approach toward managing these elements in your trading. It doesn't limit itself to addressing risks that may negatively affect value. It also considers opportunities that may have a positive impact on your business. Anything and everything that may affect the success of your trading career goals is somehow incorporated into this approach. One key element in your ERM plan is to determine your risk appetite, or the level of risk you are willing to absorb to achieve expected gains. Again, this is not about setting a specific risk on a trade. Although rarely written in trading plans, every trader has a risk appetite level. Ask yourself, what is the impact of your capital, business, and personal life if this venture fails? Risk appetites will vary greatly from an experienced and wealthy trader using 2 percent of his or her entire wealth to try trading before getting into another venture versus a beginner who leaves his or her job and takes most of his or her capital to start trading in hopes of immediately supporting a mortgage and a new addition to the family.

There are many factors that make up an individual's risk appetite. Education, capital, goals, family support, organizational skills, and level of desire are some of the components. Individuals who identify risks (pre-assessment) as high impact generally have lower risk appetites as opposed to having a majority of risks one is willing to absorb. Using the five-step process, enterprise risk management allows traders to understand the level of risk they are willing to accept before attempting to be successful.

Some traders have high expectations when starting to trade. A common example is expecting riches to be generated from a small trading account with little experience. Their appetite for risk is equally as high as their rate of failure. Low appetite can also be detrimental for success as a trader. Setting stop losses far too tight, uneasiness about graduating share, or contract size higher after a continued display of success are some examples of this. Some who just have a conservative upbringing could have low appetites for risk and may result in falling short of plan goals. Taking this holistic approach allows one to set realistic goals within one's own risk tolerance framework.

A second aspect of risk that is often overlooked in more traditional structures is that of emergent risks. The ERM approach also considers future risks that may not be anticipated or find correlated relationships between various risks. Traders, like most performance-based roles, look to the past to determine what to look out for and what to learn from. You often see top pro traders give examples about their struggles early in their career. Many have spoken about how many accounts they had blown prior to getting to their current success level. For example, stopping one of your current losing trade setups so as to focus on the current top performer could have an overall negative effect on the long-term trading performance. Also consider the impact from neglect of potential future regulatory tax changes to your trading product.

ERM is an anticipatory approach to risk that considers past lessons learned and potential future roadblocks down the road. Firms located in the World Trade Center during 2001 may have anticipated a prolonged business disruption due to their prestigious address. Evacuation drills and the concern of fire and terrorism were surely included in many emergency response plans. How were separation and segregation issues considered for companies who held their entire operations at the WTC? When constructing your plans, it is prudent to consider all possibilities of potential loss during the risk identification process. One thing for sure, if history continues to repeat itself, the current standards will often be replaced by the "new normal." The ones who really optimize the process discussed in this book are those that have an anticipatory mind-set. They look at their trading, tolerance, and business objectives to create an individualized but holistic framework and often ask themselves, "What can go wrong?" They capture the big picture and continuously take steps back to compare at any given moment where they are in their trading journey and what needs to be done to reach their ultimate business goals.

Summarizing Risk Monitoring

You now have a better understanding of the scope of risk monitoring and how it encapsulates the previous four steps. I'm sure you'll agree that there is a lot more to it than just placing stop-loss orders on trades. The enterprise risk approach is intended to convert such a mind-set to thinking about your entire trading business rather than just a series of trades. Don't expect your monitoring program to be built overnight. As you develop and grow, so will the dynamics of not only your trading business but also your monitoring framework.

SUMMARY

The preceding section discussed the foundation principles of risk management and how it can be applied in trading. The framework of these principles is the five-step process involved in managing risk: identification, assessment, control, measuring, and monitoring of trading risks and the risks inherent in the trading profession. If you understand and put into practice this process, you are well on your way to becoming a better trader. We also discussed the different types of risks and exposures that you are likely to be confronted with. Remember that focusing only on specific risk of loss on a trade is undermining your exposure in trading. You should consider risk in a much broader or enterprise scope.

Since the identification process is the most important step in the risk management process, be sure to know the different methods of identifying your specific areas that not only subject you to loss but prevent you from being at the top of your game. Sources used to identify developmental areas may be found in your trading plan, trade journal, and from review findings completed during the assessment process. Furthermore, you should have a good base of knowledge on constructing your trading plan, an essential piece of framework that statistically improves your chances of success. Before actual trading, you should know the common components of a trading plan and be able to develop rules and filters that should be implemented in a live trading environment.

Determining the potential impact of an identified risk is completed in the risk analysis step. Here we used frequency and severity as an initial exercise to bring to the surface exposures in your trading processes, trade selection, or execution and allow you to prioritize your exposures to loss and survivability as a trader. You may not be able to control or manage these risks, and the control process brings to light the areas of potential or actual loss that you can have an impact on. Before continuing with the text, understand the different types of risk controls (avoidance, prevention, reduction, separation/segregation, duplication, and hedging).

Lastly, we discussed, at an introductory level, the basis of measuring enterprise risk using key performance indicators. Measuring and monitoring of KPI dashboards for the individual trader can be implemented using the same framework as larger institutions in their approach to measuring risk and performance.

Take a few minutes to determine your understanding of these applications and theories by going through the following review questions. Trading like a risk manager and empowering your trading business via a culture of analytics requires the understanding of these risk principles prior to moving forward. See if you can provide examples in your answers other than the ones provided so far in this text. This outside-the-box thinking approach is a common trait among the best traders who continue to keep pace with the ever-changing environment of the trading world.

 REVIEW QUESTIONS

1. Name the five steps in the risk management process and provide an example of each in your current trading environment.

2. List and explain five basic core principles of risk or risk tenets.

3. Provide some examples of how one can identify risks in one's trading.

4. Explain the different risk control techniques and provide an example of each.

5. Explain the benefits of a trade journal and the ability to track trade-related data.

PART II

Managing and Measuring Risk

CHAPTER 3

Predictive Analytics Using Quantitative Analysis

I have reviewed countless trading plans in conjunction with audits of trade activity. Every trader is unique and requires an individual approach on how to improve his or her game. Of course, there are common characteristics of traders in the early and intermediate stages of their development that would allow us to discuss a generic approach to development. The use of quantitative analysis in trading is one of those areas and the focus of this chapter.

There is a wide range of approaches traders can take for using historical trade data and assessing their performance. In many instances, a qualitative approach is justified. Teaching an approach of anything solely reliant on data would be a detrimental and limiting proposition. Traders generally require more than just past performance data to make decisions. Do we make the decision to start a family or choose a partner based on historical data? Not even a seasoned risk manager would do that. Before we dive into quantitative approaches to help improve trading results, let's review a bit more about what quantitative analysis is and the importance of using it in our data-driven approach.

WHAT IS QUANTITATIVE ANALYSIS?

Look up any definition of quantitative analysis and you probably would nod off sleeping before you could finish reading the definition. In broad terms, quantitative analysis is a process of measuring things using data and statistical information. We can quantify the results numerically, thus the term's root name. It can lend purpose to determining past performance and common elements of any type of result as well as help one forecast or predict future results. Any trader who uses technical analysis or charts to determine trading activity is practicing a form of quantitative analysis. Charts are merely a visual to communicate historical data. Even technical indicators such as moving average convergence/divergence (MACD), moving averages, and candlesticks are taking quantitative data and presenting it in a format that allows us to allegedly determine buy and sell opportunities.

One of the true benefits of a quantitative analytical approach to trading is the opportunity to generate greater consistency in your trading decisions. In other words, "quant" traders do not base decisions on what they think will happen to future price movements. They solely rely on historical data to provide information and direction to future trade decision making. When used effectively, data-driven decisions can aid in taking the emotional elements of trading out of the trading plan. Trading with the human elements of fear and emotion has brought down the best of floor traders in addition to not allowing the eager beginner to ever see consistent profits. Executing trades based solely on setups that are quantified to provide a valid edge, at least historically, can provide you with the tools to circumvent the good portion of the emotional risks that play into every trader at one time or another.

Some of the best risk managers in the world are found neither in the trading pits nor behind electronic trading platforms. Nor can they be found in the corporate financial sector's mergers and acquisitions departments. Some of the best examples of risk management in a live setting can be found at the professional poker tables in Las Vegas, Macau, and on the pro circuit. World Series of Poker champion Greg Raymer discussed his approach to risk management and how it helps him remain at the top of his game. "I don't play poker to gamble, I play because I have an edge and only put my money at risk when I have an edge." In one sentence, Raymer defined how we as risk managers trade the markets. His use of knowing the statistical possibilities that present themselves, understanding his chance of loss, and executing when favorable has made him one of the top professionals in poker.

Quantitative analysis allows the trader to focus, or at least provide data on the big picture; a challenge found in many day trades where the analysis and profit objectives are determined by minutes and ticks. Data can be generated and assessed on a macro level to determine if a setup meets the result characteristics that will allow a trader to meet his or her goals consistently and in the long-term. At the same time, we can detect changes in performance or validity of a trade setup before it has a large impact on the trader's bankroll. Most importantly, quantitative analysis allows us to measure anything about our trading numerically and provide direct answers to the following questions:

- How did you perform last week, month, or quarter?
- Is this setup meeting the goals set out in your plan?
- Which part of your trading plan is most beneficial to your P&L?
- What has been the weakest performing setup in your plan over the past week, month, quarter?
- What is the most profitable part of your day?
- What is your win percentage or average gain/loss for each trade setup?

In the trading world, a common introductory phrase among traders is not, "How are you" or "How have you been?" If it is, then it is quickly followed by, "How is your trading going?" A simple question that may not demand a specific answer but rather a suggestive nod to start talking about the profession we love so dearly. How do we answer that question? "Good, hangin' in there." "Just taking what the markets give me." My favorite was a trader I knew who commonly responded, "Just cruising along!" Still to this day I haven't a clue what that means. Answering the simple question of "How are you doing?" in a quantifying state allows you to clarify not only to the questioner but more importantly to yourself. Answering trader status questions quantitatively can be a tremendous asset in the risk identification process, too. "I am meeting my trading goals so far this month with the exception of one trade setup that is well below my expectations. I have been getting hammered in the last hour of trading recently." The first phase of moving into a data-driven world is to start speaking in data-driven terms.

Data-Driven Trade Talk

The following dialogue takes a look at how to gear the mind toward thinking like a data-driven trading professional.

Question 1: How did you perform last week, month, or quarter?

A: Hanging in there.

Quantitative Answer: Last week I had a 63 percent win return, right on target and my P&L and risk-to-reward scenarios were also aligned with target overall.

Question 2: Is this setup meeting your goals set out in your plan?

A: I love my #2 setup.

Quantitative Answer: This setup is slightly below target results, but I neglected to take this setup all the time last month due to the lower summer volume. All is on track, and I continue to maintain this valid setup as an integral part of my plan.

Question 3: Which part of your trading plan is most beneficial to your P&L?

A: My #4 setup is killing it!

Quantitative Answer: My #4 setup continues to outperform all other setups for the seventh month in a row.

Question 4: What has been the weakest performing setup in your plan over the past week, month, quarter?

A: Market (expletive) lately.

Quantitative Answer: My #4 setup. Since the increased volatility in the Euro/U.S. Dollar currency pair (EURUSD), my data suggest my stops may need to be widened due to the increase in stop-outs this past quarter. I have identified it as a risk, and I am running it through the risk management process to determine the necessary actions I need to take.

Question 5: What is the most profitable part of your day?

A: Morning sessions.

Quantitative Answer: My data results show Tuesday and Friday are the best performing days with the 10:15–noon time slot continuing to be the best time frame this past month, quarter, and YTD.

Question 6: What is your win percentage or average gain/loss for each trade setup?

A: Pretty good, I think?

Quantitative Answer: YTD I am averaging 61 percent successful trades with an average net gain of 2.5 points in the S&P 500 index futures. More importantly, I am over 97 percent compliant in regard to taking the setups in my plan when my plan tells me to execute them.

This exercise at first may appear to be futile. But by starting to communicate quantitatively, you are taking the initial steps to continuously think in the same manner and framework. Of course, any audience requires responding in a manner that is acceptable and comfortable. Expressing quant data to grandma who pays a holiday visit would come across as inappropriate, to say the least; of course, unless she trades the grains. My premise here is to get you in the habit of asking these questions and answering them quantitatively. You can also practice when communicating with other traders or at trader conferences. Notice how they react when you answer with such clarity.

One of the first steps of trading like a risk manager is to get an understanding of the importance of quantifying anything that is quantifiable or measurable. Dr. Brett Steenbarger, a popular trader psychologist and coach, encourages traders to measure everything in their trading journey. I could not agree more. Start by not only thinking quantitatively but also by speaking in the same manner.

THE DATA-DRIVEN RISK MANAGER

Successful traders or those seeking success make business and trading decision that in their view will lead them to their expected trading goals. A risk manager's role is no different. We implement a plan using a decision-making process based on knowledge that has historically provided an anticipated result. We forecast what our projected result will be and attempt to execute business decisions to reach those results. Forecasts are nothing more than a projection of a future result. That result can be a trade outcome, a business decision, or an overall business plan goal. Sounds easy, right? But what separates forecasts from actual results? Noise? Distractions? Lack of discipline? Sure, all of the above. These are all immobilizers that prevent anticipated results from occurring. Immobilizers are in essence the brick wall that separates a trader from forecasted results vs. actual results. A primary principle of risk management is that we are surrounded by unpredictability. Things happen; stupidity happens, surprises happen, unforeseen events happen.

The mind-set of a risk manager is to anticipate unpredictability in many forms. We thrive on it as if it is part of a journey. When negative outcomes don't occur, we actually get concerned. During winning streaks when it seems you can do no wrong, traders tend to feel invincible, particularly the novice traders. Their euphoria takes over, and they coin themselves the kings and queens of trading. Risk managers think quite differently. They often anticipate the market dragon coming with a 5–15 win/loss record on perfectly executed trades. I'm quite the positive person, but the risk manager inside of me understands that randomness and unpredictability always loom in the markets and will eventually play their hand. All we can and need to do is to continuously manipulate edge from our data. That is our role in trading. It's nothing more and nothing less.

Predicting outcomes requires detecting consistent evidence of results in the past that, given similar circumstances, will provide similar results in the future. Since the participants and events that comprise a market and its continuous price movement are always different, the ability to predict with an exact level of precision is virtually impossible. News events, scheduled or unscheduled, are released in real time or an institution will unload a dog stock that they finally have given up on. This list of unforeseen events is immeasurable. Once an immeasurable event becomes measurable, another unforeseen event occurs to assure market randomness. But what we have to bring home is historical data. It's not a perfect science, but it's what we have. It's what we can dissect and manipulate to determine if it will aid us in our journey. This combination of quantitative data plus the understanding of market uncertainty is all we really need to possess in order to be profitable. The most important and essential element to quantitative analysis is our trade data, contained in the following elements.

The reality is that rarely will you have trade data history that meets all of these requirements. We accept this as traders and certainly as risk managers. Your data set does not have to be perfectly complete, consistent, or cover all bear and bull markets since the Reagan administration. The hope is that this book will inspire the need to start tracking trade data and then improving in each category. All that is required is that it is growing in its depth and effectiveness as you develop as a professional trader.

If you currently are not tracking your trades or do so in a limited manner, take the time now to think about what data elements you currently track or would like to know more about. We will shortly take a more in-depth look to discuss specifically what minimum data elements you should be capturing, how we obtain trade data, and how we set the assurances that we can meet the above data criteria within a reasonable level of quality and compliance.

REVIEW QUESTIONS

1. What is the definition of quantitative analysis?
2. What is an example of a trading immobilizer, and how can it impact results?
3. What are two examples of a forecasting result in a trading business?

CHAPTER 4

Statistical Edge and Its Impact on Risk

T hroughout the book so far, the term "edge" has been referenced several times. Statistical edge, mathematical edge, trader's edge, everything edge. Traders use the term quite often as a synonym for advantage. When referring to specific trade setups, *edge* is used to define any trade that has a greater than 50 percent (perceived) chance of reaching a certain price target, or having one outcome occurring over another during a valid sample of trades. Corey Rosenbloom, a successful trader and author of *The Complete Trading Course* (John Wiley & Sons, 2011), uses the concept of edge as a dominant principle in his trading success. Risk theorists and data-analytical traders base their trading plans on a similar theory. Rosenbloom defines edge as the "inherent price levels that a pattern provides as an entry, stop-loss, and target, where the target is always larger than the stop-loss." In his definition, notice how the author incorporates the element of risk-to-reward into his defined criteria to allow you an edge in your overall success as a trader and not just on any given trade. In summary, you can have a statistical edge on any given trade but can have your account depleted if the elements of risk and reward are not properly incorporated into your trade decisions.

Let's look at the following example comparing generic edge on a trade, its impact on trade outcome, and your overall success as a trader. For this example, outlined in Table 4.1, we will use a historical winning trade success rate of 55 percent.

As you can see in Table 4.1, edge is a powerful concept in trading; however, it is a recipe for failure if risk management concepts such as risk-to-reward are not factored in. Here we have a trader who "won"

TABLE 4.1   Comparing Edge and Trade Outcomes

Purchase	Target	Stop
100 shares @ $100.00	$105.00	$90.00
Statistical Win Rate: 55%	Profitable Trades: 550	Stop-Out Trades: 450
(1,000 trades in sample)		
Total Gain:	550 × $5.00	$2,750
Total Loss:	450 × $10.00	−$4,500
Net Gain/Loss:		−($1,750)

55 percent of the trades but lost account value overall. This dominance of winning percentage as a stand-alone measure of success is vastly overstated in many individual trade reports and in conversation. It is so merely because win percentage in a vacuum tells us little about the overall success of the trader. This is the one of the more common mistakes new traders make. Having a trade setup with a winning edge is virtually meaningless and quite dangerous if the risk components are not considered. Measuring win percentage is an excellent internal indicator of setup validation; however, as a stand-alone, it is a poor performance metric. If this is so, then why is it spoken about and touted so often? Trader education firms often use this promotion of edge in their marketing materials. "Eighty-three percent winning success rate! Average 70 percent winning trades over a five-year period!" The results are meaningless if the risk components are not considered. Buyer beware!

Regarding risk to reward, I have worked with successful traders who have a 77 percent winning trade rate and also some options traders whose 25 percent winning trade rate allows them to support their families equally alike. Both are successful, not specifically due to their winning percentage, but their ability to manage their risk using proven setups that provide them with an edge. The options trader has a tremendous edge if the one winning trade out of every four pays for eight losing trades. Conversely, traders with 1:1 risk–reward ratios (for example: $5 targets with $5 risk) can lead nice lifestyles with a 60–65 percent historically successful win rate. You would expect a risk-based trader to promote more of a 3:1, 5:1, or even 10:1 risk-to-reward ratio or at least require a 2:1 ratio. I have often received banter on this subject that no trader should risk more than the profit potential on any given trade. At first glance it does make sense. Of course you wouldn't want to risk more than you can gain. Table 4.2 shows how to consider using historical win percentages in the analysis to determine valid risk-to-reward ratios. Notice how it paints quite a different picture than those requiring extreme ratios in order to be successful.

TABLE 4.2 Risk-to-Reward Ratio Comparison Chart

Setup #	Reward	Risk	1:1 Reward	Win %	Wins	Losses	Gain
1	4	1	$100.00	25%	24	76	$2,000.00
2	3	1	$100.00	30%	30	70	$2,000.00
3	2	1	$100.00	40%	40	60	$2,000.00
4	1	1	$100.00	60%	60	40	$2,000.00
5	1	2	$100.00	70%	73	27	$2,000.00
6	1	3	$100.00	80%	80	20	$2,000.00

Notice that in this example, six different setups with different win percentages and six different risk-to-reward ratios provided the same overall profits. Minimum risk-to-reward ratio discussions are continuously debated, and as long as there are traders, the debate will probably continue. For those in the developmental stage trading stocks, indexes, or futures, it is important to follow this maximum risk-to-reward principle:

Only at the professional level and with near 100 percent compliant trade execution should you be risking more than 1:1 risk-to-reward. In other words, you are risking no more than $1 to potentially gain $1. Once you have achieved a level of execution consistency and are continually generating trading revenue, you can then explore a different mix of ratios on trades with consistent win percentages exceeding 60 percent.

FINDING EDGE

Now that we have a clearer picture of what this edge or advantage is in trading, how do we search for it? Where do we find it?

When asked this question at trading expositions, the number one answer I receive is, "From the charts." Chart patterns are an excellent visual source of potential edge. Remember our definition: one outcome occurring more than another outcome over a series of attempts. Any chart pattern using similar parameters that result in price movement in one direction greater than the other direction can be a solid source of edge. Here are some other areas where you can obtain or detect this advantage:

- **Education**—A trader's experience and knowledge in itself can provide an edge that results in more favorable outcomes over a negative outcome. There truly is no substitution for knowledge of the markets and perfecting your craft as a trader. This development is a continuous process, and there never is a graduation day as a trader. The markets continue to evolve, and the best traders, like most other successful people, continuously strive to develop and improve.

- **Price movement**—Chart patterns in its simplest form are price movements plotted in a visual form. Market price moves merely because of more buyers than sellers or vice versa. Price movements and even stagnant prices often forecast future movements in price that can produce a predictable direction, thus providing trader edge.
- **Inflection points**—For any given series of reasons, price tends to react at areas of inflection. They may be at prior support or resistance, a point of control, a moving average, or at a price area generated from one of many technical tools, such as a Fibonacci price level. Applying predictive analytics at these inflection points often presents several opportunities that provide a trader with an advantage.
- **Trader panic**—Often there are occurrences where the market participants themselves can create opportunities that provide edge. Small-lot traders tend to panic out of markets that test their patience. These levels of panic are often the time of price peaks or exhaustion, thus creating opportunities for consistent positive outcomes. The most common products to prey on using such panic can be found in individual equities with relatively small volume and in the index futures markets.
- **Trade history**—A majority of risk-based trade opportunities will be generated using your own trade data. This valuable pool of information is used to detect opportunities that historically have provided a consistent level of edge for the trader. The following chapters of this text focus on generating such data-driven trading strategies.

Edge, by definition, has a binary outcome. Either you have a statistical edge, as defined as the greater chance of something occurring rather than not occurring, or you do not. A core component of the edge principle for a trader is of course the probability of such an edge during a trade. Even more prominent is the determination of the frequency that such edge is expected to occur. Does a trader have a set advantage on a trade setup each time it is entered? Is the advantage lessened during times of higher or lower volatility or during news events? Does the time of day have an impact on edge and to what extent?

Probability analysis is a technique that can be used in an attempt to forecast the likelihood of a trade being successful. Given the nature of the markets (the randomness theory comes to mind again), the ability to predict trade outcomes and its relative accuracy is limited. It's important to understand that any type of forecasting or projecting the probability of anything occurring in the future has its limitations. Quarterly earnings forecasts from top companies with teams of financial analysts, not to mention independent Wall Street analysts with the best forecasting tools, often miss the mark. Some of the largest casino houses in the world can miss an earnings forecast because of one wealthy individual who bucked the house statistical edge at the baccarat table one lucky weekend. A proverbial flip of a coin rarely alternates between sides in any given series of attempts.

For the average trader or firm, all we can do is use the information we have and principles of edge to predict outcomes within an acceptable variable range, given a valid historical sample and normalized trading conditions.

Let's dig deeper into this statement to understand what we are up against. The combination of using past data to predict future results is very powerful and effective. Risk-based traders using data analytical concepts can be found in a plethora of successful black box and algorithmic trading programs that exist in the marketplace today. Their ability to take advantage of (and some will argue to manipulate) edge is the success model of many institutional and hedge fund firms. One of the most challenging concepts to grasp is that edge is generally determined within a series of trades. I have dealt with many traders who struggle because of their inability to understand such variability in their trading. Of course, having a continuously consistent edge in trading will lessen the concern of the average trader, even during a bad stretch. But even the best of traders have periods when their edge has not only diminished but also disappeared. Sometimes it was a fault in their own business and trading process, other times it was the market variability and randomness that takes hold, similar to the casino that now regrets sending the complimentary invitation to the baccarat customer noted earlier.

One of the barriers of success to many new traders is their lack of acceptance to such variability beyond their expected parameters. Sometimes the best trade under the most optimal conditions will not provide the expected outcome. Other times you will forego on a valid setup for a variety of reasons, and price easily reaches your target without you. There needs to be an understanding and acceptance that probability analysis is not an exact science in an environment with such variability and randomness. Our goal as risk managers is to use the tools and information available to us to forecast our outcomes, not to predict an outcome but to determine an edge. Each time we press the entry button, we do so because we have a range of expected probability within a level of confidence dictated to us over a period of time. When this edge and probability is detected, our role is that of a task manager—to execute continuously to obtain the rewards of such edge when the markets are ever so kind as to present them to us.

Unlike in casino or other games of chance, the challenge we have as traders is determining a clear and accurate advantage. In casino games, where the definition of speculative risk (chance of loss or gain) applies equally, casinos use theoretical probabilities to assure a house edge. For example, slot machines are programmed to produce an edge to the house. Roulette is a great example where the casino pays 36–1 when the ball lands on a specific number. Unfortunately for the player, the board has 37 and on some boards 38 numbers. These odds are not implied per se but mathematically set since they are based on theoretical probability principles of mathematics rather than based on a historical database on past spins. This separation of probability theorems is important for the trader to understand and distinguish. A discussion with a group of traders rarely goes by without the analogy of trading and gambling. There are many similarities due to their similar capital risk for reward standards. The commonalities should cease there and not be inclusive of theoretical probabilities.

Trading falls under a more empirical umbrella, or probabilities, which are deducted from historical data. Unlike theoretical probability, these probabilities can vary over time as new information is added to the data pool. Given these differentials and variables, such as in the financial markets, empirical probabilities can and often do change, whereas theoretical probabilities are generally fixed. Placing a chip on a roulette wheel has an instant theoretical probability vs. one who places a trade. The trader must rely on probabilities based on past results in a similar environment. How one would define "similar" in a marketplace is challenging since by its own nature it presents different variables and participants at any given time. This differential in probability is what makes the job of a trader much more difficult to succeed in the long term as opposed to a player in theoretical probability, such as in a casino. Granted, houses of chance have other operational challenges that many traders do not, such as staff, entertainment, and industry competition. From purely a probability theory standpoint, trading would be a much easier and profitable venue if only theoretical probability principles applied.

REDUCING VARIABILITY IN EMPIRICAL PROBABILITY

Now that the doom and gloom theories have been set upon us, there are still some methods for using historical data to determine the probability and edge with relative accuracy. To move forward with a trading plan to include trade setups that can be expected to provide edge, we need to review history in order to plan a strategy. The common trading phrase, "Look to the left in order to be right," applies perfectly here. Its meaning stems from viewing a price chart to determine the next price movement. Let's take a look at some of the concepts that will help detect edge and the amount of advantage on any given trade opportunity.

Continuing with our simple coin toss example, each of the two possible outcomes has an equal probability of occurring. There are only two

TABLE 4.3 Probability Distribution of Total Points on One Roll of Two Dice

Total Points	Probability
2	1/36 or 2.8%
3	2/36 or 5.6%
4	3/36 or 8.3%
5	4/36 or 11.1%
6	5/36 or 13.9%
7	**6/36 or 16.7%**
8	5/36 or 13.9%
9	4/36 or 11.1%
10	3/36 or 8.3%
11	2/36 or 5.6%
12	1/36 or 2.8%

possible outcomes on any given flip, heads or tails, or whatever imagery lies on your particular coin. No magic here. There is a 50 percent chance of either outcome on each flip. It is expected that 50 percent of the time, heads will come up, and 100 percent of the time heads or tails will result, since there are only two potential outcomes.

What happens to our ability to project future results when there are more than two potential outcomes? Let's expand this probability using two six-sided dice commonly used in the casino game of craps. You do not need to know the intricacies of the game in order to grasp the concept of probable distribution. What you need to understand is that on any given trade, there are more than two potential outcomes, as in the coin flip.

Let's review the statistical probability of the total points when throwing both dice (Table 4.3).

Notice that the number 7 is the most common outcome when rolling both dice simultaneously. The theoretical outcome is 16.7 percent, or on average a 7 will come out 16.7 times for every 100 throws of the dice. The reason the number 7 has the highest frequency is that regardless of the first die outcome, there is a one in six chance that the second die will land on a number that will result in the combination of both dice totaling 7. Outcomes of 6 or 8 have a lower probability of 13.9 percent. This is the result of having one side of the initial die eliminating the chance of these totals occurring. For example, if a 6 is rolled on the first die, it eliminates the chance that 6 will be the total result of both dice. If a 1 is rolled on the first die, then any number that is rolled on the subsequent die cannot total the number 8. This reduces the potential of these numbers occurring and thus the lower probability of occurring when compared to the 7. You will notice similar reductions in probability for the dice rolling outcomes for the

5 and 9, 4 and 10, 3 and 11, and 2 and 12. The game of craps incorporates higher payouts on these combinations to attract wagers even though their likely outcome is less than a 7.

How does this concept affect a trader's ability to gain edge on a trade? Let's look at our coin toss example using two trade setups that have a theoretical 50 percent success rate. We know that if we continuously trade this pattern, price movement, or event that describes the "heads" trade setup, we should be successful 50 percent of the time and be unsuccessful the other 50 percent. As you can already assume, this will not get you too far in your trading career unless, however, the rewards of each are greater than the risk. In our dice example, suppose we had 11 setups, each represented by our 11 potential outcomes. At first glance, it would not take long to choose setup #7 as your setup with the most potential. Unlike the "heads" setup, this trade only has a success rate of 16.7 percent. The amount of expected reward would have to be at least six times the amount of risk placed on the trade before you could even consider it a trade with edge. Successful options traders make their living taking advantage of such risk-to-reward on actual trade success rates similar to the 16.7 percent discussed.

The challenge with these distributions is that they are done in a theoretical environment. Flipping coins and shooting dice have fixed precalculated outcome formulas commonly found in games of chance or casino games. The foundation for casino gaming risk management is to provide a fixed theoretical environment and a payout structure to assure a house edge. For example, perhaps on a coin flip game, the house pays out 95 percent of the wagered amount or $1.90 for every $1 wagered. Or perhaps in the craps game, the casino only pays out a 5:1 reward where the theoretical payout should be 6:1. There's a reason why casinos have nice chandeliers hanging from their ceilings.

Unlike the trading environment, casinos have an extremely accurate mathematical ability to forecast probable outcome. How can that be? The reason is that these examples provide theoretical probabilities and not empirical probabilities. Does the outcome of the coin toss change if it is done using a heavier coin or perhaps in a bright room? Does the probability distribution of dice change when thrown on a craps table vs. a kitchen table? A nervous coin flipper worried about profit and loss? These variables have no impact on theoretical probabilities.

Wouldn't it be nice to be able to project trade outcomes with such accuracy? The simple answer is that it cannot predict to the exact degree of theoretical outcomes, but it can improve your ability to predict outcomes nonetheless. Trading is not a theoretical probability game. You can compare the luck of blackjack to a good trading run, but the endless beginning trader attempts to replicate a trading system in continuously different market conditions is needlessly futile. Trading is different in that it is affected by external factors: the number of traders, the volume, market sentiment, computer programs, support/resistance, and news, to name a few. In fact, while almost nothing outside theoretical probability affects the ultimate outcome, empirical probability activities such as practically every form of stimuli imaginable does affect trading. Human psychology such as fear, money supply, news events, and even weather affects price movement and ultimately trade success or loss. So what can a trader use to help achieve a level of predictive results when theoretical probability methods will not work? Let's discuss some of these ideas.

Before we discard the theoretical components, let's use some key concepts in the distribution method to help predict outcomes. The law of large numbers theory states that the more frequently an independent occurrence occurs, the closer the actual result will be in relation to the theoretical result. Simply stated, a larger sample size will generate a more accurate probability, thus allowing one to predict an outcome (and edge) with greater confidence. Back to our coin flipping: It's not impossible to have 4, 5, 10, even 15 flips land on the same side consecutively. Rarely does a coin flip result in an alternating heads then tails fashion. The key component of determining theoretical probability is volume of trials. The greater the sample of flips, the greater chance that the result is a 50–50 split between heads and tails. Go to any craps table and you will almost never see a 7 rolled precisely every six rolls. Streaks of "no-seven" go more than 20–30, even 50 rolls at times, only to be followed by 7's six times in a row. The law of large numbers confirms that the larger the number of trials, in this case dice thrown, the greater chance of the 7 occurring 16.7 percent of the time.

CRITERIA FOR DETERMINING EDGE

The greater the quantity of our sample size, the better chance we have of accurately determining our edge. Sample sizing is a powerful component to determining a probable outcome and is an essential to any valid back-testing plan. The law of large numbers goal is not intended to precisely predict a future outcome but merely to reduce the differential of the expected outcome vs. the actual one. Just because the ever-changing variables of the market are at work, providing a variance that even the best traders cannot detect, we can use a valid sample size to aid in detecting edge. In order for a historical sample to be considered eligible for possible detection of edge, we must be sure our historical tests meet the following criteria:

1. The historical trades used in the sample have occurred under nearly identical market conditions.

    Since market dynamics are ever-changing, this places strict limits on how accurate historical trade data can truly be. As risk managers, we can take trade activity during "normal" markets and optimize the ability to help predict future outcomes. We can eliminate trades that occurred during announced news events or other times of extreme market volatility unless you are looking to establish a historical outcome using such parameters. In this example, you can create a sample from trades that only occur during news events. In this case, the news event is the normal market condition that we are seeking. On the flip side, extracting historical trade data during extreme conditions such as those taking place during the September 11 event or the "flash crash" day in 2010 is prudent in obtaining identical market conditions.

2. Similar trade outcomes can be expected to occur in the future under those same conditions.

   It is not just similar market conditions that are required for historical performance to reflect future performance. Other variables such as trader psychology can result in a variation from expected results. Traders perform very differently when their bankroll is diminished or when they are on an adverse losing streak. For the laws of large numbers concept to add value, the expectation for similar results to occur must be in place. A change in exchange policy or taking historical data on one index and anticipating similar expectations from history will diminish any law of large numbers considerably. Remember that market randomness alone can minimize and even negate any trade history with a trading edge even with similar market conditions.

3. The trades must be independent of one another and be a part of a valid sample.

   The large number principle implies that as the number of trades increase, the actual result distribution more nearly approaches the historical distributed result. Once again, not only is it is imperative that the historical trade data is gathered from market conditions similar to that which is expected in the marketplace but the sample contains a minimum quantity of transactions, allowing the sample to be considered valid.

OBTAINING A VALID SAMPLE SIZE

A general principle of sample sizing is that the larger the number of records in your database to measure, the greater level of precision you will obtain. This sample does not have to be limited to your trade history logs. A sample of chart patterns, candlestick bars, price reactions to stochastic extremes are all examples of items that can be back-tested in your quest for success. All things considered, access to a large database of transactions in all market conditions does not always provide a realistic or optimal result. For one, reviewing such a large number of records, even with the use of analytics software, can be time consuming. Your time as a trader is precious and can be used performing other tasks related to your business. It can also be costly if you have a coach, auditor, or risk professional perform these for you. Rarely should your entire trade database be used or should you backtest a pattern over several decades. To the contrary, a small sample such as the one in our coin flip test may provide a wide range of results if we only flipped it 10–15 times.

For a hedge fund or proprietary desks, it is suggested that extended stratified sampling methods be considered. The reason is twofold. Since the assets at risk are commonly higher and from multiple investment sources, such entities should have the advanced tools to support the capital at risk. Furthermore, these infrastructures often require more scrutiny and reporting to multiple stakeholder levels, auditors, and perhaps regulatory agencies, whose level of compliance is higher than that of the individual day trader. Without getting into an in-depth course on statistical sampling, stratification, or extended standard deviation methodologies, we will focus on how you can determine the optimal size of records to review in order to have confidence that your results provide support in your edge discovery process.

Our primary goal in determining our sample size is to obtain an adequate number of records for review that contain the three components that will provide us at least 95 percent certainty that these results will occur in future samples. Having a confidence interval with integrity allows the best traders to stay focused after a series of negative outcomes because they are willing to let the probabilities play out over time. Should the situation require a higher confidence rating, such as 97.5 percent or 99 percent, you would be required to increase your sample size. In summary, having an adequate number of trials to validate the proper testing size allows us to assume with relative assurance that that the expected result will occur. The challenge is to have a large enough sample size to give you an accurate result but not too large so that it costs you lots of capital and time should you test it in a live environment. Too large a sample is also of little value since the extra trials will have little impact on determining your average edge and variance of the sample result. Insurance companies and actuaries use the law of large numbers to ensure a normal distribution when determining premium rates for their products. Traders should do the same but within a more manageable scale using reasonable sample sizes. All that traders need is a large enough sample size so their edge has the expectation to repeat a similar result with minimal variance. Table 4.4 provides a basic guideline sample size reference based on a 95 percent confidence interval. If you are not performing risk analytics for a hedge or proprietary firm, the 95 percent confidence sample should suffice nicely.

TABLE 4.4 Determining a Value Sample Size

Number of Trades or Opportunities	95% Confidence Level
30	28
50	44
75	63
100	80
150	108
200	132
250	152
300	169
400	196
500	217
600	234
700	248
800	260
900	269
1,000	278
1,200	291
1,500	306
2,000	322
2,500	333
3,500	346
5,000	357
7,500	365
10,000	370
25,000	378
50,000	381
75,000	382
100,000	383

In this example, using a database of 5,000 trades, one only needs to sample 357 of them to obtain the average results with a 95 percent confidence level.

Based on the sample size chart in Table 4.4, if the sample size was 400, we would only need to sample 196 records to assure with 95 percent confidence that our sample results would equal the total population. In conclusion, this sample size diagram is designed to provide a guideline as to the number of records required to review in order to obtain a valid sample size.

Let's now take this information and apply it to the trading desk. Let's review a simple trade journal to determine how we can predict with 95 percent confidence that a similar result will occur in the future. Our first task is to obtain some basic averages. In Figure 4.1, we use a basic

	No. Shares Purchased	Trade Results	Reward	:Risk
1	100	1.00	2	:1
2	100	−1.00	2	:1
3	100	−1.00	3	:1
4	100	1.50	1	:1
5	100	1.35	1	:1
6	100	−1.00	2	:1
7	100	1.00	1	:1
8	100	1.40	2	:1
9	100	−1.00	1	:1
10	100	−2.00	1	:1
11	100	1.20	2	:1
12	100	−1.00	2	:1
13	100	1.25	1	:1
14	100	−1.00	3	:1
15	100	1.00	1	:1
16	100	1.50	1	:1
17	100	−1.00	3	:1
18	100	1.00	1	:1
19	100	1.00	2	:1
20	100	2.00	1	:1
21	100	−1.00	1	:1
22	100	1.65	1	:1
23	100	−1.00	3	:1
24	100	1.75	1	:1
25	100	1.00	1	:1

Net Pts.	8.60	
Ave. Trade	0.344	
Risk:Reward		1.6 :1

Wins	14	56%
Loss	11	44%
Total Trades	25	

FIGURE 4.1 Finding Averages in a Sample Trade Journal

arithmetic mean or traditional average by taking the sum of the point results and dividing by the number of records.

In Figure 4.1, notice our series of twenty-five trades resulted in a net positive gain of 8.60 points, or on average, 0.344 points per trade. Our win rate was 56 percent with an average risk-to-reward ratio of 1.6:1 for this sample series.

In our attempt to determine central tendency, or a single outcome that is the most representative of all the outcomes in the sample, it is often more revealing to calculate the median rather than the traditional mean average. The median is simply determining the value "in the middle" of the data set (half of the figures lie below it and half lie above it). Thus in the sample of 25 in Figure 4.1, we choose the trade result that ranked 13th when sorted highest result to lowest result. This can be easily accomplished with one click by using the sort functionality on an Excel sheet as shown in Figure 4.2. For traders, it is often of more value to use this method of calculating averages since it tends to limit its effect on severe trade outliers, or those extreme trade results, positive or negative, that can skew the averages and provide a less accurate representation of the sample.

In this example, these trade results show an average gain of $0.34 per trade and a median gain of $1.00 per trade. In addition, the win percentage, although not as critical in value as point gain/loss, showed a win result of 56 percent. From a performance standpoint, this win percentage is not extremely important; however, it is important from an edge standpoint since it validates that the components that comprise the setup do have a positive occurrence outcome, or at least it does in this modest sample. Also note that the average and median risk-to-reward was 1.6:1 and well within the range of compliance on setups with a positive outcome and positive occurrence. This example shows a positive edge in results, risk-to-reward, and positive occurrence outcome, or the number of times it was successful vs. a stop-out trade. When all three of these powerhouses are finding their way into your trade results for a particular setup, you clearly have detected edge and should focus more efforts on taking advantage of these market opportunities.

Now let's look at these same results and compare them to actual trading opportunities. The challenge and limiting effect one has when auditing one's trade journal is that the sample size is limited to outcomes based on the trader's decision to implement them. They take no consideration for any trades that should have been executed. Did you bypass a trade due to fear? Perhaps you left the desk to take a break? A true risk manager not only measures outcomes but also compares them to opportunities provided. A majority of the work of a risk manager in trading encompassed these assessments to determine "gaps" in not only trading performance but also trade execution compliance.

Trade #	No. Shares Purchased	Trade Results	Reward	:Risk	
10	100	–2.00	1	:1	
2	100	–1.00	2	:1	
3	100	–1.00	3	:1	
6	100	–1.00	2	:1	
9	100	–1.00	1	:1	
12	100	–1.00	2	:1	
14	100	–1.00	3	:1	
17	100	–1.00	3	:1	
21	100	–1.00	1	:1	
23	100	–1.00	3	:1	
1	100	1.00	2	:1	
7	100	1.00	1	:1	
Median 15	100	1.00	1	:1	**Median**
18	100	1.00	1	:1	
19	100	1.00	2	:1	
25	100	1.00	1	:1	
11	100	1.20	2	:1	
13	100	1.25	1	:1	
5	100	1.35	1	:1	
8	100	1.40	2	:1	
4	100	1.50	1	:1	
16	100	1.50	1	:1	
22	100	1.65	1	:1	
24	100	1.75	1	:1	
20	100	2.00	1	:1	

FIGURE 4.2 Finding the Median in a Sample Trade Journal

Let's look again at the same results but compare them to the actual opportunities that were provided in the market during this time period. For discussion purposes, all trades listed here were in compliance with the trader's trading plan and were required to be executed (Figure 4.3).

As you can see, this data set using market activity rather than trade results shows a different picture. Notice how seven trades were missed during the same period. What we can determine from this comparative analysis is that the current plan components that generated the actual results appear to be a valid plan setup with positive confluence of results and risk-to-reward. Inconsistency in trade implementation, however, is also detected in the assessment, resulting in an additional 4.50 points in profit

	No. Shares Purchased	Trade Results	Reward	:Risk
1	100	1.00	2	:1
2	100	−1.00	2	:1
3	100	−1.00	3	:1
4	100	1.50	1	:1
5	100	1.35	1	:1
6	100	−1.00	2	:1
7	100	−1.00	2	:1
8	100	1.00	1	:1
9	100	1.40	2	:1
10	100	−1.00	1	:1
11	100	−2.00	1	:1
12	100	1.20	2	:1
13	100	1.50	1	:1
14	100	−1.00	2	:1
15	100	1.25	1	:1
16	100	−1.00	3	:1
17	100	1.25	1	:1
18	100	1.00	1	:1
19	100	1.50	1	:1
20	100	−1.00	3	:1
21	100	1.00	1	:1
22	100	1.00	2	:1
23	100	2.00	1	:1
24	100	1.00	1	:1
25	100	−1.00	1	:1
26	100	1.75	1	:1
27	100	1.65	1	:1
28	100	−1.00	3	:1
29	100	1.00	1	:1
30	100	1.75	1	:1
31	100	1.00	1	:1
32	100	−1.00	2	:1

Net Points	13.10		
Ave. Result	0.409		
Average Risk-to-reward		1.5	:1

Wins	19	59%
Loss	13	41%
Total Trades	32	

FIGURE 4.3 Determining Results for a Specific Trade Setup

that was left on the table. In addition, the average risk-to-reward dropped slightly to 1.5:1, showing the additional gains came at less overall risk than the initial 25 trades. Clearly there are developmental opportunities for this trader; however, one might not have known that solely based on the sample results. Reducing this deficiency and optimizing your trade execution parameters so as to implement your plan with near 100 percent compliance is what separates the pros from the newbies.

PROBABLE EDGE VS. POSSIBLE EDGE

It is common for those outside the trading arena to talk about this profession in the same realm of casino gambling. In fact, there are many similarities with trading and your favorite game of chance. We discussed the relationship between the two earlier in determining edge when rolling dice and playing roulette. Both encompass the elements of placing monies at risk with an expectation of a return. There is one unique difference between a gambler and a trader that supports the core need for risk management.

Casual gamblers think about the *possibility* of something occurring while professional traders think of the *probability* of the event occurring. Do you agree? Most professional gamblers would agree with this statement too. The distinction was obvious during my work with new traders. They tend to think about the possibility of becoming rich, successful, and one day trading at their beach homes or running a large hedge fund. They grasp at every trade setup that someone else has been (or at least told others that they were) successful with. They just want setups that work. Two S&P futures points per day. That's it. In their mind, it allows them the possibility of becoming successful.

If you talk with professional gamblers or traders, you immediately notice they have a worklike attitude when describing their craft. They wake up, go to work, and do their thing. When talking about trade setups or how they win at blackjack or poker, their answer tends to be calculated and includes the use of probabilities. They all have their share of bad days but continue to take advantage of the edge that is provided by their respective markets.

Take a few moments to think about this distinction. Take notice of your words and conversations with other traders. Which one do you tend to reflect? This entire text is devoted to practicing the art of risk management in trading. Risk management encompasses both probability and possibility. Our earlier exercise in frequency and severity is an example of such. When determining edge, we need to focus on the probability. The possibility of a successful or unsuccessful trade exists the very second one enters a trade.

Regardless of the probability or odds, there will always exist the possibility that a trade will or will not work. Our goal as risk-based traders is to determine the probability of a trade meeting its objectives and then the extent of that probability based on historical results. The beauty of the trading profession is that the possibility of success exists on any trade once we push the entry button. Of course, the possibility of trading success is more comprehensive than pushing a button. Capturing edge at its apex reflects the greatest probability of trade success. Optimizing this repetitive process on each trade event in robotic, project management–like fashion is what we do. All we need to excel at is detecting and quantifying such edge and then executing when such opportunities present themselves.

CHALLENGES WITH CONFIRMATION BIAS

Conditional probability is defined as the chance of something occurring given an occurrence of another event. If the speed limit was raised by 50 percent, for sure there will be a greater overall increase in accidents. The markets have the same effect. Perhaps it's a simple candlestick bar trend change or price pattern that establishes a new trend or a volume spike. In fact, most who follow any form of technical analysis are basing their trading on conditional probability. In other words, when something occurs, the premonition is that another event will occur. Conditional probability doesn't tell us that it will occur, but rather that there is a greater possibility that it will occur.

Many traders tend to assume conditional probabilities when in actuality there is no long-term data evidence to support such theories. One oddity of human nature is that we tend to recognize information that supports our idea and ignore data that conflict with it. A standard part of my mentorship program was to have a trader review his or her current trade setups over a period of time using historical charts. My goal was to determine if there was any evidence of "confirmation bias" in the trader's assessment. The trader would scroll through time charts indicating evidence of a setup and eventual outcome. In nearly all cases the traders found a way to validate their findings and simply overlooked some setups where it would have had a negative outcome. I too would perform this test as the charts moved forward and often would come up with a different set of trades and results. When we reviewed them together to assure we were in sync with our historical databases, almost always an "Oh yeah, I didn't see that one" or "Okay, you're right, that one wouldn't have worked out" came up during the sessions.

Several studies on confirmation bias came to the conclusion that people are twice as likely to seek information that validates their theory rather than agree with evidence that contradicts it. Although it's part of our human chemistry, the necessity to avoid it is critical for success in trading.

Confirmation bias can have devastating results when applied in a live trading environment. It can result in holding a position too long or too short. This is why it is so important to have a truly unbiased approach to your strategies and to have confidence in your back-testing process when trying to validate a trading strategy. Accept that any trade can go wrong and determine *before* the trade where you know you are wrong. Better yet, know the factors that can occur that would cause you to alter your decision to enter a trade. Simple "if-then" statements written in your plan may be all it takes to determine this. "I know I'm wrong if the index price breaks the low of the day price or if the trade isn't working before the news announcement. If this occurs, I must exit the trade." An independent assessment generally will include that added level of integrity and accuracy during this process.

To avoid confirmation bias, be sure to look at all of your relevant data subjectively. Include the data that is most appropriate for each setup and is prevalent in similar market conditions. While it may be appropriate to not include a traditionally "normal" setup during time periods just before scheduled news announcements or other events that are excluded from your plan, it is not appropriate to exclude the losses on a setup due to unforeseen news. In summary, never exclude a portion of the historical data sample unless there is a valid plan reason not to include it.

Given this conditional probability, what specifically should we be looking for when seeking an edge in the markets? When a valid edge exists, how do we know if an even greater edge will present itself? These are challenging questions to answer when we are talking about an environment filled with randomness. First, we cannot dismiss the expenses we inherit in our trading business. Commissions, trading platform fees, and bid/ask spreads are direct expenses we encounter each day we trade. Other expenses such as overhead and technology also eat away at our profits. A theoretical definition of edge can describe any trade setup that historically produces a positive outcome greater than 50 percent of the time when it is executed properly. The realistic definition needs to be inclusive of the aforementioned required trade-specific expenses. Given these realities, what can we assume to be the minimum required probability edge? Rather than provide a minutia of value at risk (VaR) formulas, I suggest an absolute minimum 53–55 percent historical edge on any trade setup, price pattern, indicator, or other measurement to be considered acceptable. Preferably, I start to get interested when I have solid data that reveal edge in the upper 50th percentile and start validating any sample test in the 60th percentile. Let's start with discussing the following components and theories of measuring probability greater than acceptable edge.

INDICATORS THAT DETECT EDGE

There is enough market information, charting data, and technical indicators to keep a trader very busy these days. It's clear by now that the quantity of information available doesn't help traders gain an advantage on a trade or in their trading career. So how does one begin to decipher which indicator or chart to use? Before we determine either, we must gather our most important element to edge-based trading.

Historical Data

The most valuable tool we have to be able to forecast or predict future price movement is via the use of prior activity. The basis for data-driven trading strategies is reliant on the premise that history repeats itself when presented under similar market conditions. Historical data can come in the form of price movements, price patterns, or price reactions at key inflection points. Price movements can also be correlated with other market activity, such as price reaction in a stock index when a foreign currency pair moves in a particular direction or pattern. Assessing these forms of information to capture edge can be limiting in the sense that it does not factor in the human element. Traders' strengths and weaknesses are not captured in raw price data provided by the exchanges and used on simulated trading platforms. A particular price pattern may be difficult to detect for one trader, while another may detect the same edge easily but it may be difficult to allow one to pull the trigger at the optimal opportunity.

Using historical price data in a vacuum to determine market opportunity without consideration of actual trader activity in a live environment is limited since it does not factor in the human condition. This is why traders will come across a price pattern that is appealing only to find they cannot implement the strategy in a live market. A trader will hear about a strategy in a trading blog or a trader convention and rush to implement it. Often excited about finally finding their personal holy grail, they put it to the test in a live market using real capital only to find that it isn't working for them. If historical price action is followed by consistent price movement under similar market conditions, there is a good chance it can act as the basis for a potential opportunity with trader edge. Traders must accept and understand that the gap between detecting edge and executing trades when edge presents itself is often the biggest challenge and acts as the immobilizing barrier between failure and success. In summary, successful traders do not focus too much on getting the exact price. They focus more on getting an entry price that was determined historically to be the optimal entry.

Trade Entry Level

The opportunity to take advantage of edge is based on entering a trade at the optimal entry price. Traders are not psychics and will never be able to predict the best time and price at which to enter. Rarely can one enter at the best price to the tick or penny and then have it move directly to target without suffering any heat. When it does, the story is usually saved for happy hours and online blogs.

This game of edge manipulation begins and ends with obtaining such entry price. Entry accuracy truly is everything in trading. Not doing so requires price to trade through the target price that would have been if the entry price was optimal.

In Figure 4.4, we predetermined that the optimal entry price is at $15. This can be from a price pattern, support level, trade data, or a combination of factors that historically produced a trader's edge at this level. When price hits $14.75, Trader A enters as per plan. After a test of the $14.50 area, price proceeds to move higher in our favor as we had anticipated. Trader

FIGURE 4.4 Price Entry and Risk-to-Reward

B waited a bit for confirmation of such movement and decided to enter at $15.00. Given the 2:1 risk-to-reward requirement that both traders use, Trader A sets their target at $16.50, a level of anticipated price resistance. A $1.00 stop-loss at $13.50 is also entered. Notice how Trader B would still have an open position and is forced to hold the trade and increase their risk in order to reach their target at $17.00. Trader B understands that by holding for the target, they are putting their trade at risk while Trader A has successfully closed their position and is awaiting the next market opportunity. In this example, Trader B would have eventually reached their target albeit at a longer exposure time period. Attempting to "hold-through" a historical area of price resistance is actually reducing their edge and increasing their exposure. Similar to obtaining optimal entry, taking advantage of the anticipated optimal (and greed-free) exit price is equally as vital to your trading success.

Case Study: Price Probing on the E-Mini S&P Futures Using Market Profile Strategies

Assessment

Rarely does a trading day go by when I as a moderator or futures trading room member do not discuss the price mechanism at key reference or pivot areas, otherwise known as price probing. While there are many reasons why price will trade through a potential pivot area prior to reversing, one thing most agree upon is its frequency in the e-mini equities indexes.

It has become such a critical topic because it affects some of the most important elements of trading: price entry selection and stop placement. My attempt here is to assess the true frequency of such events and determine an optimum solution for the above decisions. While an analysis as to why price probes key reference areas is a topic for a more intensive thesis, this study takes a data-driven and statistically supported risk-based approach to the frequency and severity of such events.

Although equity markets tend to move in a general correlation, the most common indexes—the S&P 500 (ES) and Nasdaq (NQ)—have unique dynamics in regard to price action. While there may be little dispute about the validity of such price probing, this assessment will focus on the S&P 500 Futures (ES) index.

The key reference areas tested are the initial balance, or the price high and low from the first hour of regular trading. Of course, there are several other key pivot areas to consider; however, the ease of availability and quality of transparency of such data allows for an accurate study. Again, the findings of this limited-scope assessment can serve as the basis for other key pivot areas and other indexes at a later date.

Conclusions

The average and median length of probe has increased from three ticks respectively in 2009 to seven respectively in 2010. The trend has been consistently increasing each year for the past three years.

It is evident that using a three-tick stop on a consistent basis may not provide optimal risk loss protection in the current trading environment. The summary data found that this stop level may be too "tight" when one is using the initial balance (IB) as a support level or a basis for the trade.

Approximately 16 percent of all trades had a front-running price reversal action. This is defined as price reversing within four ticks of the initial balance with price never allowing resting orders at the IB to be filled.

Strategies to Consider

The most simple of strategic changes would be to increase the stop-loss amount greater than the average probe level. Based on the findings of this report, that would be equivalent to a stop greater than six ticks, or 1.5 points. Of course, maintaining the proper risk-reward will require the target level(s) to be increased to accommodate such a modification. One also has to consider trading account risk and the impact that a smaller account would have on a series of adverse outcomes at the greater stop level.

An alternative to increasing a stop distance would be to place an entry order two ticks outside the IB entry level. This "play the probe" strategy would provide a better entry level, albeit at the cost of missing any front-running entries or others where price reversed right at the IB price level. This strategy may be suited for more conservative trading strategies, traders with smaller size accounts, or ones that may only accommodate a single contract entry.

A higher probability strategy is to use a scale-in approach using multiple contracts. According to the assessment, one would place one-half of the total position at two ticks outside the IB price level, the other half at two ticks below the IB level. For accounts eligible for contracts in multiples of three, one can place one-third of all contracts at the above levels and the remaining third at 1.5 points below the IB level. As with most scale-in strategies, this would reduce the overall trade risk but will increase account risk due to the increased contract exposure. All strategies would bypass the front-running effect that occurred with 16 percent of all IB level opportunities. Those with trading strategies in multiples of four may opt to place one-fourth position at two ticks in front of the IB to initiate their entry and capture partial fills on trades that reverse prior to the IB level. Although this four-contract-level strategy was not formally assessed, one should consider this strategy when other markets are testing the IB level and the ES price has not.

The following finding supports of such a strategy:

Only 4 percent of all probe entries with a "catastrophic" 5-point stop would have hit the stop price. The assumption is that:

The summary data conclude that 96 percent of what originally may have been considered a failed trade using a six-tick or 2.0 pt. stop will still provide the trader with an opportunity to close out the trade at the original entry or average entry price, or less than the full "catastrophic" stop level of 5.00 points. The data used in this assessment did not discriminate price action following major news releases such as Federal Open Market Committee (FOMC) data or other planned economic releases. It is the assessor's opinion that this catastrophic stop percentage would fare even lower should the trader avoid entries around such volatile events.

Market dynamics are continuously changing as did the volatility and price action in the scope of this assessment. It is up to individual traders to determine the impact to their trading risk, business risk, ability to adjust to such changes, and ultimately, trader performance. As with any strategy, greater opportunity for reward is accompanied by greater risks. Ultimately, only you, the trader, can make the decisions that will take into considerations these findings and implement a suggested strategy that meets your risk profile and trading plan compliance.

Support/Resistance

Prior levels where price reversed direction is one of the most common technical tools used by both novice and experienced traders. Whether this simple concept works effectively or not, it takes just a quick glance at any depth-of-market tool. Often you will find clusters of buy and sell orders surrounding areas of recent price support or resistance. Breakout traders place buy orders just above prior resistance in hopes of creating new resistance areas. Those same areas may be flooded with buy stop orders for short traders who believe a price breakout confirms a failure of their setup, thus potentially fueling a rally even further. Can you determine where the support and resistance price levels are in the S&P 500 futures (Ticker: ES) depth-of-market chart in Figure 4.5?

Do support and resistance areas work? At minimum, many liquid markets such as the S&P 500 and Nasdaq indexes often have price battles

BID	PRICE	ASK
	1180.00	120
	1179.75	330
	1179.50	1120
	1179.25	1460
	1179.00	975
	1178.75	12
	1178.50	33
	1178.25	86
	1178.00	130
	1177.75	290
	1177.50	420
	1177.25	865
	1177.00	960
1220	1176.75	
850	1176.50	
220	1176.25	
130	1176.00	
88	1175.75	
2640	1175.50	
1890	1175.25	
	1175.00	

FIGURE 4.5 Depth of Market Order Entry

surrounding these areas. Prior days' open, high, low, or closing prices often attract inflection activity. This concoction of buyers placing target sell orders at prior resistance areas, buyers anticipating breakouts, and short sellers looking to cover often paint a picture of a standoff battle in price action. It is the greater supply or demand that ultimately wins. When assessing your market of choice, it is important to perform your due diligence and assess the price action with the time frame you are comfortable with. A swing trader may back-test for edge of a reversal occurring within a set period of time, such as five days, or within a particular risk parameter. Day trading scalpers may assess edge opportunities provided by the immediate bounce reversal in price and not be concerned about the ultimate outcome of the support/resistance breakout outcome. Others may seek the opportunity of the failure of other trades anticipating a reversal, and then take advantage of those "sitting duck" stop orders parked right outside resistance. With so many technical traders using support and resistance as a trading strategy, perhaps reaction at these levels is a self-fulfilling prophecy. Regardless of the reason, areas of prior support and resistance can be the genesis of many opportunities that create edge in your setup. Simplicity is often a beautiful gift in this business that many seem to overlook.

Inflection Points

This term reflects the perfect description of anticipated price reaction levels. These levels act as anticipatory opportunities in price movements at predetermined price areas. Support and resistance levels can be considered an inflection point since a cluster of institutional and retail buyers and sellers is anticipated at these levels. They are predetermined in that the price level has already been established, in this case by prior price activity. Traders often use technical charting tools in a live environment such as stochastics, volume, and price patterns at inflection points in an attempt to capture an edge in the markets.

How are inflection points determined? For one, there isn't a memo that goes out to traders handing them areas where price will reverse. We wish trading was so easy. Throughout the trading day, a myriad of technical charting tools used by the trading community is put into place in anticipation of potential price reversals or a test level for the current buyers or sellers who are in control of the market at that particular time. Traders using technical analysis and charting tend to use these tools to determine entry points, target areas, and stop-losses. Since there are a handful of popular charting tools used, many traders use these price levels for "decision" or inflection points. Perhaps as a self-fulfilling prophecy, traders seek these levels to unload a position while others are willing to absorb their inventory and enter at the same price level. Inflection points can be market specific; however, there are some general universal technical charting tools that are used in most of the commonly traded markets. Let's take a closer look at some of the most popular analytical charting tools used to determine these decision points.

Pivot Point Indicators

Pivot points are derived from standard formulas based on prior period high, low, and closing trade prices. Commonly known in the trader community as floor pivots, these anticipatory support and resistance levels include a primary pivot area surrounded by additional levels of support and resistance. Calculating the pivot point price is simple.

To find the next day's pivot point, simply take the highest traded price from the prior day, plus the low price and close for the same period, and then divide the sum by 3.

Pivot Point = (HIGH PRICE + LOW PRICE + CLOSING PRICE)/3

There is no need to actually calculate them manually. Several websites such as pivotfarm.com report these inflection points on several indexes and individual securities shortly after the close of the trading day to help traders prepare for the following day. Extended support and resistance pivot levels are also widely available as well as weekly pivot numbers. Although pivot points are available on highly liquid individual securities, they are extremely popular among the index, index futures, and forex trading products.

Price Gap

In its purest definition, a price gap is a price level range determined by the close of the prior period and the opening price of the current period. Daily gaps are popular among the short-term day trading community; however, longer-term traders often monitor gaps from prior periods until these price areas are closed or "filled" and price has traded through this range area. Gaps often occur due to premarket activity that raises or lowers the anticipated opening price from the last official trade of the prior day. Figure 4.6 shows an example of a daily gap that occurred in Goldman Sachs Corp.

As an inflection point theory, the closing price acts as a magnet until price trades at the gap inflection point. While there is often debate over the validity of the gap as an inflection point, S&P 500 futures prices tends to fill any overnight gap over 65 percent of trading days. Gap-specific filtering strategies over a valid sample time period can produce an overall performance edge into the 70th percentile using acceptable risk management rules combined with the discipline to rigorously adhere to such "set it and forget it" strategies.

Fibonacci Retracement Levels

Fibonacci retracement levels are an extremely popular inflection point tool among the retail trading community where ratios are used to identify prices of inflection. Those interested in learning the history of the 12th-century Italian mathematician who popularized such golden ratios and numerical sequences can certainly do so at their leisure. From an inflection point perspective, traders often use "fib" tools to anticipate areas of retracement or where price will resume a current trend. The most popular retracement percentages are the 38.2 percent, 50.0 percent, and 61.8 percent levels; however, traders often argue their passion for other popular retracement levels such as the 76.8 percent and 23.6 percent levels.

Fibonacci tools are included in most charting software and Web charting tools. Since the live market calculation requires the use of moving swing high and swing low prices, they are rarely calculated manually. Daily, weekly, and monthly Fibonacci inflection levels are commonly found on

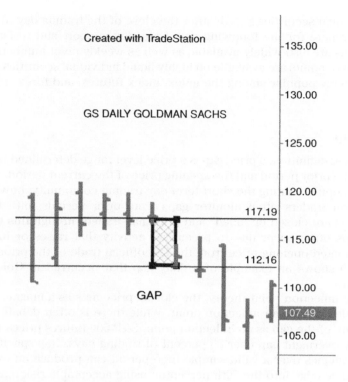

Created with TradeStation

GS DAILY GOLDMAN SACHS

135.00
130.00
125.00
120.00
117.19
115.00
112.16
110.00
GAP
107.49
105.00

FIGURE 4.6 The Daily Market Gap
Prior day's closing price: $117.19
Opening price: $112.16
Opening gap: $-5.03

the Web as well. Figure 4.7 shows a chart using Fibonacci retracement ratios on the S&P 500 Index. Highlighted are the 50.0 percent and 61.8 percent retracement levels. Notice how price reached a high of $121.59 and then retraced down directly to the 0.618 Fibonacci level price of $120.84.

Notice how sellers pushed price to the 61.80 percent fib level where buyers took over and eventually proceeded higher.

There is another set of inflection points within the Fibonacci family called Fibonacci extension levels. Extension levels are price areas of inflection drawn beyond the 100 percent level using the Fibonacci ratio numbers. The most common levels are 127 percent and 161.8 percent. Let's look at a similar chart using the same index and adding the Fibonacci extensions. Notice in Figure 4.8 how price broke through the prior resistance area at $118.15 and found new resistance at the 127.0 percent fib level. Once price

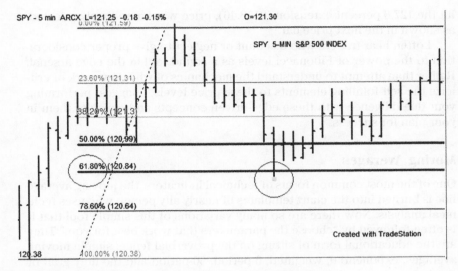

FIGURE 4.7 Using Fibonacci Ratios to Detect Edge

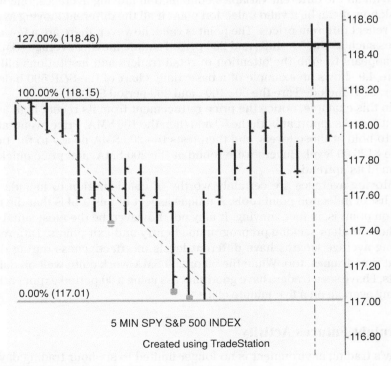

FIGURE 4.8 Using Fibonacci Extension Ratios

hit the 127.0 percent extension ($118.46), price was immediately rejected, as shown in the next price bar.

I often hear traders who discount or neglect to give proper consideration to the power of Fibonacci levels as a sound tool in the edge arsenal. Rather than attempt to understand the mechanics of why they work or criticize the self-fulfilling elements to these price levels, I suggest performing your due diligence with these edge-driven concepts and consider them in your plan for success.

Moving Averages

One of the most common forms of technical indicators, the moving average line is burned into the chart templates of nearly any person who uses technical analysis. Now there are so many variations of this simple tool that it is often followed by "choose the parameters that work best for you." They are the educational form of sitting on the proverbial fence: simple moving averages, exponential, weighted, 5-period, 50-period and the holy grail of moving averages—the infamous "default settings," to name a few.

With all the different variables contained in moving averages, one has to ask how it can be a valid inflection point if all the different moving averages reflect different prices. The point is valid; however, there are a few averages such as the 50-, 100-, and 200-period simple moving average (SMA) that appears to grab the attention of retail traders and institutions alike. Figure 4.9 shows an example of a basic daily chart of the S&P 500 index, ticker: SPY. Included are the 50-, 100-, and 200-period SMA.

In this example, notice the price retracement from its recent high and how it found support at both the 50 and then the 100 SMA. Price eventually fails to hold at those levels, and then tests the 200 SMA nearly to the tick at the $126.00 level. Buyers were found at the 200 SMA, and price quickly resumed its uptrend.

Moving averages are certainly worthy of consideration to include in your list of inflection point tools. A unique aspect of this tool is that the inflection point is, in fact, moving. It may not, however, be the most suitable for those traders seeking preprogrammed entry and exit points. Different moving average lengths have different levels of effectiveness during different time frames, too. While the 50 or 200 SMA work quite well on daily charts, I have seen traders have good success using a 30-period exponential moving average on a five-minute chart.

Overnight Futures Activity

Today's trading environment is no longer limited to six-hour trading days. While one side of the world is sleeping, the other is open for business.

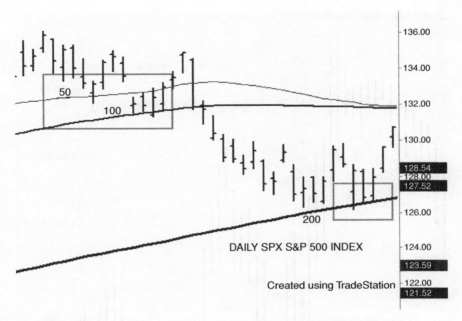

FIGURE 4.9 Using SMA Support and Resistance to Determine Trade Risk

In fact, markets in some countries, including the U.S. futures markets, are open for trading virtually 24 hours. The forex markets traditionally open on Sunday evening and continue through Friday. While the volume of activity may be lower during portions of the overnight sessions, the price activity and ranges that are produced often act as decision points for traders. Figure 4.10 shows a chart of the S&P 500 futures markets, otherwise known as the ES. The ES futures trades virtually 24 hours with volume traditionally lower in the overnight session.

In Figure 4.10, notice how the overnight range of price activity had a high of $1,210.00 and a low at approximately 9:00 am EST at $1,196.50, resulting in a $13.50 overnight price range.

As we look toward the opening of the regular session, notice how price tested the low range within the initial 45 minutes of the session. Price "probed" the lows by approximately two points, and buyers pushed price back into the overnight range. Overnight traders generally seek small retracements and tests of prior support and resistance moves. While this bounce does not appear to have broken previous highs, these minor retracements in price are worth gold to those traders who take advantage of such inflection points. Some individual securities have extended hours on certain exchanges. This is slowly changing as the world becomes more flat

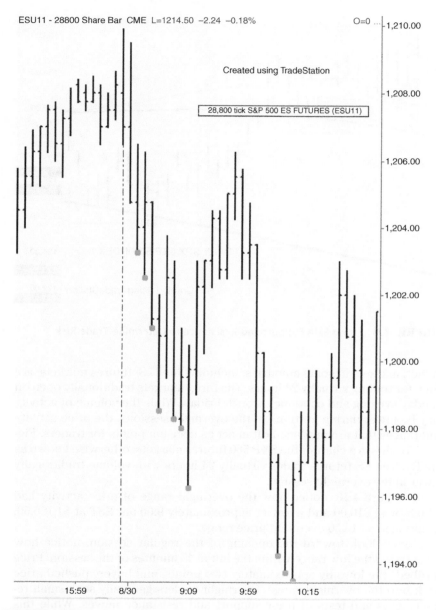

FIGURE 4.10 Using Overnight Futures Activity to Determine Support and Resistance

High price: $1,210.00
Low price: $1,196.50
Range: $13.50

and the world financial arenas become linked though technology. When performing your discovery and due diligence on which products offer overnight opportunities, you may consider starting with the index futures markets in the United States and in Europe.

Market Profile

A rapidly growing area for effectively determining reversal and target areas is the use of standard deviations. Market profile techniques include the graphical representation where the market participants perceive value. Simply put, it is the area where buyers are most comfortable buying as the sellers are liquidating. The theory is that any market that has a buyer and a seller is sold at the then-perceived value. Market price will fluctuate in an attempt to "find value" for both parties, but in the end, the price where a majority of the trades are settled is considered at value, and any range of normal fluctuation surrounding this perceived value is considered normal and in a "balanced" range. There are more unique terms associated with market profile, perhaps, than any other style of trading; however, it is important to retain not only the concept of market profile as well as its inflection points they produce and ultimately the trader's edge. It's best to describe market profile in its simplest form using the display in Figure 4.11.

In the example noted in Figure 4.11, let's assume that the entire price range of a particular day is 15 points, indicated here between the price

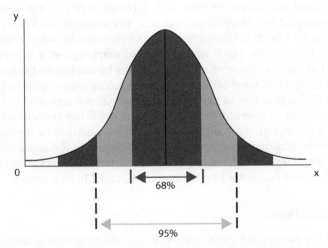

FIGURE 4.11 Using Market Profile to Determine Price and Value

at 0 and Y. Some trades will go off at one price, and while the markets fluctuate during the day, other trades will be settled at other prices. The area within the 68 percent range indicates the range of prices where 68 percent of all trading activity occurred. In market profile, this represents the balanced area, or the price range where a majority (68 percent) of the day's volume had occurred. When prices are in a consolidation pattern, price will often fluctuate within value, or between this value area indicated within the 68 percent range. When buyers and sellers have determined that value has changed, for whatever reason, price will break outside the prior value area and enter an imbalanced state. If enough activity occurs between buyers and sellers at this new area, then that range becomes the new balanced state. Confusing? Perhaps it could be at first. This activity is what truly makes a market, whether it is for stocks, foreign exchange, or the value of hot dogs. Price continuously fluctuates based on supply and demand, and market profile attempts to visually display this accepted high, low, and midpoint range.

One might ask, how does market profile project inflection points? Inflection points often occur at the high, low, and midpoint ranges where 68 percent of all market activity has occurred for a given time period. These points are commonly referred to as the value area high, value area low, and point of control. Let's look at another visual sample of one day's price activity to be sure you can capture the basis of this powerful inflection tool (Figure 4.12).

You will notice the three lines from top to bottom: value area high, point of control, and value area low. Notice how price reacted at the test of each level. In this example, the value area low acted as a nice support for price around the noontime hour as it attempted to reverse higher and found resistance at the point of control at approximately 13:45 en route to test the value area high. It subsequently was overcome by sellers and made its way back through the value range. Diehard market profile theorists live in the world of these value area inflection points by buying and shorting the value areas until the market proves them wrong. The center line, or point of control, is often a first test of price through the value range and a common place for scalpers to unwind their position or for other traders who take risk off their trade, either by selling some of their position or moving their stop-loss levels. Although not as widely used as some of the other inflection indicators, when utilized in a disciplinary environment, market profile can be one of the most consistent edge detectors available to a trader.

Market Conditions

The caveat for productive data assessment is that current market conditions are relatively similar to when the assessment had taken place. Often

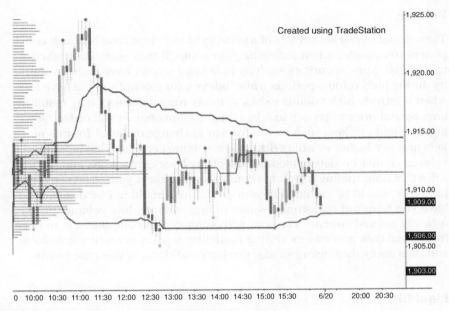

FIGURE 4.12 Market Profile Entry and Exit Points

traders will use back-tested setups in all market conditions and eventually lose their edge. I have found this caveat often is ignored by new traders. They find a strategy that they are comfortable with and confirm through sufficient audit that it provides an edge, only to have a negative outcome in a live environment. They have neglected to account for the similar market condition requirement. The markets are continuously performing with some form of randomness. These levels of randomness increase during certain unannounced times or during specific economic events. Trading during these times usually results in an increase in risk and a reduction of edge. Price activity immediately following a news event is a perfect example of a burst in random price activity. Any opportunities become more of a 50–50 event rather than a predetermined edge determined during an assessment in normal market conditions. Traders who trade the news might argue differently and rightly so. Their strategies are audited and proven to provide an edge only during these times and to exploit such edge with overall success. Conversely, these traders do not use their news event strategies during low volume activity and reserve these setups only for what it was designed to do—take advantage of edge exposed during, in this example, news events.

Volume

The amount of market activity of a security at any given time is a must component to consider when assessing your setup. It may seem contradictive to say that some securities such as individual stocks have higher volatility during high-volume periods while indexes, for example, could have less when relatively high volume exists. A thinly traded security may result in unexpected price pops due to a large institutional buy or sell order. Other highly liquid markets such as the foreign exchange or index futures markets may see higher volatility during low-volume periods. What is "normal" volume should be determined on a security-by-security basis and having rules that limit trading to volume conditions that meet your valid setup parameters should be included in your plan. This should not be designed to have you filter out opportunities due to high volume, low volume, or historically normal volume. The goal with volume as a component is to perform your data assessment during particular market condition standards and then apply them using similar market conditions, in this case volume.

Liquidity

Often discussed in the same breath as volume, liquidity is the ability to buy or sell a security at a desired price. More than ever there are more trading vehicles and products available for traders to choose from. From a risk management viewpoint, those with liquidity should be at the top of the list of consideration. When performing trade journal audits for e-mini S&P futures index day traders over a significant period of time (six months and greater), one can see the average gain or loss differential per trade from the consistently successful traders and the novices is approximately 0.29 of a point. That is the near equivalent of a mere tick separating the best from the worst. The S&P 500 futures and related index products are some of the most liquid products in the marketplace. Getting that extra tick on average can be the difference between success and failure. In order to do so, you need to trade products with the participation level sufficient to get in and out of positions at your desired price.

Even in the most efficient markets, liquidity risk increases during times of high volatility or market-sensitive breaking news. Be sure to include a rule such as this in your trading plan. An example of security risk is the price spread, or differential between the bid and the asking price of a security. It acts as an obstacle in the traders' quest to meet their trading objectives. The differential is the amount by which the ask, or the offer price, exceeds the bid price. Day traders, scalpers, and similar traders who have a relatively high frequency of trading activity are most susceptible to such liquidity and spread risk.

TABLE 4.5 Determining Spread Risk Trading Forex Pairs

Currency Pair	Symbol	Average Spread (in pips)
Euro/U.S. dollar	EUR/USD	3
U.S. dollar/Japanese yen	USD/JPY	3
Australian dollar/U.S. dollar	AUD/USD	4
Euro/Swiss franc	EUR/CHF	4
Euro/British pound	EUR/GBP	4
Euro/Japanese yen	EUR/JPY	4
British pound/U.S. dollar	GBP/USD	4
New Zealand dollar/U.S. dollar	NZD/USD	4
U.S. dollar/Canadian dollar	USD/CAD	4
U.S. dollar/Swiss franc	USD/CHF	4
Canadian dollar/Japanese yen	CAD/JPY	6
Australian dollar/Japanese yen	AUD/JPY	7
Canadian dollar/Swiss franc	CAD/CHF	7
British pound/Japanese yen	GBP/JPY	7
Swiss franc/Japanese yen	CHF/JPY	8
Euro/Canadian dollar	EUR/CAD	8
Euro/Australian dollar	EUR/AUD	10
New Zealand dollar/Swiss franc	NZD/CHF	15

Table 4.5 is a chart of liquidity risk by foreign exchange currency pair market. Spreads will vary by product and competing brokers within each market and may also widen or shrink during abnormal market conditions. For example, the euro/U.S. dollar or other major currency pairs may have a spread as low as one-hundredth of 1 percent while others in the same forex market, such as the Australian dollar/New Zealand pair may have a 10 pip spread. At minimum, one needs to consider these spreads as not only a transaction cost to trade but an addition risk imposed on your success. Trading can be such a challenging venture, and by choosing securities and markets that provide lower transaction costs resulting in lower trade risk, you increase your edge in trading.

These are just a few examples of how the market and the trader can generate a reasonable edge that provides the probability of a favorable outcome on a trade. Notice how some examples are obtained by way of technical indicators, others by market price values already determined by prior price action, and some by trader execution precision. Deciding from this list or generating your own is ultimately the decision of the trader. Consider markets that you will be comfortable with in a live environment and would find easy to track in your trade journal. After all, you are in search of the ultimate tools to provide you a consistent edge in the markets. Tracking which component or components were used on each trade will ultimately produce a valid sample size that produces evidence of those that work the best with your strategies and setups. Experiment and be innovative. Most of all, measure, measure, measure.

LEVERAGING EDGE USING CONFLUENCE

The short list of edge components discussed each has its own unique contribution to the concept of discovering trade advantage. One of the most powerful concepts that provides this essential edge is an overlapping leveraged portfolio of all of the above components and others in use. Simultaneous usage of these components and conditions exponentially provide some of the greatest opportunities to succeed in trading any market.

Confluence is the leveraged support of multiple and various edge-based components that support your decision to enter a trade. Confluence theory states that the greater the number of components to support your trade, the greater the edge. Stated differently, the greater the confluence of support, the greater the probability that the trade will be successful. Let's show an example using a few of the edge components just discussed.

Figure 4.13 shows a trade setup in our plan that calls for a long entry when price pulls back between the .50 and .618 Fibonacci retracement area. Again we are using the S&P500 futures contract in this example. This is a historically powerful reversal area and works well as a stand-alone setup or with an added layer of edge using confluence of support. Notice how price retraces not only to the desired Fibonacci area but also lands right on both the 50-period and 100-period simple moving average support lines. All three setup indicators are lined up in the same entry area. You have this trade in your plan because historically it has provided you with a positive edge over a long period of time with a valid sample of trades. This multiple, overlapping area of edge components denotes confluence of support for your trade. Both components are listed in your plan as valid and are required to be taken when no other rules or market conditions prohibit such. Let's say that your historical records show a similar edge of 57.5 percent when price tests this Fibonacci area. So what is your edge on this trade? Based on the confluence theory above, we know that it is at least 57.5 percent, or some level of edge greater than the Fibonacci component alone.

Think of confluence of support as added levels of risk protection to support the premise of your trade. When you are sick, you don't just take medicine and then go running in the freezing cold, right? You do everything you can to break the fever, stuffy nose, and cough. You take a fever reducer, wrap yourself in a warm blanket, and perhaps make Mom's proven

ESU11 - 28800 Share Bar CME L=1214.50 -2.24 -0.18%   O=0 ...

1,215.00
1,214.50

0.00% (1,212.89)

1,210.00

1,205.00

50.00% (1,203.11)

50

61.80% (1,200.80)

100   1,200.00

28,800 tick S&P 500 ES FUTURES (ESU11)

Created using TradeStation

1,195.00

100.00% (1,193.32)

FIGURE 4.13 Detecting Confluence of Support and Resistance

chicken soup recipe. Will implementing confluence-based setups make you successful as a trader? Trading using proven confluence-based supportive setups alone will provide you with an edge that can at minimum provide the opportunity to be successful. However, without proper risk management, discipline, and trade execution, confluence may at best deplete your trading account at a slower pace. What it does do is increase a trader's edge in combination with other arsenals. It also allows for increased probability, if managed properly, resulting in a successful trade. This distinction of knowing the tools and concepts for a trader to be successful versus the ability to be successful in a trade is completely different.

So if confluence theory is valid, is it safe to assume that the more supportive components as confluence is used, the greater my edge on the trade? The level of edge is determined by a combination of components, their historical percentage edge recorded in the trades you had tracked and/or have taken, and their results when all components and market conditions were similar. Other factors, such as randomness, still exist whether there are two levels of confluence or five levels. The edge curve, if you will, flattens as the number of valid stand-alone components increases.

Many tests conducted on my behalf showed that there was a powerful increase in edge when two confluence components were combined. Some tests noted an increase after a third component was added. Greater than three components revealed that the edge factor flattened out over a valid sample of trades. Why would this happen? If confluence is evident and is shown to increase my trade success, one would think he or she should trade setups that include as many areas of confluence as possible. The reason that increases in edge are limited is primarily due to market randomness. This uncontrollable variance that is a staple in the market is such a strong force that it limits the edge a trader will have on any given favorable setup. The truth is that regardless of our search for the holy grail of setups, market randomness is always present and often works to assure we do not get too good of a result over a period of time, regardless of our precise execution and risk compliance.

The other concern is from the risk side of trade setup management. Opportunity risk increases exponentially as setups are used with multiple components of confluence. For example, I may have a trading plan setup where I execute when price retraces to the 61.80 percent Fibonacci level. If my setup requires a second level of confluence such as the pivot point level as indicated earlier, there is much less chance that both components will line up simultaneously at the same price. Throw in a third confluence component, and the opportunities shrink even lower. I am a big proponent of confluence trading and always am grateful to see those practicing my methodology as a means to success. I do raise a concern when I see near perfect opportunities being passed by because a third level of confluence did not support a particular trade. The opportunity edge was provided by the market but was lost due to nonexecution. Traders who use confluence as their primary basis of trading edge need to understand that if edge is present under conditions of expected risk, it is a lost opportunity if not executed. Passing up on a 62 percent edge because a third level of confluence would have provided a historical edge of 63.5 percent is not representative of a sound trading plan. Having two solid levels of confluence that can be easily detected, tracked, and executed is more than enough components if they historically provide a sound edge that can be benefited from over a consistent series of trades. If a third happens to fall in the same confluence zone, even better.

The power of confluence of support can only be truly realized by using such strategies over a period of time. The strength of a confluence of resistance, however, is equally as powerful. Let's say we have a long trade at

SPY $114.25, and based on our risk-to-reward parameters, we have a target price of $118.00. Prior to execution, we notice that we have confluence of resistance at the $116.00 level. Confluence theory is powerful, and in this example, it can be used against you with the same level of strength. In fact, you may be able to justify taking a short position at the $116.00 price area if your plan supports such. But with this trade, success requires you to hope that price breaks through a known resistance level. Given this new information, should we take the trade? We have determined that the $114.00 area is a valid support level with confluence. In summary, in order to execute a trade with effectiveness, a trade should have confluence of support for the trade *and* no known barriers of confluence prior to the target price.

Let's go one step further. How about our stop-loss order to minimize risk? Remember our $114.00 confluence area? Was it not the reason we placed our order there because the $113.75–$114.00 area provided the multiple components to support our trade? We need to give our trade some reasonable price action volatility so we do not take an unnecessary stop loss; however, it is safe to assume that having our stop at minimum below the $113.75 is necessary. We have detected the market's gift of technical or price support and we need to allow the opportunity to test these support levels. Failure to do so will result in price penetrating those support levels, thus allowing us to take our stop with pride. What we do not want to do is to have our risk limited within the support range. It is critical to always place any stop order BELOW recognized support levels. Always remember that risk management is not the art of minimizing loss. It is the art of optimizing loss given a known potential reward.

SUMMARY

There are so many market variables that come into play on nearly every trade. As traders, we need to take advantage of every numerical opportunity in the edge discovery process. Experienced traders often have an advantage in sampling since their history is large enough to generate a sample review size. When performing risk audits in the financial and corporate fields, I am required to adhere to specific accounting or similar standards when compiling my sample sizes. Failure to do so can immediately discredit my findings and recommendations. In trading, such rules can be a bit relaxed, especially for the individual traders who trade their own capital. Using a practical approach with strong sampling and audit principles is often best. After all, we are traders looking to profit from a detected edge. A paralysis by analysis over the top formula to determine the number of records you need to review should be left to the corporate-sector risk management teams. You will often be forced to sample data outside your personal trade history. Sample size theory will help in this regard, too. When reviewing chart patterns, price data, and technical analysis tools, consider the similar market conditions rule discussed earlier as equally if not more important that the size of the sample. As market conditions change, setups having edge will lose their luster while others start to appear. Results using perfectly valid samples will sometimes not show true in your live trading. Human and market elements make determining edge a tireless quest similar to that of a weatherman. As traders, we can only work with the elements available and the understanding of the markets. This is why the risk component is such a crucial element to your understanding, acceptance, and success in trading.

Now that you have a deeper understand of several edge concepts and have the ability to leverage them with confluence theory, there is one important question to ask yourself: "What is the data telling me about my performance, and what changes do I need to make in order to improve?" In the next chapter, we'll take the data and allow it to produce eye-opening results that will allow you to bring your trading to the next level.

 REVIEW QUESTIONS

1. List the different methodologies in which a trader can detect edge.

2. Explain the relationship between sample size and expected value.

3. How can confirmation bias negatively affect a trader's performance?

4. Explain the principle of market profile and its ability to generate trading edge.

5. Define the terms *volume* and *liquidity* and the difference between the two.

CHAPTER 5

Embracing a Culture of Analytics

One of my favorite parts of this business is that of having the opportunity to help others improve their A game by transitioning their focus toward risk analytics. Common questions I get from fellow traders are, "Is there any part of trading that incorporates intuition into the equation?" and "Is it truly only about the numbers?" The answer, of course, is no. If it were only about analytics, every trader, regardless of experience level, would be on an equal playing field. Trader A with 15 years of market experience would have the same overall edge as the newbie who just opened his or her first account.

While this book focuses on data analytics as a method of optimizing risk and success, it would be demeaning to the best traders to say that developing a feel of the market is worthless. If you have extensive experience in trading, you recognize that sixth sense that pops up right before a statistically perfect setup telling you not to participate. The data nut that I am, I attempted to track my intuition-based trades that in some way altered my decision to execute a +60 percent edge trade-up. During that time, I was 54.5 percent correct in making the right decision. This was fairly respectable given the fact that a majority of them were bypassing valid trades with a defined edge. Similar to someone who stands on a soft 16 with a blackjack dealer ace showing, sometimes there is that signal that comes from that other powerful spreadsheet called the stomach.

In trading, our strategies need to be based on a more credible source, at least in the beginning of your career before any market muscle is built up. Sure, you will have winning streaks based on intuitive notions. Any arena that includes an element of variance will allow for such. Just as a coin flip will end up heads 12 times in a row, so will your trade activity contain streaks both good and bad. This irrational behavior of the markets will often have a positive effect on your trading account. It will at times have an equally negative effect. Every trader, regardless of experience or execution compliance, will experience this in his or her journey. John Maynard Keynes said it best, "Markets can remain irrational far longer than you or I can remain solvent." So you can blame Mr. Keynes for the push to incorporate some data analytics into your trading plans. Our goal is for the probabilities to overcome the market variance over an acceptable sample of trading activity. For those who may be a bit intimidated by data analytics and any discussion about mathematics or numbers, please don't be. They are merely informational guidelines that will allow you to become successful using an analytical approach to risk management. Let's discuss these analytical mantras, if you will.

RISK MANAGEMENT RULES FOR THE TRADER

First is to wholeheartedly accept market variance. It is a powerful force in the markets and not only must it be accepted but also understood. Variance will test your confidence in a particular setup or even as a trader. Often there will be times where you will have multiple losing sessions during times of peak execution and plan compliance. I can offer you an opportunity to pay you $2.00 every time a coin lands on tails and you pay me $1.00 every time the coin lands on heads. Let's say we take 20 sessions with 10 flips of the coin. Most would jump at the chance, especially if the contest included as many flips of the coin as I could tolerate. One sure thing is that I am confident I will win at least a few of those sessions, even though statistically the odds are clearly in your favor to have a better dollar win outcome. The markets work in the same way. If we started this contest and after four sessions of 10 coin flips I was actually ahead, would you give up and complain that the "system" doesn't work? Of course you wouldn't. Now if you only brought $20 to the game, you would be in dire trouble. In fact, you would be a loser in a game with an obvious edge on your side. It can and does happen in the markets every day. New traders with a minimum bankroll cannot overcome the Keynesian quote mentioned earlier. To overcome this variance, one must overcome the short-term fluctuations of the markets. It must be overcome not only from a trade execution standpoint but also from traders frantically adjusting their successful plan when in the end it was only the variance effect causing the temporary disappointing results. One of the key aspects of trade journal auditing is to dissect poor execution or plan noncompliance vs. mere variance of a well-executed plan.

Secondly, one must understand the importance of sticking to a long-term commitment to a plan. Because of our aforementioned variance friend, we need to execute our setups using a large enough sample in order to reduce the outcome variance. Since your overall edge will be rather small, you will need a rather large sample of trade opportunities to realize the edge and for it to be reflected in your trading account. Train yourself to ignore short-term fluctuations in your performance and focus on executing your trading plan to perfection. You are a risk manager implementing a plan. Holding yourself up through rough stretches of negative variance will require superior risk and money management as well as psychological discipline. Equally as important, you must have enough bankroll to start with to get yourself through these inevitable divots and adjust your trade size to a level that can absorb such random events.

Patience and discipline during an account drawdown is critical to your success in trading. We have all experienced drawdowns due to several reasons ranging from variance to negligent activity. It's very challenging to continue to trade a setup that is generating loss after loss. The value of a historical edge generated from a trade journal is of little comfort when losses are mounting. We will discuss how to manage such risks when these droughts occur. As risk managers, one thing we know for sure: They will occur.

Lastly, traders need to have developed a superior level of confidence in their strategies and their approach to trading that has provided them with the trading advantage. There are several dynamics all taking place during your trading career. Market randomness, changing market conditions, trader experience levels, and the ability to execute a plan effectively are just some examples. During the development phase of a trader, confidence is one of the key elements that will support growth as a professional. All other elements aside, if your confidence does not improve, it is likely that neither will your chances of success as a trader. As market dynamics change, so does the need for the trader's approach to trading. Perhaps a trade setup has not worked as well recently as it has historically or the ever-increasing use of computer algorithms by the trading institutions forces you to reevaluate breakout-based setups. You must have the ability to reevaluate your strategies when market conditions change. By tracking your trade activity, you now have the ability to assess and check for changes in results early and place yourself in the forefront of professionals who take the necessary actions to alter your plan using analytics from credible data. Constantly checking and testing your strategies is a standard part of any risk management plan.

For me, I live and die by the numbers. It's part of my culture as a risk manager. I see myself as an expert in detecting conditional probabilities in the markets. Although I don't ignore the human elements in trading, the human condition is more prominent in corporate risk management where you have teams working with other departments in an effort to establish corporate "harmony" among the people in these departments. In trading, it really needs to get back to the basics of executing a plan when an edge in the markets exists. This by all means does not allow one to ignore all emotion or mind games that battle the very best of traders at one point or another. What it does do is continuously remind me that my data is king and that my fate as a trader will always be traced back to my data. It is all that really matters. Economic forecasts of higher interest rates, unemployment figures above expectations, or a friend telling me that the business channel said AAPL was going higher is really of no value to the risk-based trader.

THE DATA COLLECTION PROCESS

If you are just getting started in your trading venture, you probably do not have any data available to you and certainly no home-grown trading results. While reading about the need for what seems to be reams of endless data, you may be overwhelmed about the task that confronts you. It may appear to be a huge mountain of work, but once you set the framework for collecting the important data, the actual recording is quite easy.

The investment in time and effort to collect the correct data and record it accurately is the first step toward making better trade decision making. You do not need years' worth of data in order to get started. Most traders will back-test six months or so and then validate it live in simulation or at a very low exposure rate for a month or two prior to actual plan execution. Going back several years to capture data may have limited value. If you recall, the theme of this book is to reduce risk by expecting similar results from past history given similar market conditions. When we go back several years to assess data, we are exposing ourselves to a market that may not have the same characteristics as today's market.

Secondly, even the law of large numbers has its beneficial limits from a value standpoint. Two questions you need to ask yourself during this process are: What information do I need to know to enable better trade decisions? How do I go about gathering this information?

DATA ASSESSMENT

Once we have collected the data, we next need to know what we should do with it. Data acts as the pathway toward finding and understanding the advantage or disadvantage of making trading decisions based on similar occurrences. It acts as the catalyst to help you make the correct statistical decisions. Poor execution of such information has vaporized many a trading account. What is the data telling you about this particular setup? What is the data telling you about you? Using information to tell a story is rather easy and only limited by the capabilities of the data management software used.

Using information to determine the human element is much harder to assess, largely due to the high level of psychological components involved in the human mind and how one reacts to any given set of circumstances. When assessing the human element in trade history, I want to consider a wider scope of data in my assessment. For example, if I were looking to hire a trader for my team, I probably would seek information about their entire career, educational achievements, and other pertinent experiences and skills. Since their most recent skills better correlate to the position at hand, I may put more weight on that experience. This does not mean I neglect their prior achievements at earlier jobs or their overall level of ethics from their entire work history. The same goes for assessing trade histories. I may only need six months of credible market data to have a general understanding of a particular event and a determination of edge within a reasonable margin of error. For the same edge determination using a trader's trade history, I would seek a larger journal sample in order to capture the trader's ability to be compliant with trade execution and management.

If you dedicate yourself to data assessment with the fullest integrity, you understand the law of large numbers and expect variance to occur. Big winning streaks and even losing streaks are part of the game, and you must embrace them. Your focus is on the inherent edge that exists even after the biggest losing streaks, and you have the responsibility to execute the next market opportunity providing a similar edge without bias. It may not feel comfortable, but it is part of the execution plan we are being paid to implement. Any data set you review will never be perfect. There are volumes of in-depth analysis on the approaches to determine proper sample sizing and the assessments that follow. NASA or perhaps scientists seeking the drug that cures cancer need to adhere to the ultimate published standards. We are traders mixed up in a game with lots of randomness and a margin of error that is larger than most corporate forecasting departments. My advice is to try to keep data assessment relatively simple, if there is such a thing. We are not scientists or even data analysts, so don't try to replicate them. We are traders who understand that the data we maintain or even our assessment capabilities will never be perfect. What we do know is that the data we have will allow us to make reasonable trade decisions based on sound analytics. If there is a margin of error in your assessments, the market results will let you know relatively quickly, thus normalizing your results even further.

I have encountered some who are a bit obsessive with gathering the largest sample size before executing a strategy. I raise my hat to them but suggest they seek a valid sample rather than the largest. Assuming it is in fact a valid sample, the results will not vary so much as to dramatically impact your business. I have seen the desire for perfection reduce execution risk to near zero. This is because they passed on valid trade activity due to their belief that their data set was not fully complete. Remember to focus on edge, not perfection.

How we summarize our data is also an important element in the data-driven process. While performing risk management in the corporate sector, I am usually asked to summarize a process, quantify it, and then perhaps add some summary commentary to the analysis, such as lessons learned and process improvement ideas. When I perform risk management in the trading sector, I immediately notice the shrinking verbiage and commentary being replaced by statistical summary numbers or results, as if an entire setup or trader's performance can be summarized in a percentage. Sure, many components such as compliance, risk-to-reward, or even trade frequency can be summarized numerically, but often I find more complex processes with multiple variables represented in its simplest form. Perhaps the result requires a weighting element or an indication that certain elements do not apply. Trading index futures during the day and then overnight is a perfect example of why not to summarize trade histories since these markets conduct themselves so differently with both having many different variables.

In the end, we want to know what decisions we should make based on our data. What should I be waiting for? When do I execute? What share or contract size should I use? Do I have an edge? In risk-based trading, it's all about edge. Let the numbers do the talking, even if the numbers aren't perfect. Trying to quantify anything that involves a group of humans making decisions on the fly can be a daunting task, not to mention quantifying it with a single summary number or effectiveness percentage. Overall as a society, we tend to hunger for simple in-your-face statistical summaries. I am as guilty as the rest of us. Give me the number and be done with it. Wall Street dumps a stock because a company's earnings were the largest ever, but forward-looking numbers are 2 percent less than expectations. Television networks cancel shows because of a Nielsen rating generated by a small (however valid) sample that says they watch shows slightly less than the heavily advertised pilot.

The very statistical "measure everything" approach I have been preaching so far has its drawbacks when summarized in a single number. Perhaps there was a period during the sample where a trader had some personal challenges outside the trading arena or a period of having to watch too many valid and successful setups at once, resulting in missing more entries. Using summary results to communicate performance is a sound approach, but always look to support it with key information relevant to the decisions at hand. That supportive information will provide huge value to the lessons learned and development plan that we will discuss later.

BASIC PRINCIPLES OF MEASURING DATA

Your trading goals and particulars about your trading style come into consideration as to what you will be measuring. Ask yourself what the key variables are that, if successful, will give you an advantage in trading and thus allow you to meet your business goals and objectives. The infamous win-loss percentage is a popular measure and comes under much criticism in the trading community. It can be misleading since it does not consider any risk factors in the process of obtaining an attractive number. I have seen many traders go out of business with a 70 percent win percentage due to their disregard for risk. Their losing trades more than wiped out their winning ones even though the latter were in the majority. Win-loss percentage can be and is an effective measurement when used in combination with other measures, such as risk-reward and execution accuracy. My personal primary measurement for success is plan compliance expressed as a percentage of total trades. The belief is that if traders follow their plan effectively with little or no errors or emotional decisions, such as intentionally passing on a valid setup in compliance with all rules and filters, they would be successful over a valid sample size of trades. While profit and loss is the most common measurement for most traders, there is a direct correlation between plan compliance and success. Failure to implement a plan correctly results in greater losses and results below expectations. P&L and win percentage are the metrics of value to determine if your overall trading results are consistently flowing in the right direction. Certainly you cannot be meeting your objectives with consistently negative P&L. Win percentage, however, can paint different pictures for different trading styles. A 30 percent win rate can be reflective of a stellar options trader while 80 percent winning trades for a stock trader without risk considerations can result in failure.

The metrics are limited in that they do not show the complete picture of your actions. Let's use the example of a 60 percent win percentage and a P&L of $250 per trade. For this example, let's say that $250 is your expected average win per trade with the 60 percent win percentage. What does this tell you? If your goal was to achieve 60 percent and $250 per trade, did the market provide opportunities to generate such a metric? Perhaps the market allowed 70 percent winners during a period. Does 60 percent now seem acceptable? What if each trade averaged a chart resistance plan exit area at a level equivalent to $400 average gain per trade? Although you may have met your personal goals, did you leave opportunity on the table? Compliance metrics bring to light not only performance results but also activity in relation to total eligible market opportunities. Ultimately, a combination of performance metrics will form an optimal blend, allowing the trader and support team members to answer the question, "How am I doing?"

Statistics should be stated in a format as simple as possible. Summary data in a percentage of 100 or risk-to-reward information in relation to one (i.e., 2:1, 5:1, etc.) are common and reasonably understandable. They should be reflective not only as a stand-alone metric but within the entire key performance metric report. Using the win percentage example above, you should include an average risk per trade component to support each metric. Having a compliance metric may include several subsets of metrics including rules violated, missed entries, or filter avoidance.

These measures should also be something that is useful and not just something that is easy to measure. I often see a metric that measures the number of trades taken during a reporting period. A potentially valuable metric for those who have noted their tendency to overtrade, it also can have little meaning as a stand-alone figure. What adds importance to the number is the ratio to the overall number of opportunities provided in the market during that same time. If you are seeking to keep your trade count a bit lower but the market is for some reason providing a higher frequency of opportunities, then a rising trade count may not be such a bad thing. Perhaps adding an additional filter may be the proper adjustment, rather than getting dinged for allegedly trading too much.

Lastly, there should be a standard level of ethics when working with your summary statistics. This means not only being accurate with your information but presenting it in a format that is not misleading. Having results sorted in a logical order with dependent metrics in the same summary section is a good example. One visual that can be easily manipulated is chart visuals when attempting to show a trend of results. A chart can make the worst numbers look good. Some of the worst-performing companies have annual reports that make them look as if they are leaders in their industry. Be honest with yourself and the people who have an interest in your success. Whether it is a coach, auditor, investor, or even a spouse, stakeholders in your success can only assist if provided information presented in a format that allows them to perform their roles in assuring such success.

PERFORMANCE MANAGEMENT: WHAT IS THE DATA TELLING ME?

Just looking at the result of a trade should not be the basis of judging if it was a good trade decision. Good trading decisions can have negative outcomes, and bad trades can work out. It happens quite often in trading. If a win was good and a loss was bad, there would be little need for trade reviews or trade audits. There would be one metric: wins vs. losses. Our data can tell us so much more, and the best in trading and in other businesses use data to bring their game to the highest level. It is unfortunate that many new traders do not understand this concept of good trading vs. poor trading. Just ask a trader, "How did you do today?" Almost always they will base their day on their P&L performance. There may be a few digs about missing a few trades or a couple of bad beats or even that runner that just kept going. For the most part, the response will end with some reference to their points or dollars gained or lost. Generally, when a trader makes good decisions based on historical data and not from emotion, he or she will generally receive better outcomes over a large sample size of activity.

Being able to interpret what your trade data are telling you is an art that breeds value for a trader. It allows one to pinpoint deficiencies or areas of development. It may further confirm a belief that a setup has a valid edge or it may invalidate it. Assessing data can also bring out psychological deficiencies that need to be overcome. Now that you are hopefully sold on the importance of trade data, it is time to put it into action. For this to take place, we need to first track certain trade information and follow it up with solid data assessment.

DEVELOPING A TRADE JOURNAL

Risk-based trading is founded on the basis of using historical trade data to make future trade decisions. Having an easy-to-use record repository for this data is essential for performance assessment. Many track their trades with a simple date, security symbol, number of shares or contracts, win-loss result, and dollar impact on the trading account. It is a much better foundation than one who doesn't track activity at all, but what exactly does this simplistic journal tell you? Win-loss percentage? Average number of trades taken per day? Overall impact to your trading account? Perhaps all three. In order to use your data effectively, we need enough data to be able to track specific aspects of plan compliance and risk. A trade journal could be quite deceiving if you have a great win percentage and some initial profits but execute a poor risk management plan. If you have a good record but continuously break plan rules to do it, your plan will not tell you that you are on a path to trader destruction. For an effective plan that adds value to your business, you need to be able to obtain summary data in the following areas:

1. **Trade results**—Of course, this is one of the more logical benefits of a journal. The ability to track each plan setup independently is also important. Other factors such as time of day, market conditions, and the daily trend are also data points that can add value and improve your trading.

2. **Detect plan compliance**—Data analytics is more than just the ultimate outcome. Since plan compliance is one of the most critical success factors in trading, a solid plan must be able to generate statistics on a trader's ability to follow a plan with precision. Such data will assess your ability to execute a plan.

3. **Bring to light deficiencies**—Trade journal development is that of a process improvement project. Like any professionals, we all need to continue to improve our skills and reduce our deficiencies. Using our data to detect such opportunities is essential to your success as a trader.

As you construct your trade journal and its components, be sure to evaluate its core functionality and ability to meet the above requirements. There can be minor variations in your style and in the specific components you are tracking. Many change their tracking components several times during their trading career. As your business develops, there is a good chance your appetite for valuable analytics will also grow with your mission to become a better and more profitable trader.

Your journal can have different components depending on the type of securities you trade. Stock traders may have an indicator that segregates after-hours trading. Forex traders may wish to determine if their trades are trend-based trades that correlate with other currency pairs. Options traders often seek to include "Greek" premium or expiration data to measure the differentials in results when compared to these variables unique to the options market. Here we discuss the more common and effective data points to consider in your journal. Just remember that any data point that is retrievable and is able to be tracked can be included. Keep it simple in the beginning and be sure your journal can meet all three value objectives.

Common Components

Your collection of trade information is the backbone that allows the ability to determine your trading business production and compliance. Your trading style and the securities you trade allow you to add or omit certain components; however, these components should be considered staples in your trade journal.

Date The date field will not only track the obvious "when," but also allow one to show results within a variety of reporting time periods.

Account For those with multiple accounts for strategic or product-driven purposes, you may have different needs to keep summary results separated. For example, one account might be an IRA, so you want to segregate accounts for your tax professional. One account may be an individual account, while another may use external funds or a partnership structure. The most common purpose for individual traders is for them to have separate accounts to accommodate their broker's requirements: one for stock, one for forex, and one for futures, for example.

Time Commonly recorded in an hourly period, time can bring to light specific periods within a trading day when a particular pattern's results may differ depending on the time the trade took place. Generally it is most appropriate to record time of entry as the proper time category. Rather than just using hourly trade brackets, consider replacing them with those that reflect common market behavior. For example, have one bracket that captures the initial open or a common time period for news events. Lunchtime has its own market behavior, so I recommend the 11:00 AM–12:30 PM CDT time bracket for equities and stock futures traders. Commodities and bonds have unique price and volume characteristics that are product specific. In order to allow your data to speak the loudest, try to be innovative in having your trade journal time frames reflect your product's market behavior.

Setup Having more than one edge-generating setup is a key driver in the risk-based approach. The ability to generate information specific to each setup is critical for your success. One should know how each setup is performing against others and against all other data components in your plan. Consider your setups like thoroughbreds all racing against each other. Wouldn't you want to know who keeps winning the races and at what time of day or under which market conditions they are winning them the most?

Trend Certain execution strategies or setups tend to shine in different markets. Some are designed to take advantage of a trending market, while others gather confluence at anticipated market inflection points in an attempt to "fade" the move. Knowing how your setup is performing in different market conditions will allow you to focus on the conditions that allow it to shine. Even with a 60 percent setup success rate, wouldn't you like to know that the setup results have a 67 percent edge when faded versus a 53 percent edge when going with the trend? This data point acts as a filter to allow you to focus on the best conditions to trade a specific setup. Consider it a form of confluence providing you with additional edge.

Setup Pattern Time Frame   When you start to build your initial setup list, you will spend a majority of your time back-testing chart patterns and other data and events in hopes that it will provide an edge over a valid series of trials. If some of those setups are discovered from chart patterns, you need to nail down during which time frame your pattern is most effective. A day trader may use a 5-minute chart while a swing trader may initially seek 60-minute or daily charts to see if their pattern is effective. Often a pattern is effective by only using a particular chart time frame. Only back-testing and continuous trade journal management and assessment will eventually lead you to the ultimate time-frame nirvana. Many beginning traders give up on a setup only to realize that the chart pattern was a moneymaker on a particular time frame that they neglected to validate.

Quantity/Size   As you build your business, you will not be trading more but trading larger size as you build your confidence as a trader. Building your trading capital account can be challenging during the trading discovery period. Building your business in a systematic fashion by trading higher share or contract amounts is imperative for an effective business risk platform. Recording the quantity allows one to measure performance variations when size is a factor. It also allows you to determine a psychological "scarcity" level that is required to move to the next level. We will discuss shortly how to systematically graduate your business to higher share quantities as you become more successful.

Initial Risk-to-Reward   One of the key auditing tools for any trader is to determine your success in relation to the amount of risk placed on the table. Tracking reward is relatively easy. Mark each trade by a win or loss or even the net dollar amount gained or lost. How much you are risking is often overlooked. Recording the amount of points you are willing to lose in relation to the trade success target will allow the trader to determine optimal risk levels that should be taken before deciding to enter a trade.

Primary Confluence   In our earlier definition of confluence, we seek to use multiple layers of nonrelated factors to support our trade entry premise. Each setup should have a preferred minimum of two forms of confluence to trigger a trade after a setup pattern has been detected.

Tracking this data will allow one to determine not only if a setup is creating the desired edge, but also if a greater edge is being found when using specific forms of confluence. Often you will be trading a generic chart pattern setup. Once you determine that the same chart pattern generated an even bigger edge when occurring at a major market profile support level or Fibonacci inflection price, you may seek to enter that trade only when all three come together. Trading off such information often separates the surviving trader from the future pro.

Result—Win/Loss One of the core staples of any tracking program is the infamous win/loss metric. It is certainly valid to track such information since it provides a good snapshot over time if a pattern, setup, or even a trading business is successful. It's easy to track, and that is why most traders do it. Most conversations among traders refer to this metric when asked, "How is your trading going?" From a risk management perspective, it is highly overrated and generates little value overall if one is not in full compliance with the trading plan. For example, one who continuously exits winning trades too early only to capture the "W" in the journal will have a high win percentage, only to be out of business because the exorbitant losses could not be offset by the small gains. Only when a trader is in complete plan compliance does a win-loss metric have any validity. Nonetheless, it is a staple in nearly all journals, and we can include such in an attempt to add validity to the plan-compliant trader.

Costs Any business has costs, and for a trader there is no cost more visually depressing than transaction costs. Brokerage fees generated each and every time you push the button attempt to slowly eat away at your hard-earned gains as well as the painful losses. While not as obviously visible, it is opportunity cost that is the greatest cost to your business, but it is rarely tracked. With the exception of transaction cost containment efforts, these data provide little value within the trade journal. Performing a cost comparison assessment among service providers should be performed from time to time; however, tracking these costs line-by-line is often futile and unproductive.

Uncommon Tracking Components

A trade journal by definition is a data warehouse that stores actual trade activity. As we'll see shortly, you can use this information to make data-driven decisions to improve your trading results. Its limitation is that it only tracks the executed opportunities that you decided to trade. What about the ones you decided to pass on? Weren't they valid setups?

Executed vs. Nonexecuted If one of our goals is to determine if a setup is generating the proper edge, shouldn't we be tracking the result each time the event occurred? Having this additional data allows for more precision with less variance per the law of large numbers theory. One can still track such information by adding a component such as "not traded." Why was it not traded? If it did not meet the valid criteria for the setup, then it should not be recorded. This would apply only if it was valid and should have been acted upon. It's an incredibly valuable piece of data since it not only allows for a more accurate summary of how the setup is doing, but allows you to track the results of the ones you opted to pass up. Over time, traders regret not taking these opportunities on a more consistent basis. Whatever scared them away from entering usually ended up costing them in opportunity cost. One annual audit performed on a "successful" trader showed that his success would have more than doubled if he had executed on only 25 percent of the missed setups he decided to pass on for whatever the reason.

Tracking Phantom Trades

Having a trade journal is important, but tracking the right data is imperative. Auditing "opportunity risk" is equally as important as measuring your actual trades. You simply cannot afford to overlook it.

Since I started trading, I have kept some form of records in a trade journal. The actual data components I track and the structure have changed several times since my spreadsheet days, but the information gathered from the journal still acts as the basis for my trading decisions.

I applaud those who maintain a trade journal in any form and use the information to develop solid strategies that provide a consistent trading edge. Even the best-kept journals, however, miss the mark on one of the biggest risk exposures to the trader: opportunity risk. Simply put, it is the appropriate market opportunities that you don't execute—the ones that never make it to the journal— that create a gap in your performance.

In all the risks associated with trading, I find opportunity risk, whether in the form of unexecuted trades or pretarget exits, to be the difference between traders who reach that much-talked-about top 10 percent in the profession and those who remain in the novice pool, struggling to keep their heads (and P&L) above water.

To overcome such risks to your trading business, the first step is to acknowledge that your source of trade data should be expanded to include eligible, yet unexecuted, valid setups.

Actual trades executed are only a fraction of the total population where the market provided you with such legitimate opportunities. For example, let's say you had several trades for the week with one of your favorite setups and you recorded them precisely in your trade journal. It's your favorite setup, of course, because it produces consistent gains, and you are proud of your ability to execute them. You assess your journal regularly, and the results confirm your positive variance. So far so good, right?

Good, perhaps, but how many opportunity dollars are you leaving on the table? Perhaps your daily goal is relatively low, and having a few good trades forces you to close up the platform early.

Or maybe you get a bit timid after a green morning and pass up the afternoon opportunities that would have provided you with a similar historical edge. Let's also not forget all those setups that were perfect but for which you stood aside because of your personal beliefs of where the market was heading.

As traders, we need to continuously remind ourselves that we are playing an opportunity game. When the market kindly grants us that historical edge, we as traders are paid to take advantage to optimize our reward for taking such predetermined risks in the marketplace.

So how do we overcome this opportunity gap? First, don't assess your performance based solely on the actual trades taken. The data assessed should be based on the actual valid opportunities when the market presented a particular trade setup in your plan.

After all, your trading plan doesn't tell you to trade only some of the opportunities that are giving you an edge over the market. Consider adding a plan-compliance ratio to your performance reviews that captures executed trades versus total market opportunities. This will allow you to pass up legitimate setups that your plan rules may not allow you to trade, such as setups just prior to news events, or setups during periods of high volatility. If a valid setup that has historically provided a trading edge is working for you, and you are only executing it 50 percent of the time, you are leaving good money on the table. It's like winning a horse race and neglecting to cash in some of the tickets. It takes focus, desire to succeed, and of course, discipline to execute your plan in robotic fashion.

As you develop and improve your trading skills, be sure to consider your execution compliance as a developmental metric and measure it consistently. You and your capital account will be glad you did.

—Source: Michael Toma, www.TWCFutures.com, 2010.

Emotional Status   One of the few non-numerical data points is recording a psychological element of a trade. Since it is such a dominant factor in the success of a trader, it is only fitting to record a metric that brings out trader emotion at the time of the trade. You should be commended if you already record such information. My question to you is, "How are you using that information to help you improve your trading?" Many include free-form text information that cannot be assessed on a large scale. To assist in measuring this data, consider a numerical drop-down or combo box that includes the most common emotional feelings that you encounter while trading. Here is a list of some common emotions that traders deal with:

1. Worried that the current trend was over
2. I had locked in profits for the day
3. Scared to take the valid trade after loss
4. Left the trading desk
5. Didn't feel in connection with the markets
6. Market analyst on TV said the market was going down
7. Trading room was short at the time of my long setup

When you include a number with the emotion you now can generate valuable data to help alleviate emotionally based trading decisions. For example, you may find that you would have had a 62 percent success rate if you had overcome the emotional element listed as #4. To assess further, using an average share size, you can quantify in dollars the amount of money left on the table due to this emotional barrier. Our attempt with this exercise is to enable the ability to track our emotions in a data-driven format and allow us to ultimately measure plan compliance.

Compliance Factor   For the risk manager, this is the most prominent metric that should be tracked in a trade journal. No one single piece of data is more valuable. This is a binary metric that asks the question, "Have you followed your plan rules on this trade?" A simple yes or no is an acceptable approach. If you can assume that your trading plan is designed to capture edge and profit from it, then measuring an execution compliance rate is the key piece of data to ultimately measure success. In essence, your trading plan states, "If you do this, you will be successful." The compliance metric answers the question, "Did you do this?" If there is only one piece of information you obtain in an effort to incorporate risk principles into your trading, it is measuring plan compliance.

Noncompliance Reason   You will have trades that you simply should not have entered into, entered at a price less advantageous than your plan allowed you to, or perhaps exited earlier than the planned stop or target price. When the compliance metric is "N," one can generate valuable data to assist in improving plan compliance in future trades. Recording the "why" will lend focus as to the area of development needed in order to improve.

Every trader makes mistakes. It is the ones who learn from them that become successful.

Here are a few examples that you can add to your drop-down box menu:

1. Executed too late.
2. Executed perfectly but needed to get back the last few losses.
3. I scaled-out too early to be sure I was green on the trade.
4. Right setup; wrong time of day.
5. Didn't check to see if trade had valid confluence of support and got stopped out.
6. Traded on "tilt" due to personal matter.
7. Valid setup and entry but did not have proper risk-to-reward minimum.

Keep in mind that noncompliant trades and profit/loss results are two separate and unrelated data points. You can and often will have noncompliant trades that make you money and compliant trades that lose money. Allow for the compliance component to be determined based on your plan rules. Never, ever allow trade results to be the component that determines trade compliance.

MEASURING SUCCESS THROUGH A KPI

You may recall being introduced to the key performance indicator (KPI) dashboard concept earlier in the risk management process section of this book. Here we will go one step further and custom build your KPI dashboard so you can manage your trade quality and compliance. A standard introduction in any Western world culture is simply, "How are you doing?" In the corporate risk world, different stakeholders want to know about their respective interests in areas of productivity, quality, compliance, and of course profits, to name a few. How do traders know how they are doing? How do they measure their success? How do they define success? I once had a trading group that told me that they use only one gauge to measure success: profits. "We really have only one goal and that is to make money for our traders and the company." Do you use the same in how you measure your success?

The argument is quite valid given that you can't buy clothes for the kids with plan compliance measures nor pay the mortgage with risk-to-reward stats. The critical difference is to measure the components of your business that ultimately generate profits or whatever else your other goal in trading may be. Taking this approach allows you to take a magnifying glass to expose the strengths and weaknesses as a trader and set the stage to take the necessary actions to improve in a respective category, thus affecting the ultimate goal or desired outcomes. Measuring our decisions and other processes is quite powerful in creating effective positive change. One of the mantras in risk management is "If it isn't measured, it doesn't get done." If you measure the most important areas of trading, you are building the platform for improvement and allow for the risk identification process to be conceived. Measuring performance exists in almost everything we do and is a staple in almost every work environment imaginable. Companies use performance metrics to evaluate individuals to determine their value as employees. Many are compensated based on the very results of such measurements. Trading is no different. There is no better example where the salary model of "the higher the scores—the better the pay" applies.

So what can we measure that provides us with the information we need to determine how we are doing? First, we need to measure our business activity. This is not our profit and loss but the activities we perform as traders to generate such profits. These measurements or metrics are the key processes that are aligned with our core trading strategy. To assign a value to the measure, we need to establish performance indicators that quantitatively allow us to measure the result numerically. Key performance indicators or KPIs and their management have become extremely popular and effective as a method of measuring performance and risk. The biggest and the best of IT consulting companies have endless competitive products to allow an individual or the largest of companies to measure their performance. Combined with a business intelligence framework that assists in the improvement of key metrics, today's traders have all the tools available to help them reach their goals.

Each key performance indicator that we seek to establish will have several attributes. For one, KPIs should always be linked to a core strategy. For example, the consistent execution of a trade setup is a good example of a core strategy. The KPI measurement may include the quantitative scoring of how compliant we are in executing our trades when these setups present themselves in the market. KPIs also have a specific target that represents successful implementation of the process and a range of acceptable performance. Some targets may include a desired result, such as a number where rule-compliance KPIs may require a near zero-tolerance range of 98–100 percent. These ranges are areas of acceptable practice that should contribute toward your core strategic goal and not trigger an identified risk or required action plan.

The optimal risk performance plan is one that is relatively simple to use, simple to understand, and can be interpreted easily by an outside party. Reading them should be rather straightforward. The trader or person reviewing the KPIs should be able to look at the summary information and know whether a measured process is within the expectations set out in the plan. One should also be able to determine at an immediate glance how the result compares to previously measured results. This allows one to trend the results and determine if a red flag may be approaching even though the results may be within an acceptable range.

My personal preference is a visual KPI display option, often referred to as a dashboard. A good KPI dashboard will highlight the metrics being assessed at a high level. Consider it your ship's instrument panel or indicators on your car's dashboard, thus the name. It should provide the status of the result in relation to the expected result. The dashboard should also have a column where the net differential in the target and actual results, or variance, is noted. A metric such as the average number of trades per day, for example, is a numerical KPI and so it will have a variance measurement. A metric such as a simple trade win percentage will of course be displayed as a percentage in the KPI and variance.

The level of complexity can vary depending on the size of your trading operation, the number of metrics used, and the desired amount of data you wish to measure. Having a dashboard for an individual trader starting out compared to a 20-person prop firm will vary due to many factors, including the number of stakeholders who are interested in the data. Proprietary firms may seek additional metrics from outside stakeholders such as partnership owners, consultants, or perhaps the firm's risk manager. A misnomer is that the bigger the operation, the bigger the dashboard. Of course, larger firms may have drill-down data structures where management can review metrics by individual trader, by product, or by specific categories of risks. In measuring key performance indicators for a trading operation, the principles discussed above still should remain as the standard for any size operation.

So how do we choose our target and acceptable range? There is no exact science to setting these parameters, but you do want to assure that the targets are achievable. Setting a KPI target that is more wishful thinking than reality will only disappoint. Secondly, are the targets reflective of your trading goals? If one goal is to average x points per day but reaching that target will not result in reaching longer-term goals such as self-sufficiency as a trading professional, your performance indicator will not be effective. KPIs should also be measured against a benchmark that reflects an initial challenge to improve results and performance. Experienced traders who may have kept a trade journal can use historical results to determine an approximate target. Logically, we seek to improve our results from one period to another. The following simple formula should be considered when determining future target measures:

Prior results $\times$ (1 $\times$ improvement factor rate) = Future target

You may consider reaching out to others in the industry that have benchmarked against similar metrics. These groups can range from trader education firms to brokerage houses, and even the exchanges. Many of my initial benchmarks were refined by mentors and by inquiring of professionals at the end of webinars held by trading firms and at trading conventions. You can determine your ranges using the same historical data or outside sources. The most important factor in determining ranges is acceptance. Initially consider what results would still be considered an acceptable threshold that would not require you to add it to your risk identification list. As you develop your risk management plan and experience as a trader, these benchmarks and ranges will be modified to more accurately reflect your current performance level and experience gained.

Most of the trading performance indicators will be quantitative in nature. We measure trading activity by quantity or an average of some figure, such as win/loss results. Qualitative results may include feedback from mentors or consultants. These consultants may assess historical performance aspects of your trading but also may comment on the development of your psychological toughness. Recall the trading pyramid. The top achievement of fulfillment is extremely difficult to measure quantitatively. While a majority of our KPIs will be quantitatively measured, please keep your mind open for qualitative methods to assess not only trading performance but any personal inhibitors that could impact your ultimate trading goals.

General Rules

Constructing a performance management platform is more art than science. Using the components discussed here will provide a solid framework that allows the trader to monitor and measure performance in relation to the trading goals. Please consider these guidelines when constructing your KPI dashboard.

Keep it simple—Less is more, specifically with individual or two–three-person trading partnerships. Too many performance and compliance measurements dilute the attention required for the ultimate measurements. Stick to five to eight measurable items at first. You can always increase them as your business expands. The more you measure, the more you must track and record. This also results in more identified risks that require assessment via the risk management process. Fifty-page reports may have the "wow" factor in the corporate world, but not in trading. Remember, they call them *key* indicators for a valid reason.

Understandable—The dashboard summary page should be reasonably understandable by other traders and nontraders alike. I have come across highly complex ratios and calculations with formulas directly out of an MIT calculus course. Not only are they difficult to understand but also a challenge to address. A nontrading spouse can be an excellent litmus test to determine if your KPIs are too intricate.

Adds value to your trading business—Performance metrics are measured because they are a valuable indicator of your business. Having a goal of mimicking a moderator's trading room calls will have little value if the room closes down. KPIs should be able to detect a change in trend or noncompliance with a quick look and be accompanied by a known corrective action plan that can be implemented immediately.

Balanced in scope—The indicators should represent a balanced monitoring synopsis of performance, compliance, and business metrics. A common gap in KPI programs is that it is completely dominant in trade result metrics. A measure that detects rule breaking is far more indicative of trading success than a KPI that measures current win percentage over a small time period.

Transparency and integrity—Reportable KPI figures should be generated from spreadsheets or other software that cannot be manipulated. It may be asking too much for an individual trader to adhere to the latest Sarbanes-Oxley internal controls standards regarding audit processes and reporting controls. Proprietary firms, however, should consider these standards as the norm. For traders that manipulate data (ever have a losing trade that didn't count?), in the end they are only hurting themselves.

Not overly sensitive—Measured data points can have a dizzying effect if they do not account for normal variance within a particular time period or number of events. My own trading plan includes 10 setups that are part of my plan. Eighty percent of my trades are generated from my top three setups. This leaves some setups with proportionately less trade activity, thus requiring a greater acceptable risk variance for the same measurement period. The results often would be scattered in every direction—one month making me look like the greatest trader in the world and the next on the precipice of shutting down. How should one handle this? One option is to measure these setups once they have reached an activity trade level that would allow for a smaller margin of error. Always have a standard minimum of 30 trades as a starting point. If your outcomes on some setups have a large range, consider measuring them once you have a series of 50 or greater. If during your assessment period you do not have such activity, just place a note in that KPI result field advising that you will assess once a minimum count of the activity is attained. Another option is to widen your acceptable range so it does not continuously trigger unwarranted risk warnings.

Ability to cascade—The above also serves as a simple example of KPI cascading. Using a "master" KPI of trade performance of all setups should also have the capability of measuring each component for your trading plan valid setups. You will quickly notice that performance will vary from the averages of the entire setup group. This allows the trader to drill down to perform risk assessments on trade setups that warrant such, even though the overall high-level metric may have met or exceeded targeted standards.

Data is king—The entire concept of KPI, and in fact the risk management program to trading, is mandated on the concept of clean data. All recorded data and other business information must be clean, valid, consistent, and accurate. The trader and any other part of the trader's coaching team must be able to trust the data. A predominant factor in performing risk analytics is the ability to not only understand a trade group's data but also be convinced of its accuracy and integrity.

There is no official rule book when constructing a KPI dashboard. Regardless of the guidelines followed or omitted, the best dashboard is an effective dashboard that plays a critical part in allowing you to achieve your goals.

Dashboard Metrics

The following section will provide you with several key performance indicators that you can use to monitor your progress as a trader. Again, the purpose is to identify areas of development as well as confirmation that a setup or aspect of your trading is meeting the expectations set in your trading plan. You can use the KPIs listed here or an offshoot of them that you customize to fit your trading plan and style. You have lots of flexibility with this assignment, and you should make every attempt to make it your own.

1. **Average Number of Trades per Day**

    Formula: Total number of trades for a specific period divided by the number of periods.

Purpose: Designed to alert the trader if there is a significant increase or decrease in trading activity when compared to other time periods. If you are averaging 2.5 trades per day and then it jumps to 6.0 trades, this might indicate overtrading or be a result of overconfidence. This also may simply indicate that there are more opportunities presenting themselves in the market, or perhaps you are simply identifying them better. Conversely, a drop in this metric below a historical average may reveal a hint of fear or an intentional pullback in activity due to a trader going into "tester" mode during live trading. Perhaps you are closing up shop early after a green morning. This isn't a bad or good metric. What one should be seeking is the variation in the frequency of trades. This metric is often measured in combination with a compliance indicator. For example, a reduction in average trade volume combined with a metric that measures the percentage of a setup taken in relation to the market opportunities indicates a potential fear component that needs to be addressed.

2. **Average Quantity of Shares (or Contracts) Traded**

   Formula: Total number of shares divided by the total number of trades.

   Purpose: To indicate proper growth of your business according to your trading and business plan. Traders create more wealth not by trading more, but by repeating the same trading activity with increasingly larger share size. This gradual increase in size must be in congruence with your graduation plan, where you increase size after a series of successes and reduce after a time of negative results. While many traders tend to get too aggressive with share size too early, your business is at even greater risk when you are required to increase size but opt to stay at the current level. This opportunity risk may be supported by psychological components that are often faced when moving to a higher share or contract level. This is frequently observed even during times of trading success. One's inability to grow as the trading plan defines growth can be a critical barrier to trading. This KPI metric is a must for the dashboard to indicate you should slow things down or bump up size.

3. **Ratio of Trades Reaching Target vs. Trades Hitting a Stop**

   Formula: Total number of trades reaching target vs. total number of trades taken.

   Purpose: Rather than track wins and losses, this KPI adds a compliance element to it. The metric only includes the trades that stayed the course until target or stop. Any trades taken off too early, regardless of outcome, are not included. This will allow the trader to get a true sense of edge on trade setups. It is encouraged to display each setup separately within this metric to determine which one of your horses is continuously winning the race.

4. **Trades Reaching Target vs. Total Trades**

   Formula: Trades closed out prior to target or stop vs. total trades.

   Purpose: A pure compliance KPI enabled to detect early exit noncompliance. There will be rules in your plan that allow you to close a position early. This indicator helps surface noncompliant trading decisions and the potential opportunity cost for them.

5. **Opportunity Risk**

   Formula: Number of missed trades vs. total opportunities.

   Purpose: Best when tracked for each setup, the indicator places a point or dollar amount on trades that were intentionally or unintentionally neglected. The data point may indicate that the setup is more difficult to trade live than when tested in simulation. It also may reveal a fear component. Regardless, any money left on the table is lost money and would indicate the need to develop the skills to optimally execute trades when the market provides the opportunity.

6. **Performance Consistency**

   Formula: Number of time periods of account growth vs. total number of periods.

   Purpose: To determine your ability to produce profitable trades on a consistent basis. A common indication of new trades is to have three or four weeks of positive trading only to see this mass devastation in the fourth week. While the metric may not be a tell-all, the indicator could alarm the trader or team of deeper root cause issues, perhaps trading too much size when overconfident or chasing a losing week with greater size. The number of periods used can be days, weeks, or another standard. If you are preparing an annual summary, a monthly period may be best. Consistency is king in trading, and this KPI will provide early indication if such consistency isn't meeting the minimum quality standard.

7. **Risk-to-Reward Ratio**

   Formula: Average risk taken in points vs. average reward expected in points.

   Purpose: To provide an average risk-to-reward for your entire trading portfolio and for each trade setup. Contrary to what most believe, a good risk-to-reward ratio does not have to be 3:1, 5:1, 10:1, or greater. A 1:1 risk-to-reward with a consistent 65 percent success rate will make you a very successful trader over time. This metric is to alert you to changes in your risk-to-reward parameter. If you have historically noticed 2:1 risk-to-reward success on a particular setup but find it dropping to 1.5:1, this KPI will alert you to perform a risk assessment. Perhaps it's a trade setup that just isn't capturing that 2:1 as in the past. It also may be a sign of taking profits too early, thus maintaining your historical trade success edge, but at a lower profit margin.

8. **Number of Days in Full Compliance**

   Formula: Number of trading days of full compliance vs. total trading days for the same period.

   Purpose: The quintessential compliance metric to measure one's ability to follow a trading plan. The metric takes the compliance column data in your plan and summarizes it into a percentage. Market randomness can determine many a trade outcome, but regardless of result, you should be reaching for 95–98 percent compliance with this metric. Root cause assessment is required when any given review period sheds results less than near perfect. This KPI is vitally important to your success since those that do not follow their plan rules almost never become successful traders.

9. **Performance Edge by Setup Opportunity**

   Formula: Total quantity of net points gained during a specific time period or series.

   Purpose: To determine which setup in your trading plan is providing the most value and opportunity. Notice how the KPI does not measure trade results only. It measures total opportunity. While one can substitute trade-only data, obtaining the net points of total opportunities and then comparing them to their setup peers is the ultimate apples-to-apples job fair. Several applicants apply for the job, and you need to determine who will produce the best results. Consider this KPI a comparison of your employees. This metric not only determines who gets the job, but who gets the raise (in share quantity).

10. **Peak Performers by Day and Time**

    Formula: Net point results sorted by day and then by time period.

    Purpose: To determine peak days and times of the day when you are generating the most opportunities (and hopefully profits) for your setups. Sorting this data in reverse order could indicate the best time to step away from the markets, too. Such analytics can allow you to hone in on the best times, at least historically, when the market is giving the best opportunities. This is one of the few times when even a simple win-loss data metric will help alert you to high priority trading times.

TABLE 5.1	Displaying Trade Results by Time Frame					
Setup Number	Premarket	Open– 10:15 AM	10:15 AM– 12:00 PM	12:00 PM– 2:00 PM	2:00 PM– 2:45 PM	2:45 PM– Close
1		4–2	1–0		0–1	3–2
2	3–1	2–2	12–4	6–4	5–3	11–7
3		5–5	3–2			
4		2–5	3–3	1–0		
5		2–4	4–4	1–2	1–0	4–0
Totals	**3–1**	**15–18**	**23–13**	**8–6**	**6–4**	**18–9**
Win Percentage	**75.0%**	**45.4%**	**63.9%**	**57.1%**	**60.0%**	**66.7%**

Table 5.1 is a summary chart of win-loss trades broken down by time frame. Notice the challenging environment during the opening time frame. While some of the time frames surrounding lunch were profitable, the number of opportunities was much lower than in the 10:15 AM–12 noon EST and 2:45 PM–close time frame. Including such information on your dashboard tells you to be at total focus during this time frame. No phones, no e-mail, no distractions. Take a long lunch to refresh your mind for the last 1.25 hours of trading. They are your money-making time frames. Be prepared and ready to go.

Use a similar model to incorporate days of the week into the mix. The dashboard will highlight not only the best times of day but also the best performing days of the week. Using actual trade data will surface information personal to you. Perhaps a setup has the best opportunities on a Monday morning, but your ability to get into trading mode after a weekend might not be as compatible as you would have hoped. Consider adjusting to the market opportunities, but also let your data tell you information that cannot be overlooked.

The dashboard KPIs generally reference three categories: quality, compliance, and setup-related data. Many will have a flavorful element or two, if not all three. You may notice that most of them have little to do with profit detection. This is modeled precisely from the risk manager playbook. Risk professionals truly do not place much of a priority on measuring profits. A rising capital account is really all that is needed to detect such. Risk professionals are focusing entirely on trade compliance and then drilling down to the setups and trader qualities that enable trading success. Most importantly, these indicators bring issues to light early so you can mitigate the risk exposure each data point addresses. Adjust these samples to your liking or create your own key performance indicators. As long as they alert you to areas of development or internal issues that are preventing your success, they truly live up to their "key" performance acronym.

Tools and Vendors

As data analytics and the importance of measuring data have become more prominent in the business world, so has the desire to do so in the trading world. The availability of different software vendors and their charting capabilities has never been greater. As business needs for transparency and precision increase, so does the availability of tools and software for the data-driven trader.

The data and software industries have created some interesting products that are appealing to today's trader. Some focus more on the high-end trading operations such as hedge or proprietary funds where there is a need to capture data and include advanced reporting and accounting features. For individual traders, the choices are rather limited, but much greater than in the spreadsheet days of old. As if the high-tech risk manager wouldn't be caught dead with a spreadsheet as his or her trade journal of choice, many ask what high-flying Silicon Valley–produced version of trade journal management is on a risk manager's desktop?

The choice you decide to make should be based purely on your operation's needs and budget. Individual traders can perform most analytical tasks using the latest spreadsheet version. The most popular database software packages will also allow you to perform the analytics as well as generate summary reports.

The latest tool to accommodate the trader and any other risk professional, for that matter, is business intelligence software, or BI. The Cognos line created by IBM has many features that allow the ability to perform powerful analytics or intelligence mining. Since most are used in the business sector, they include root cause analysis and the ability to generate flashy summary charts and reporting features. Alert indicators allow you to develop acceptable ranges of compliance or performance and set off alarms when these valid areas are breached.

The most important decision in KPI management is the commitment made to tracking and assessing your data. While certain charting software has some impressive bells and whistles, some traders put the cart in front of the horse and seek the flashy features that take their mind away from the core purpose of KPI management: detecting edge in the market. Coming from the world of 80-page corporate business plans that provide little about the business, I'm somewhat of a skeptic when handed large trading plans and high-tech business intelligence (BI) software. My suggestion is to keep it simple, especially in the beginning of your trading venture. Many tools will provide gadgets that you may never use, thus consider those with a simpler and cleaner design. As your business develops, you can slowly move toward more complex business solutions. One thing for sure, there will be plenty of vendors awaiting the opportunity to sell them to you.

TRADE REVIEW AND REPORTING ETHICS

Your summary findings that your auditing efforts produce are the pipeline that will fuel your development as a trader. Your consistent time investment into assessing your performance provides a value-add that most traders do not seek to pursue. Some entities are required not only to report results and supporting KPI information, but also to produce ethical attestation statements and disclosures reflecting accurate and unbiased information. These reporting and conformity to ethics standards are becoming more the norm in the hedge fund community as it continues to migrate toward a more regulated environment. For the most part, there is no regulatory body overseeing individual traders' reporting processes, hence the reason most do not perform any formal assessments or analytics. The one continuous theme throughout this book is that your investment in data and risk assessment will provide exponential value to your trading and your trading business. Regardless of any entity or individual forcing you to do so, it is a best practice that should be considered.

Throughout my consulting career, I have performed assessments on many traders who were eager to succeed. For one of many reasons, they did not. Their passion to succeed existed as well as their effort, but there was a common theme among many: Their strong desire could not lead them to actual trading success, however they defined such a term. When starting in a simulated trading environment, I would often receive comments next to trades, such as the following:

"I didn't mean to take this one."
"I wouldn't have taken this one live."
"Other than those rule breakers, at the end of the day I still managed to get green."
"Didn't see the conflicting signal. Considered no trade."

It's comical, but these are actual trade journal comments seen during my arduous reviews. It was as if a fairy godmother with a liberal eraser would come and wipe them clean off the brokerage statement. In real trading, once the button is pushed, there is no delete button. While I'm a fan of simulation as a learning tool, it can be quite forgiving when it comes to learning and development. It's too forgiving for some. When summarizing your key performance information, stating lessons learned, or completing your trade journal, you need to conduct yourself voluntarily with the same ethical standards as the regulated entities.

You might ask why you would need to do that if you have no particular stakeholders to address. What you do have is the biggest accountability for the number one stakeholder: yourself. Building your trading business requires you to take critical information as you develop to generate valuable performance improvement ideas. Fabricating or neglecting to include valuable trade information only limits the powerful capabilities of your data. The fabric of risk-based trading is the ideology of data-driven decision principles. The integrity and independent assessment of such data is vital for one to make the journey toward success.

Clearly this book is not about corporate ethics in a risk management environment. We'll leave that discussion for the other business texts. In regard to maintaining data integrity and reporting that holds up to the same standards, here are a few principles all traders should adhere to:

- **A trade is a trade**—Filtering out entries that you believe should not have counted or that you realize didn't meet the criteria of a valid setup will hurt you more in your career than any loss on any trade. Even the trades that went away by way of technical error, lightning, or the cat stepping on the buy button ultimately count. It's all factored into the valid data that allows you to improve your performance.
- **Sim is not sim; it's live trading without money**—Almost all new traders start out using a simulated platform in some form during the initial stages of their trading career. Using simulated platforms is one of the most effective methods of learning to trade without putting real dollars at risk. Today's simulated platforms are virtually the same as the live parallel, allowing a trader to develop with little transitional difference when moving to the live platform. Once you have mastered your execution platform and are implementing plan setups in simulation, you should be tracking all activity. This must include the good, bad, and ugly mistakes as well as those out of your control, such as technology-related failures. The reason is because these same errors will happen in a live environment from time to time. Neglecting to recognize such developmental opportunities is only pushing you backward in your quest for success. Remember, the most experienced traders probably have made the most mistakes. The difference is that they looked at them as opportunities to learn and minimize them from happening in the future.
- **This is not trading but more a business of trading**—Trading is not a video game activity, as many new traders describe it. It's hard work that takes thousands of hours of dedication, study, and mastery.

It requires networking with other successful peers just like any other business. Using data to reveal anything other than actual results would be considered ethical misconduct, misleading, or even fraud in the corporate world. The same should apply to the micro-account new trader as it does for the largest of managed funds.

Trading your own account has the benefit of your not having to answer to anyone. This lack of required business structure or enforceable ethical standards does more harm than good for many traders. Treat your trading like a business that you are accountable for. Having an independent person such as a coach tends to keep traders in check and is a highly recommended investment.

BENCHMARKING

Now that you have the framework to track key trading performance data, you may be asking yourself, "What does it mean? What does it tell me? When do I know if I am at the performance level I should be at?" After compiling your results, you need to be able to compare such results to another metric to truly determine what the results mean. What should we measure or compare our results to? The art of benchmarking, or comparing a result to another metric or other standard, is a very valuable practice to bring perspective to your results. Here are a few approaches to benchmarking:

Previous results—A very effective comparison to determine advancement or progress in your business development. It is one of the more common benchmarking techniques if one records accurate trade data.

Plan expectations—This benchmark brings an element of compliance to the mix rather than just a quality comparison. A trader can have improvement in results over time, but one cannot be meeting his or her business goals if gaps exist between actual and plan results.

Best in the business—The ultimate comparison is that against the best traders. Best-in-class benchmarks are used in all industries to determine how one stands in relation to one's peers. Everyone wants the J.D. Power or Good Housekeeping seal to show they are the best at what they do. Many corporations include these benchmarks in their mission statements, thus validating their importance and effectiveness in motivating one to strive to reach an elite level.

How should a trader benchmark himself or herself? There are so many dynamics in trading, thus making it difficult to compare your trade results to others in the business. Another hurdle is the actual availability of other traders' results. Trade journals posted on the Web can have questionable integrity and not be perfectly correlated with any individual's particular trading style. Trading goals set in your plan are a relatively easy metric to compare to since they are officially recorded and are often sought as the ultimate benchmark.

For any trader to be successful, he or she must be in complete compliance with his or her plan rules. Thus, the ultimate benchmark is your trade compliance and comparing it to a 100 percent compliance goal. Honoring and implementing your trading to your plan rules should be the ultimate quality comparison. Rarely does one become self-sufficient as a pro without having near perfect compliance with one's plan. It is the ultimate risk metric and a must in the benchmarking world.

 REVIEW QUESTIONS

1. List the two core competencies required during a series of losses or drawdowns.
2. List a benefit of having the ability to interpret trade data information.
3. What is the primary benefit of tracking "phantom" trades?
4. List five components required for a trade journal to be effective.
5. List and explain five guidelines regarding key performance indicators (KPIs).

PART III

Qualitative Elements of Risk

CHAPTER 6

The Human Element: Psychological Risks of Trading

T he emotional elements of trading are often undetected in basic trading plan reporting. Perhaps a comment such as "exited trade due to fear" or other abstract free-form text is often added to a journal and never reviewed again. The business model of trading in itself is relatively easy. We detect a pattern or indication that an edge exists and we push a button. However, when emotions such as fear and greed are present, it can be the most difficult task you will ever take on.

The beauty of trading is that we should be on the winning side given our discovered edge. We should not be afraid to lose because the probability and odds tell us that we should succeed. We should execute each trade as if it will adhere to the probabilities set out in our trade history. Fear is a great separator between expected results and actual results. It immobilizes the best of traders at times and prevents them from being successful. This fear of loss is a prominent risk in trading and is prevalent in nearly all aspects of the trading community. Like any other identified risk, we must run it through the risk management five-step process.

LOSS AVERSION

Let's face it—nobody likes to lose. Loss aversion risk refers to the bias that we as people are more affected by a potential loss than we are by a potential gain. Risk management professionals often probe loss aversion risk in initial consultations, and you should seek such an evaluation if your coach or other professional has not discussed it with you. How to avoid or reduce loss aversion risk is vital to trading success if you are struggling with such matters. It may cause you to hold on to a poorly performing trade or give you the desire to close a position early to guarantee you are "right." The biggest loss aversion exposure is that of risk avoidance. Simply put, the trader's fear of loss forces him or her to bypass a valid trade opportunity provided by the markets. Some may argue that the definition includes those who stop trading during the week in order to lock in early gains.

Experts in psychology suggest trading "in the moment" without reservation. You may be happy that you had a good start to the week but need to convert that thinking toward the greater need of continuing to make good decisions in order to grow according to your business plan. There are two primary types of decisions that most often result in noncompliance with a trading plan: errors of incorrect or inaccurate action and errors of inaction. Studies have shown that inaction occurred several times more frequently than did the decisive errors. One study assessed how the average blackjack player makes calculated decisions. The study concluded that the error of inaction was four times greater than an actual decisive error. In other words, most people were too conservative in their play and afraid of busting over 21. Rather than take the chance, they waited (and hoped) that the dealer would bust. The results showed that this inactivity was rather costly. The players who made the optimal decisions won 20 times more often than the conservative players who were scared to take the proper card, potentially break 21, and lose their hand. This omission bias, or choosing the less active choice, will psychologically cause less pain or regret if the trade, or in this case, the blackjack hand, failed. Just this information alone should alert you to consider the opportunity cost risk exposed for not taking planned action.

A robotic approach of entering and exiting trades with an edge sounds easy to accomplish. Those who focus on the opportunity cost of risk avoidance and their need to continuously perform as per the plan are the ones who eventually get the worm.

THE RISK OF REGRET

Regret risk is a similar exposure where you seek to take profits prior to a set and known target or if you hold onto a trade seeking additional profits only to see price reverse direction. It is important to understand that in both cases you are losing. In the first case it is the opportunity cost of not holding to the historically optimal target. In the second, you are losing profits that should have been taken at the known target. From a trader's perspective, he or she may not see either as a loss since both can be recorded as a win in the trade journal. From the risk manager's eyes, both are losses to some degree and more importantly, plan violations.

Traders are not superheroes. We are not psychics nor are we perfectionists. All we have is a plan, and our role is to implement that plan. Traders are paid to make the best decisions with the most accurate data available that exposes edge in the markets. We need to be experts not in actual trading but in the ability to analyze situations using statistics. Many a successful trader's foundation is based on these ideas. When the human element comes into play, the purity of the above principles becomes diluted and is replaced by many forms of psychological risks. In this chapter we will discuss several risks, including the inability to accept loss and risk associated with using improper share size, and steps on how you can master each of them.

INTUITION TRADING

Intuition Trading   Style of trading that is dependent on what the trader believes will happen rather than relying on pure, data-driven, statistical decision making.

There should never be a point in your trading when a decision is made without the use of statistical edge as the primary decision factor. It should not matter if you feel lucky or unlucky. Nor should you be concerned if the setup is occurring after three previously successful trades or in the midst of a dismal losing streak. After several years of trading, I still rarely use my intuition about a trade. Measuring trades where I opted to use my intuition rather than historical data often proved victory on the data side, at least over a period of time. I still use intuition on occasion. After all, I'm a human trying to trade like a robot, not a robot trying to trade like a robot. In the end, there may be a spot for intuition to be a part of your trade executions. A viable solution is perhaps a hybrid, having intuition with the backing of some form of statistical data or some other factual information. Intuition is used more often in my corporate risk management side, since the human element is more of a factor. The best poker players will often consider intuition in their risk-based decision. Coaches in sports often look to their stomach during pressure situations. They may call it intuition, but there probably is some form of past experience that is giving them that stomach pulse. Tracking your intuition-based trades could shed light on to how often you actually use it in the future.

THE SUCCESS FORMULA AND DISCIPLINE

Discipline means that you have to overcome variables such as loss aversion, confirmation bias, and variance. You should embrace variance, which is a product of the markets, since at times of variance in your favor it will produce results that are well above expectations. You cannot remove this risk unless you choose another profession, so focus your development on the acceptance of such uncontrollable variables. Along with accepting it is the practical ability to manage variance risk appropriately within your precious bankroll. Taking a broader "enterprise" viewpoint using trading as a long-term business will help build discipline in regard to market variance or other quirks that the market dishes out. No trader should define success based on the last trade. A disciplined trader always looks at the big picture; the ability to detect edge and execute trades directly impacts the pace of his or her development as a trader.

So how should we define success? Is it winning trades? Is it perfect trade execution? Implementing a plan with precision and compliance? Perhaps a piece of each would suffice. When asked this question I often find the "winning trades" response to be the most popular. It logically makes sense. Winning trades equals profits that lead to living a life of obtaining the things that you expected when you set your trading plan goals. The risk-minded trader defines success a bit differently. Since we know and accept the reality that losing trades will occur, we should consider losing trades as part of the success formula. In fact, no trade that follows your plan should be considered a losing trade. It merely is a trade that did not have the outcome that you would have desired. Discussing psychological elements of trading can be difficult to absorb on the first read. Books such as *Trading in the Zone* by Mark Douglas (Prentice Hall Press, 2001) are seen as more of a reference book rather than a one-time read. If there is one key psychological concept you retain, understand, and preach throughout your trading journey, it is this: Losing trades are part of the success process.

Our ability to accept loss must be overcome before advancing to the next level in trading. In other words, your psychological capital must be in place and nurtured prior to attempting to grow your trading capital. There are so many who fail to prepare as a trader in this order. They have capital, open up an account, and somehow figure that their accounts will continuously grow without a solid psychological foundation. Douglas refers to it as the "trader's mind-set," and it is even more essential to possess than any amount of capital. This gap between what you expect to earn as a trader and the reality of doing it without such psychological preparation is an identified risk that you need to consider seriously. Those that have achieved success have overcome several obstacles, including the ability to close such a gap. Let's discuss this risk gap and how one can overcome it.

RISK ACCEPTANCE

Nearly every trader reaches a threshold where he or she is challenged to move toward the next level. They may be treading water or even mildly successful thanks to solid risk management and discipline. They start to increase their share size gradually, which starts to generate an increase in fear or other emotion that immobilizes them. What appeared to be mild risk-taking at a low share level now starts to be seen as taking bigger risks, even if they are implementing the same strategies as in the past with the same proportion of financial risk to their capital.

The best traders not only accept risk but thrive on it. They see risk as an opportunity, not a threat, and accept the uncertainty that accompanies every trade. Psychological risk is minimal since they know the numbers that provide them with the edge and are only concerned about execution compliance, not about the what-ifs about the trade not working. In the end, if you cannot accept the risk, you will avoid the risk. This is what most beginning traders do. What in essence they are doing is avoiding the golden opportunities provided by the market.

Expecting Loss

When we play games of chance in a casino, we tend not to express fear. The nature of casino games is that most of us expect to lose, and we hope that our entertainment value makes up for our expectation of loss. Also, the amount of monetary loss can be much less in placing a $5 chip on a blackjack table as opposed to the amount on a losing trade. When we do lose, we don't sweat anything. Our outcome was expected and we go home. In trading, we expect to win. We have an alleged edge and we should win. When things don't work out over a trade or a series of trades, fear starts to take over. Why? We should be winning. Our edge says so, right?

When playing in a casino, we tend to blame outside elements for our loss. "The dealer beat me!" In poker, it is "The cards beat me" or "I just couldn't get a good hand." In trading, we blame the markets. I cannot tell you how many times I've taught in trading rooms and find a trader saying, "This volume is pathetic," or "What did you expect, it's options expiration day." The inability or desire not to blame ourselves is a common immobilizing trait that is not only evident in one-on-one sessions but is communicated in many a trade journal after a losing trade. It's natural to not want to lose anything or to be the one to blame on a trade.

Even after several years in the business, I still find myself thinking or even saying out loud reminders to be sure I accept the risk I am about to take. My favorite and personally most effective saying is the three most beautiful words before I enter a trade. Of course, "I love you" works well after a nice winning trade that included a stress-free runner, but that may not be the most appropriate thing to say out loud on a prop firm trading desk.

"I Don't Care"

One simple method of risk acceptance is to repeat this simple phrase. It's a way of desensitizing your emotions as a trader and focusing on execution at the most optimal entry level. If the market wants to show its randomness during the trade, say words like, "Go right ahead; stop me out!" "Do what you have to do." "I am on my way to becoming a professional trader, and I accept market randomness." "I don't care. I really don't care." "In fact, if this trade doesn't work out, statistically I have an even better advantage next time my historically winning pattern shows its hand." If you are trading in a group, you may get some strange stares and perhaps a chuckle or two. The pro traders probably will respect you and may even applaud you because they know that this is the attitude to take when challenging the risk acceptance demons.

MASTERING INCREASES IN SHARE SIZE

Pure trade data information all the way up to refined KPI reporting statistics should contain both risk and compliance elements. This should be the framework of your success model. If I am compliant with my plan execution and within my risk-to-reward parameters, I know I will be successful over time. As an expert in managing risk, one needs to follow an extremely rigorous risk management plan, which is part of your overall trading plan. Contract size should be based on the concept of the Kelly criterion, which supports strict progressive-style criteria when successfully increasing trading capital and reducing risk during periods of drawdown. It also factors in the amount of edge to consider. Generally speaking, the greater the historical edge on a particular setup, the greater the odds for success, thus allowing an increase in share or contract size to use for the trade. The basic formula for the Kelly criterion is as follows:

$$f^* = \frac{bp - q}{b} = \frac{p(b + 1) - 1}{b}$$

where $f^* =$ is the fraction of the current bankroll to wager;
$b =$ is the net odds, or risk-to-reward received on the opportunity, quoted as "b to 1";
$p =$ is the probability of winning;
$q =$ is the probability of losing, which is $1 - p$.

Rather than provide a lesson in risk analysis and statistical analytics, the objective of the principle is quite simple. When you have historical setups with a positive edge, you apply a percentage of your risk capital to the opportunity. The greater the edge, the greater the share or contract exposure you should take while maintaining a similar percentage risk to your trading capital. Likewise, if there was no historical edge, you should not apply any risk to the opportunity. If there was a negative edge, you should take the opposite side of the opportunity, which is the founding principle of the casino gaming industry (at least from the "opposite" side of the player). The Kelly strategy generally applies to gambling strategies, but I have found the concept applicable to any risk framework where there is a potential reward, such as in the investment arena, trading, building a business, or even your family card game.

The key to the Kelly criterion from a risk perspective is $^*f$. In all cases, any trade amounts are to be made within a percentage or other ratio in proportion to your risk capital allocated for trading. When the bankroll shrinks, the formula tells us to reduce our share size based on the lower bankroll. Although one should never load the boat on any trade, share size is increased as bankroll is increased. Should there be a significant or at least a consistent increase in your historical edge, the formula allows for an incremental bump in exposure as well.

It sounds so simple. But how many traders actually follow this principle? It can be explained and understood by a 10-year-old in less than a minute: Increase when winning and decrease when losing. How many traders not only avoid following this principle, but actually do the opposite? They increase the size of their risk after losing a series of trades or, even worse, they do it after each losing trade. Remember what John Maynard Keynes said: "Markets can remain irrational longer than you or I can remain solvent." The key to this principle is to be able to ride out the times when the market or even you are not producing the anticipated results. The strategy does not consider the emotional pain factor during the initial experience of negative variance prior to reducing your share/contract size. As risk managers, we must be continuously focused with the worst-case scenario in mind. In fact, managers of risk wake up every morning thinking the worst-case scenario will occur and manage their capital accordingly even though we understand the minute possibility of such a scenario.

THE GRADUATION PLAN

The emotional challenges with raising your share or contract exposures when your plan is successful are often underestimated. Many traders find an emotional comfort zone that is difficult to penetrate even though their results are telling them to continue to raise quantity levels. This actually will increase your risk of failure to reach your plan goals. In order to capture a method of managing trade risk while eliminating the intricate process of the Kelly criterion, I've developed a rather simple approach to meeting the same objectives. It contains the increase as you win–decrease as you lose format but factors in the emotional elements and market randomness associated with the inevitable drawdowns associated with any trading plan. The methodical elements and smoothing of quantity increases the opportunity to allow for share and contract sizes to adjust along with your comfort level. The unique component of the graduation plan is that it works independently for each valid setup in your trading plan.

Your responsibilities include tracking your trade results for each setup that was traded. While the Kelly strategy assumes we have a positive edge in our trading, we know that reality (and market randomness) says that any trade or a series of trades over a period of time can result in a negative outcome. The graduation plan also considers the level of confidence you've accumulated during the back-testing process but does not have historical trade results that factor in your actual trade activity in a live environment. The graduation plan attempts to capture the realities of the trader.

Figure 6.1 is a summary chart of a typical graduation plan for a given time period. You'll notice the data elements include:

- The setup number (or name)
- The current share or contract level
- The graduation "count"
- Win/loss record
- Win percentage or edge on each setup

As noted earlier, the graduation plan works independently for each setup in your plan. Notice on setup #1 there is a positive edge of 74 percent

TRADE PLAN TRACKING AND GRADUATION GRID: S&P500 INDEX (SPY)

Month Year Setup Number	Size Level	−10	−9	−8	−7	−6	−5	−4	−3	−2	−1	0	+1	+2	+3	+4	+5	+6	+7	+8	+9	+10	+11	+12	+13	+14	+15	16 Points	W	L	Tot	Win%
1	2																											54.00	14	5	19	74%
2	2																											18.50	5	2	7	71%
3	1																											0.00	0	0	0	0%
4																												0.00				
5																												0.00				
6	1																											−10.00	1	6	7	14%
7	1																											0.00	0	0	0	0%
8	1																											0.00	0	0	0	0%
9	1																											0.00	0	0	0	0%
10	1																											0.00	0	0	0	0%
Other																																
TOTAL																												NET 62.50	20	13	33	61%

FIGURE 6.1 Graduation Plan Grid

given the current sample of 19 trades. The win/loss record of 14–5 has a net positive trade result of nine positive outcomes and is reflected in the "count" section as a +9.

But what if some of the setups do not graduate or, even worse, reach a net negative result? Setup #6, for example, shows a current negative variance with a 1–6 record over the initial seven trades. This is quite common when trading a portfolio of multiple setups over a relatively short period and simply normal variance at work regardless of a historical positive edge. The net −4 trade result is recorded in the graph as indicated.

There are two options to consider in using the graduation plan. First, if you promote your winning setups, then you should alienate the ones that do not. The hidden value of this method is that they are based on actual results of your work in a live environment. Perhaps there was a setup that had worked extremely well in back-testing or in simulation but, for whatever reason, it could not be executed effectively during live trading. It could be a particular setup that was historically positive but is no longer working effectively during certain market conditions. Surely this is an alert for possible development or focus on fine-tuning the trader's execution. Regardless of the why, the results are the results, and if they continue to provide negative outcomes, it will only draw down your capital account further.

This plan alert works well with trade setups that traders swear by as effective but in real time are not producing effective results. Traders sometimes get attached to certain setups, even during times of changing market dynamics. My audit work using a similar assessment tool attempts to bring to light such setups where the results just aren't there. You will also not be as comfortable with some types of setups as with others. Some will just not fit your trading style. All of these will affect your trading of these setups and ultimately the end result. Fortunately, the graduation plan framework will shield you from exposing yourself to a large number of losses for a particular setup. In fact, it is naturally common to stay away from trading these setups knowing the results are not as profitable. In my experience, if a trader has 10 setups in his or her plan, a majority of all trade activity will occur using two or three of them. Traders tend to execute trades they are most comfortable with, that are easy to execute, and, of course, that are most consistently profitable to their bottom line. Those setups that do not perform consistently will continue to show negative results, similar to setup #6 in this example.

So what if you are a beginning trader and do not have a formal trading history? Can the graduation plan be of benefit to you in your back-testing process? How about trading in simulation? The process can benefit the trader who is testing a new setup that may have shown positive results from another trader. The back-test may have shown a positive edge over a large number of trades, but what about the drawdown phases? Were they manageable given your current capital account size? Were you able to withstand the emotional variance? Using the plan while in simulation will provide a level of confidence in your setup prior to graduating to the next size level. Try running any setup you are considering through simulation using the graduation plan before going live. Have the setup graduate the first two levels before introducing it to live money at the first level. Not only will you have actual results that, at least during the simulation sample, provide a positive edge, but they should provide that essential confidence when you first start to apply real dollars to any trading strategy.

Having a trading coach can assist in determining your trading style and which setups match your personal profile. Profitable setups and comfort with setups generally will go hand-in-hand. Traders simply will trade the setups that are making money for them, so going this route is also a good option to initially consider. All the information needed to support your graduation plan grid should be gathered directly from your trade journal data.

Constructing the Plan

In constructing the initial base graduation plan, there are a few assumptions that you need to consider. Each trade setup assumes a standard risk to reward. Of course, there is never a standard risk to reward in any trade setup, but regardless, you should add a win percentage goal column to your chart to visually see your win results versus a goal that may be less than 50 percent. For example, if you have a trade that requires a 2:1 risk-to-reward, then performing at a 45 percent win rate would be quite impressive. You also may wish to record the net points gained instead of the default $+1$, -1 structure in the graduation grid. There is no magic formula for tracking in your graduation plan. Most important is that the results are transparent and that you are increasing quantity in your trades as your setup proves successful and reducing size when it is not.

The plan defines a win or loss as a trade that reaches a determined target or stop-loss. While it is encouraged to stick to predetermined targets and stops, a live market can suggest otherwise. Perhaps a target was set that did not recognize resistance lower than your initial price. Market activity during the trade may suggest that you exit the trade immediately, and your plan rules may allow such decision making to take place. Most traders will encounter these situations quite often. The markets allow such discretion and reward those who use it but don't abuse it. So what if we bail on a trade prior to reaching its target or stop? Aside from the compliance aspect of the decision, we record the trade just like any other trade in the grid. You may wish to place half a win if you closed the trade halfway toward the target and vice versa. When taking scratch trades (breakeven), you can record the trade as a B/E column next to the W-L if you so desire. Remember, the graduation grid is merely a tool to determine contract or share size. It is not a compliance or audit document to determine if you are entering and exiting properly. If you have a slight profit or slight loss (the equivalent of a two- or three-tick profit or loss on a trade), you can also consider those trades at breakeven if you wish. As long as you are consistent with documenting your results in your trade journal or graduation plan, you are considered in compliance. Conversely, recording scratches that may have squeezed out a tick or two, perhaps to pay for commission, should not be defined as a win. The reason is that it did not meet your overall trade objectives. Unless your intention on a scalp setup was to generate two ticks on a futures contract or $0.10 cents on a stock or index trade, you should not consider that a W. Doing so will skew the results to promote greater contract or share size when the results truly did not reach the level of achieving such promotion. The same, of course, goes for losing trades or breakeven trades that resulted in a slight loss due to exit slippage or similar. Remember, your discretionary decision was to prevent a losing trade, and you should not be penalized for making a proper risk decision even if it resulted in a few pennies' loss plus transaction costs.

The Plan in Action

The relative simplicity of the plan also contains one key challenge for most beginning traders. The success of your setups will trigger your contract and share sizes to increase. Your goal as a trader is to achieve such nirvana with all of your setups. Unfortunately, your psychological capital may not increase at the same pace as your trading capital. There are times when the statistics are telling you to graduate, but your mind is telling your trading finger to take a rest or at least continue at the current level. Since each setup will work independently, some of your other trades may be struggling and depleting your overall capital, even at the lower quantity. This is quite common among newer traders or those with relatively smaller accounts. This inability to increase your quantity according to the graduation plan will eventually limit your ability to reach your ultimate capabilities as a trader and your trading business. How does one overcome such a welcome challenge? You can extend your requirements for graduation for each setup, thus allowing your plan to require more net positive trades prior to graduating a setup. This should also help increase your confidence in the setup, thus allowing the transition to a higher quantity to be less stressful. One risk control strategy would be to retrace back to the second level after successful completion of the third graduation level. Once that level is completed, the trader "goes for it" and considers any deviations a breach of plan compliance. Similar to a baseball player using a heavy weight in the on-deck circle so as to have the bat feel lighter when at the plate, this deviation benefits not only the capital account but also the trader's state of mind and comfort zone. That comfort eventually will need to be at a top endurance level to succeed in trading. Better to groom it while taking a pause in your trading journey at a relatively lower trading level in hopes the psychological investment pays off in the future when it will be tested even further.

In my years of using this method and teaching it in seminars, many have suggested using points gained as a tracking barometer. For example, you can graduate to the next level after a setup reaches a net positive +40 points. This certainly takes away any adjustments needed should your setups have a variety of different risk-to-rewards associated with them. Do whatever is most comfortable for you. The grid is meant to take the decision of share and contract size off your plate and make your trading day and business documentation easier. Others have recommended that they adjust the count or the number of successful trades needed in order to graduate to the next level. No arguments here as long as you are sure to adjust the count on both positive and negative sides of the count. When looking to raise size after a +10 count, then you must reduce size after a −10 count. After you have succeeded in reaching the second or third levels, you should consider reducing your negative count to a 2:1 ratio in relation to wins. In this example, if you are seeking to graduate contract size after a +10 count, then use a −5 as your threshold to revert back to the prior level. This is a more conservative approach but should be of little influence on your trades that are consistently producing good results with little variance. After all, isn't that what we are ultimately seeking?

Any of these variations or other creative ones you come up with are acceptable as long as you adhere to the basic principle of the graduation plan—increase size after a series of positive performance results and decrease when the opposite occurs. The key is to understand what trading size you should be trading at any given time. There is little guesswork with this progressive framework. There are very few risk managers who would discredit such variations as long as you could show this was occurring. This robotic approach to graduating share size will reduce the exposure of the psychological and emotional barriers that every trader confronts at any given time in his or her trading career.

SUMMARY

The graduation plan is just one of many examples of step 3 in the risk management process: risk control. You can implement this plan immediately on your first day of trading, and it will work equally as well when trading in simulation. By reducing exposure during poor performance, you are controlling your ability to preserve your business capital. One thing that is certain, there will be times when loss occurs, and this plan is designed to mitigate such loss. Now that our risk control plan is in place, Chapter 7 focuses on how to prepare for those times when periodic losses will occur.

REVIEW QUESTIONS

1. Define loss aversion and the associated risks for the trader.
2. Give an example of how a trader can practice risk acceptance.
3. Explain what is known as the trader's mind-set gap.
4. Explain the key concepts of the graduation plan method.
5. How does the graduation plan overcome the psychological and disciplinary challenges of increasing share size?

CHAPTER 7

Preparing for Risk and Loss

W e've discussed several types of risk that you will encounter prior to trade execution and how to address them. Now we'll discuss whether there are different risks to consider once you are in the trade and how they might be handled differently.

MASTERING RISK DURING A TRADE

Here's how it usually goes: Once you detect your setup at the price that gives you your plan-prescribed edge, you enter the trade in accordance with your trading plan guidelines. Then you wait for the market to do its thing and produce its edge-based results (preferably at the historical win rate or even a bit more if the market is in a giving mood). It sounds simple to wait it out. We often wait at red lights, train platforms, and at the dentist. So why do some traders have so much difficulty doing it during a trade? I find traders have the *most* difficulty simply doing nothing. Sitting and patiently waiting for a trade to pay out is often the most difficult thing for some traders. The flashing platform lights and price movements create an arcade-like atmosphere that engulfs the trader in wanting to do something when simply doing nothing is the only decision that is warranted.

Why do traders do this? Why do we close a position before target? Or before our proper stop? The answers can be quite numerous, and sometimes the reasons are valid. Perhaps the trade is still open, and a news event that will rattle the markets is ready to come off the wires. Maybe the trade has not reached target or stop, and your rules require you to close or at least reduce the position before the close. These can be valid reasons supported by your trading plan. They are predetermined decisions that if not adhered to will result in noncompliance with your strategy.

Rarely will a trade start immediately in your favor and continue directly to your target price. It's a great feeling to watch price movement that provides little or no heat on a trade, and these market gifts will come if you trade often enough. The randomness of market movement rarely allows such gifts, and pro traders neither expect nor get rattled when price fluctuates between stop and target. In their eyes, it's just market randomness and price action as a result of buyers and sellers battling it out. So how should we approach managing a trade that had a clear edge at execution but lost a portion or all of the edge during the trade?

Let's look at this from a gaming perspective where the edge or odds are known prior to placing your wager. In blackjack, your odds of success are about 49 percent with near perfect basic strategy play, that is, making the correct decision to hit or stand based on optimal play. Certain strategies in the game of craps come with odds of 49.3 percent of winning at any given time. These games have a defined beginning, middle, and end. The dealer executes your card decisions, then draws or stands his or her hand as per the defined rules, and then an outcome is determined. In dice games, a 7 or reshooting the "point" normally concludes a craps game, with a few defined exceptions. Once you decide to put your chip down, it generally means that you are playing until the outcome is decided. The gaming industry refers to blackjack bets, pass line wagers on a craps table, and virtually any other game of chance as "contract" bets. Simply put, you are risking your money until the outcome is determined. Even a slot machine is in essence a contract bet. Once that coin goes into the machine (remember the days of coin-operated slot machines?), you are contracted to play the game until the outcome is determined.

This is not true in trading. You have complete control at any time after your "bet" has been made. You can take it all off, add more, take a portion of it off, and even leave the money on the table after you have "won" your trade or have reached your target. The contract-based wagering philosophy simply does not exist, and you are free to make whatever decision you wish within the confines of bankroll and exchange limitations.

While a trade is open, a variety of emotional factors may pop up that influence your decision. You may start to get nervous about a trade that isn't working out. Perhaps you get excited after a trade hits your target, and you decide that greed is the best option. The ability to have this open-ended flexibility to change your mind appears at first to be the biggest advantage for traders; however, it often is their biggest nemesis. Imagine if at any time you were allowed to take away your blackjack bet during a hand. In some venues, the house does allow you to reduce your risk in the middle of hands that have an obvious disadvantage for the player. The "surrender" option can be one of the best risk management tools for a professional blackjack player, and many play only at venues that allow such a risk-reduced option. In dice games, one can theoretically determine the change in odds when one die lands on a number and the other is in the process of landing. For example, if a player is seeking a total of 6 to roll and the first die lands on a 6, the player knows he or she has a zero probability of winning on that toss. Although dice are thrown simultaneously, it would be a player's dream to be allowed to take the bet off in this example. Casinos, of course, would throw you out if you attempted to do such a thing. In trading, you are welcome to do so any time you'd like.

If this flexibility is such an advantage for a trader, why do we often fail to address these options effectively? Having complete control sometimes acts as a double-edged sword. It allows us to make decisions in an environment where there are no house rules or a contract-betting structure to curtail behavioral decisions. Other than a few stock or futures exchange limitations, we only need to rely on our own trading rules and boundaries. As any trader knows, those rules often are from the broker, and unlike the casino that throws you out of the place, our trading platforms invite you in for more as if they have a "don't worry about it, try again!" invitation at the door. This business where the house doesn't set the rules often causes more financial loss than in a casino that is based on contract-based rules.

THE NEED FOR PLAN COMPLIANCE

In my work with traders, I have seen many who back-test their strategy before implementing an identified holy grail strategy in a live environment. One characteristic flaw of novice traders is that they implement their strategy differently live than in their back-testing. I'm always asking myself questions when performing trade journal audits. Why did they miss this trade? Why did they hold past target? Why did they take profits too early? Why did they not follow the plan or "contract bets" that I assessed and validated? It's this determination of root cause that is the value offering of any auditor or coach that is worthy of their fee.

Ultimately, it is the trader who assumes responsibility for every trading decision he or she makes. It is a common response found in trading books, convention presentation disclaimers, and coaching articles. I find the response somewhat cynical when a trader is told this. Back when I started trading, I would have a confused glaze on my face when told about my trading responsibilities. "Why, of course I am responsible for my decisions! How does that make me a better trader?" Only later as my trading improved did I truly understand what I originally considered marketing psycho-babble. For my first few years of trading, I was of the belief that it was my responsibility to be a "winning" trader. It was logically defined as having winning trades and "beating" the market. I even defined my trades as winning or losing. An executed stop was a losing trade. A trade where I took profits too early was considered a winning trade. A simple column in a spreadsheet simply noted as W or L defined the basis of my success. Only until I understood the true meaning of what I am responsible for did I turn that psychological corner that originally prevented success. Rather than take responsibility for the outcome of a trade, I graded my responsibility solely on being compliant with executing my trading plan. The market is what it is; a house of edge, odds, and opportunity for those who risk their capital. The randomness of market movements is something a trader cannot predict or be responsible for. So why do so many traders have a W/L column in their journals? Your ultimate responsibility is that of consistently implementing your trading plan. The plan advises you to make the proper risk decisions at any given time when you are provided with a historical edge. If you are not thinking like this now in your current trading, please make this mind-set change your biggest priority before moving forward.

The hunger for winning should soon be replaced by the hunger to simply comply. Fear of loss tends to subside since you are no longer focused on winning trades based on a positive dollar outcome. A trade that did not have the outcome as planned is now considered a plan-compliant trade. In essence, it now has become a winning trade since you executed your plan effectively. When successful traders make a mistake or two, it is often reflected in a compliance metric, such as 95 percent plan-successful implementation followed by an action plan to work on areas of developmental execution. Do not get frustrated if this concept does not get absorbed in your mind after the first read. If it did for every trader, this business would be like riding a bike. You can overcome your fear of falling off the bike and reach a level where you sprint out of your driveway without any thoughts of falling.

RISK PARTICIPATION AND LOSS ACCEPTANCE

One of the reasons I suggest reducing the emphasis on keeping a Win-Loss column in your journal is because of the relatively small value the data provide in regard to identifying compliance risk. It serves as more of a satisfaction to those with hunger pains for the desire to win. Recall that the term "loss" is in our simple definition of risk. We define it simply as a chance of loss. In other words, when we accept risk, we in essence are accepting loss or at least the chance of loss in hopes of gain.

So why do traders often get frustrated when they lose? The primary answer is obvious: loss of capital. We also get frustrated because we simply do not want to lose. It is a characteristic of our being. A common element in my analysis of trade journals is the ratio of trades considered a win in proportion to those that have reached a predetermined target. Often, there may be reasons to take a trade off early, but a consistent pattern often denotes a desire to win or be "right." The best traders aren't concerned about being right on any given trade. The challenge is that we chose a risk-filled business where we cannot control a lot of the activity being conducted while our money is at risk. We also cannot control the outcome. Traders are always between a rock and a hard place with their desire to be right, understanding the reality that often you will be wrong. By changing your definition of being right or winning, we strengthen our psychological capital and shift the focus from our desire to having winning trades to being a trader in compliance with our trading plan.

This battle of not only understanding risk but expecting it in an environment that is based on putting capital at risk is essential in overcoming risk acceptance. When we accept risk we are in essence anticipating and allowing the chance of loss to occur. We understand that in the big picture, any unplanned outcome is really not that important to our overall success. We embrace it like a fisherman who doesn't get a nibble on any given day. This being the case, there is little reason to incorporate any emotions that would normally follow an event that most would define as a loss.

So how does a trader overcome this? One is to work on your psychological capital in risk acceptance. Never believe that the market is out to get you or your money. It doesn't know you exist and doesn't make your trading decisions for you. Remind yourself before each trading day that the market is not a threat to your business. It is a vehicle that provides you with the ability to be successful. It is not an ugly monster or a demon that reaches into your pocket. The market is your best friend, because it facilitates your successful business, just like your best employee or machine that produces the best-quality product. The market is the production machine for your manufacturing business that facilitates production of, in this case, revenue. Your goal is to simply know when to start and stop production.

Ask any successful trader in the futures pits in Chicago, and he or she will likely agree with this scenario. They look at the market as a sea of opportunities, not a threatening monster. I was speaking at a trading conference, and one man asked several skeptically toned questions during my presentation. I often embrace all questions since they are normally the same questions others want answered but refrain from asking. I try to keep an upbeat, positive tone to teaching; however, I could tell this gentleman was attempting to turn the session into a pool of skepticism and that you cannot "beat the market." His last reference was that the market will eventually get you, and any risk management scheme will only get you so far before the market wins. I merely replied, "That is a very profound statement, sir. We both probably have similar desires; the desire to succeed in trading; the desire to provide for our families; and to allow this profession to give us the things that we want in life. There really is only one difference between us in that one of us perceives the market as a threat. The other sees it as a vast sea of opportunity." The gentleman was honorably silent the rest of the session.

Trader psychologist expert Denise Shull, author of *Market Mind Games* (McGraw-Hill, 2011), notes that the research actually shows that fear of loss is not on the top of the average trader's fear list. In essence, the fear of regret or the fear of missing a trade is higher on the list. The fear of being left behind is a stronger fear than losing money. Perhaps this explains why certain trades are entered late or at least not at the optimal entry point as defined in the trading plan. One way to audit fear focuses on entry compliance. In other words, did the trader not only enter the trade but was it done at the time it was supposed to be entered, according to the plan? Often you will find an overwhelming increase in noncompliance when the setup was followed by a series of trades that did not reach target. We tend to hesitate because we want more comfort knowing that the market is moving in our direction before entering. Often we will just pass on the perfect setup with edge and leave opportunity dollars on the table. The ability to treat each trade as an independent event is a skill that takes time to develop. When achieved, it is often the first sign of transition from a trader to a risk manager. Here are several ways to help build your stamina in seeking each opportunity as an independent event:

1. Have a minimum time period after each trade when you do not trade. Any setups you miss will still be in compliance, since it is part of your strategy. You will miss out on some opportunities in the beginning, but it will build your psychological ability to bring yourself into the "moment of now."

2. Keep your trade size at a level where your recent trades do not become a mind factor in the next setup.

3. Remind yourself before each trade that you currently have an edge. Think as if you have been dealt a 10 and the dealer has a 6. Your job as a trader is to take advantage of the dealer's low edge. It is your responsibility to execute this opportunity as per your plan.

4. Update your trade journal on weekends or at the end of the month. Updating your results too frequently keeps both winning and losing streaks fresh in your mind. Those five losses in the dreaded win-loss column can create havoc in a trader's mind.

5. Track each trade independently. While you may have had a bit of a drawdown of late, the trade opportunity you are about to enter may be more consistent than your previous setups. There is nothing worse than passing up your most productive setup after a few losers based on other setups in your arsenal.

Missing a trade is often the result of fear of loss overcoming the opportunity presented to you. Isn't it funny how most traders would be all-in on the same opportunity after a winning series of trades? It's only normal to reflect back to the most recent events to shape your mind over your next decision. Memories of lessons we learn make us stronger and allow us to make better decisions in all facets of life. In trading, a good memory can be a dangerous asset. State of mind is everything in trading, and focusing on the now moment, or the current valid setup, will aid in allowing the fearmonger to overcome your job as a trader. This mind game goes against how our mind is constructed, thus making it a daunting challenge to overcome. This skill is built over time and is one of the many reasons why most traders are not successful in the early stages.

PROCESS OF PREDEFINING RISK

So far we have not painted a rosy picture for traders and the psychological challenges they will face. Maintaining a strong, positive attitude after a series of losses, accepting the fact that we cannot determine outcomes, and that we will often experience something that we as people hate to do: lose. On top of that bright news is that the human mind-set was designed to remember recent pain to help us guide our decisions away from those that caused the emotional discomfort, only to be told to get back in there and do the same thing over and over again.

So what can we control psychologically? What can we overcome? One of the tasks of a trader that has little impact on our emotions is our ability to define what our risk is before we accept it or take action. This ability to filter out high-risk trades is often the difference between success and failure in trading. The best traders tend to do just a few things better than the average trader that places them in the top of their field, just as Hall of Fame batters get just a few more hits per 100 at-bats than their teammates.

Both sets of traders have the same potential to control their decisions. Both cannot control market randomness and the continuous unknown factors that come into play during a trade. The best traders accept this unknown variable while other traders expect the edge to play out in their favor each and every trade.

After factoring in all of the random events that can occur during a trade, one might be scared to even participate. A news event causes prices to hit your stop. A hedge fund unloads a block of stock just after you enter. How does one predefine risk on a trade? Let's take this scenario and look at the opportunity that the risk provides us. First and foremost, we have history that supports our decision to take action when certain patterns or other market activity occurs. Was market randomness in force during those trades? Of course it was. Market randomness is always present. What we do know is that historically over a valid series of trades, the market allowed us to profit from similar setups. What the market has done is virtually overcome all of the unknowns and events that we cannot control. A consistent positive outcome by definition predefines the risk. Using this principle alone is a powerful method of predefining our risk.

There are other components to assess that also predefine risk, even on setups that have high probability outcomes. Other factors include how the setup works during specific times of day or during periods of relatively high or low volatility. Confluence of support for a setup is an extremely valuable factor in predefining risk.

The greater the historical edge, the less predefined risk on a trade; however, that risk is never entirely eliminated on any one trade, regardless of the strength of the setup. There is not a direct inverse relationship percentage regarding predetermined risk and edge. In theory, even if a trade had an historical result of 100 percent success, the predetermined risk would still not equal zero. This is a result of the ever-present changing market that we must accept before joining this profession. When you think in probabilities, you instantly recognize your edge when each opportunity presents itself but accept the fact that each trade is unique. There will be a random distribution of positive trades and ones that get stopped but the odds of success on each individual trade are predefined. This continuous exposure to the unknown and historical results creates a potpourri of potential outcomes separated only by a little thing called edge.

Once you start to think in probabilities, you are on your way to building your psychological capital base. You begin to trade from an abundant state, since your trading decisions are edge-supported rather than what you think will happen. You stop trying to be a market analyst who predicts future movement, and you become a trader who could care less where the market is heading. Wanting to be right is the least of your concerns. You become a risk manager who predetermines risk—nothing more, nothing less.

TRADER EXPECTATIONS

Traders who have recently made the decision to give this profession a try possess the innocence of excitement that is only paralleled by watching a child getting candy. The idea of working in your pajamas, quitting your job, telling your boss goodbye, and having money print out of your trading platform is just too rich a dream to pass up. That initial high diminishes after the first weeks when one realizes the complexity of educational and psychological challenges that come with trading. Traders expect to be winners, and some expect to win on every trade. After all, that is why they are taking the trade. Of course, some know it will work since they are (sarcastically) expert market predictors.

The pro trader takes that energy, focuses on more reasonable expectations, and has the patience to ride out the numerical quirks of market uncertainty and randomness. Pro traders are much more flexible in their expectations. Expectations on any given day or week are nonexistent since the random sample is too small. It's impossible to predict what the next five trades will result in when a statistical sample may need to have 150 trades completed prior to being considered valid.

Having reasonable expectations, you eliminate any thought of what to expect, thus taking your focus off the emotional risks in being *right*. The only expectation one should have after a trade is that there will be a positive outcome, a neutral outcome, or a negative outcome. As discussed earlier, the "I don't care" attitude addresses the lack of desire to be concerned with outcome. Outcomes cannot be controlled, so why should our expectations be dictated by outcome? Doing so is a waste of energy and time, and it projects your focus in the wrong direction. Make it a practice to read the list of expectations and control elements in Table 7.1 on a daily basis until you are executing your plan with a minimum 95 percent plan compliance.

Being a successful trader is not just about accumulating successful trades. It is a mind-set, a robotic mentality that is quite boring at times. Many companies encourage cross-training to fill a void or help stimulate career development. You may be asked to sit in for someone who is not at work and perform that person's duties. Trading, however, has a monotonous assembly line–like process to it. We wait for setups with a historical winning edge, we enter, exit, and then wait for the next valid setup. When you can get to the stage where you are somewhat bored or at first less excited with the process, you are establishing a characteristic that is common among some of the trading elite. This mind-set also requires one to think in probabilities rather than predicting what will happen next.

At some point, your hard efforts in building your psychological capital will start to show in your trading results. This is an exciting step in

TABLE 7.1 Understanding the Expectations of Trading

What We Know	What We Don't Know	What We Can Control
Each trade has a random outcome.	The outcome of any trade.	The use of stop-loss orders or other risk control methods.
The bigger our sample of trades, the greater the certainty to estimate the outcome over the series of trades.	When a series of results will deviate from the historical averages.	The share or contract size of each trade or series of trades using the graduation method.
We know which setups have a historical edge and profit potential if executed effectively.	If these winning setups will continue to produce winning results under different market conditions.	Implementing risk avoidance on valid setups that do not meet our plan rules and filters.
The results of the prior trades have no impact on the next trade.	The outcome of the next or next series of trades.	The ability to detect and execute these setups effectively.
Trading involves risk of capital, and we accept it prior to entering the trading profession.	The severity of such loss of capital if the risk management process is not implemented.	Ability to limit financial risk on any trade and our trading capital.

your journey, but you may not know it is happening. Many traders cannot specifically say what they did differently when asked what that light bulb moment was when they started to trade with greater consistency. They had witnessed the change in results, felt more confident, but they were implementing more or less the same trading plan during their development phase. It is ultimately one's passion to succeed, ability to learn and develop, and willingness to make changes where needed.

When I talk to struggling traders, all they want to be taught is valid setups. They neglect to do their homework, build their psychological stamina, and learn about risk management. They make mistakes like the rest of us but fail to identify or acknowledge them, particularly on trades resulting in a positive outcome. Their thinking is that their trading plan is not good, even though they may be using trades with historical edge. More often than not, if a setup or a portfolio of setups generates a historical edge and includes solid risk management, it is usually a plan that can be implemented. It is the ability to execute the plan with precision where most traders fail. Overcoming the psychological challenges that a trader needs to overcome is a journey in itself. It's not about charts, support and resistance, or profits and losses. It's about looking inward to your ability to overcome human traits that we were born with and taught to use, and then rewiring your thinking in order to be successful.

BUILDING YOUR RISK TOLERANCE

Earlier we discussed risk-to-reward and its relationship to trader edge. It is common to have traders say they seek a minimum of 3:1, 5:1, or greater before taking a trade. This ratio would allow a trader to be successful even with a sub-50 percent success rate. To the contrary, 60–70 percent success rate traders can get away with a 1:1 risk-to-reward, or risk the same amount as their profit target. Traders spend a lot of effort studying the relationship of the two and still find themselves bewildered when their capital bleeds a slow death.

No doubt understanding risk and reward is an important part of trading. It is one of the primary principles of this book. The element that traders often overlook is that risk in itself must be contained regardless of reward. You can run simulated back-testing all year and have a positive outcome, but the game is over if one trade has a loss larger than your capital account. It is your capital tolerance and your personal risk tolerance that must supersede any back-testing drawdowns. To manage this risk effectively, we first must understand the maximum loss we can expose ourselves to on any given trade, series of trades, or time period. The ultimate goal of professional trading is to have the ability to sustain your business during periods of adversity. Understanding how to manage your business during these trying times will allow you to reap the benefits when your numerical edge reappears.

The first step to understanding account tolerance is determining the maximum amount one can lose. In essence, there needs to be a "get me out" price for every trade. While not determined by emotion, it is what we need to do to preserve our precious capital that enables us to trade another day. This tolerance maximum is known as the maximum adverse excursion, or MAE.

Maximum Adverse Excursion Measures the largest possible loss suffered by a single trade while the trade is open.

Don't be confused by the terminology that otherwise is known as the kill switch for traders. MAE simply measures the largest possible loss suffered by a single trade while the trade is open. For example, you may have a trade that gained two points but during the life of the trade, price fluctuated up and down. Let's say at one point you were down 3.5 points but bounced back and took the two points profit. In this example, the −3.5 points would be your maximum adverse excursion. Sometimes we take our stop right at the maximum loss only for it to bounce back toward our target without the opportunity to at least give us a scratch. That's trading. We have stops to protect us, but sometimes they do more harm than good. In the end, stops protect our capital and allow us to trade another day. Stops serve an invaluable purpose, but their use can often be frustrating. While valid setups provide you with a historical positive edge on a trade, MAE gives you an edge on the risk side of the trade. Let's see how this is applied using our data-driven approach.

The trade journal in Figure 7.1 shows a series of 25 trades for a specific setup (named #4 in this person's plan). This individual is trading the S&P

Setup #4

	Contract	Trade Results	Reward	Risk	Stop	Target	MAE	MFE	Profits Using MAE/MFE Stops
1	ES 500	−2.50	1	:1	−2.50	2.50	−4.00	2.00	−2.50
2	ES 500	2.50	1	:1	−2.50	2.50	−1.75	5.50	5.00
3	ES 500	2.50	1	:1	−2.50	2.50	−2.00	5.25	5.00
4	ES 500	−2.50	1	:1	−2.50	2.50	−3.50	2.00	−2.50
5	ES 500	2.50	1.5	:1	−2.50	3.75	−2.00	5.00	5.00
6	ES 500	−2.50	1	:1	−2.50	2.50	−4.50	2.00	−2.50
7	ES 500	2.50	1	:1	−2.50	2.50	−0.75	9.00	5.00
8	ES 500	−2.50	1	:1	−2.50	2.50	−4.50	6.75	−2.50
9	ES 500	−2.50	1	:1	−2.50	2.50	−4.75	2.00	−2.50
10	ES 500	2.50	2	:1	−2.50	5.00	−1.00	5.00	5.00
11	ES 500	−2.50	1	:1	−2.50	2.50	−5.00	1.75	−2.50
12	ES 500	−2.50	1.5	:1	−2.50	3.75	−9.00	5.50	−2.50
13	ES 500	1.25	1	:2	−2.50	1.25	−1.50	5.00	5.00
14	ES 500	1.75	1	:1.5	−2.50	1.75	−2.00	6.75	5.00
15	ES 500	2.50	1	:1	−2.50	2.50	−2.00	7.75	5.00
16	ES 500	2.50	1	:1	−2.50	2.50	−2.00	6.00	5.00
17	ES 500	2.50	1	:1	−2.50	2.50	−2.00	5.00	5.00
18	ES 500	−2.50	1	:1	−2.50	2.50	−4.00	2.00	−2.50
19	ES 500	1.75	1	:1.5	−2.50	1.75	−1.50	11.25	5.00
20	ES 500	2.50	1	:1	−2.50	2.50	−2.00	10.00	5.00
21	ES 500	−2.50	1	:1	−2.50	2.50	−3.50	3.50	−2.50
22	ES 500	−2.50	1	:1	−2.50	2.50	−8.00	1.00	−2.50
23	ES 500	2.50	1	:1	−2.50	2.50	−1.00	6.25	5.00
24	ES 500	2.50	1	:1	−2.50	2.50	−2.00	5.00	5.00
25	ES 500	2.50	1	:1	−2.50	2.50	−2.00	6.00	5.00
		9.75	1	:1	−2.50	2.59	−3.05	5.09	50.00
	W-L	16-9							
		64.0%							

FIGURE 7.1 Maximum Adverse Excursion Concepts

500 futures contract, simply known as the ES. Notice that for each trade, the trader recorded the profit or loss as well as risk-to-reward. Also note the maximum adverse excursion for each trade recorded in the last column. Based on the summary data noted at the bottom of the journal, the trader had a success ratio of 64 percent with a risk-to-reward ratio on average of 1:1. This is common among traders who seek to set their targets and stops at predetermined support and resistance levels. Overall, this appears to be a successful strategy with a supportive risk-to-reward ratio given the success rate.

If we dig a bit deeper, we notice the average MAE was −3.05 points while the average stop loss was 2.5 points. In fact, all losses were taken at 2.5 points, which appears to be an obvious standard stop loss used by this trader. What this information tells us is that although the trader is seeking to minimize losses, this specific setup requires, on average, a −3.05 point fluctuation point, or average MAE.

Now we look to the maximum favorable excursion, which supports the same principle but on the profit potential side. Notice in the last column, the maximum favorable exposure (MFE) average was +5.09 points while the standard target gain taken was 2.5 points. What is this information telling us? In summary, we are risking 2.5 points per trade; however, we can see that on average, price will fluctuate an additional 1/2 point below that stop. On the upside, profits are being taken at a stiff 2.5 points; however, on average, price tended to hit north of 5.00 points. Although risk was limited due to the stop at 2.5 points, the trade actually would have generated more profits on average if the stops were placed slightly higher than −3.0 points.

In summary, the trader was leaving some opportunity on the table by taking profits early and placing the stops too tightly. Notice also if we use the MAE and MFE as the stop and target, our risk-to-reward is slightly over 1.6:1 (5.09 MFE − 3.05 MAE). The total profit points were increased from +9.75 to nearly 50.00 points. This differential was from the profit risk that was initially left on the table due to the smaller target.

When we discuss risk management, traders tend to focus solely on the risk. While in principle this is prudent, it's important to seek the big picture. This holistic form of risk optimization allows you to determine on average what amount of risk to take on a trade or where to place a stop order, since historically you know on average the price fluctuation required for the trade to have the potential to be successful. *Risk management is not limiting losses. It is the art of maximizing profits for a given optimal risk.*

The MFE and the MAE are very good tools that allow the trader to find an area to consider for the initial stop and target. When these levels coincide with multiple layers of support and resistance, then you are trading with a confluence edge, which is the most powerful formula for success.

Using MFE and MAE can act as powerful parameters in your backtesting methodology, too. Run your simulated strategies and record the excursion bracket figures to determine the optimal amount of risk on a trade and its accompanied reward. Many of these tested summary figures can become the initial fixed stop and targets set in your trading plan rules. It also allows for stop-loss and target compliance where one could not extend risk or reward over a normal variance from the average excursion. This is how powerful the concept can be. The only caveat is that your capital preservation strategy cannot be compromised regardless of the integrity of MAE data. In other words, if your historical MAE is an average of 4 points and a maximum 1 percent account value loss per trade averages to 3 points, you cannot trade this setup. Capital preservation always dominates any trading business plan . . . always! The goal is to find setups with edge that support a stop-loss and target management program that can be accepted by the size of your capital account.

POSSIBLE LOSS VS. PROBABLE LOSS

Advice and experience come in many forms. The beauty about continuous lessons-learned opportunities in business is that most of them come from an experience that at one point turned sour. The value offering provided in this text is to limit those real-life business experiences with particular focus on the high-severity exposures. One of the more misunderstood and overabused concepts in trading is that of maximum possible loss vs. maximum probable loss.

The terms have roots in the insurance industry and other genres in the risk transfer business. Used to estimate physical loss due to a peril, possible maximum loss is the ultimate loss that the insurance company would ever be exposed to. Worst-case scenario quantification was the unchallenged norm for the insurance industry well into the 1960s. Thanks in part to more advanced and realistic analytical thinking and the computerized tools that came along with it, the business of insurance migrated toward what losses most likely would occur rather than assumptions of total loss.

In our business of trading, that transition of examining the more realistic exposure at times is still stuck in the Woodstock era. Even the more aggressive trading professional still thinks of a "what's the worst that can happen" theory that has been the litmus test for their decision-making process. In our insurance industry example, actuarial professionals usually consider the maximum exposure on an insured asset, such as a piece of real estate. Can the structure result in a total loss? Most structures can end up unusable, but will they more than likely be exposed to partial losses?

The benefit that actuaries have is a history of previous losses. They can review loss runs to determine the percentage of claims that were total losses and the common elements that were present when those total losses occurred. Do we not have that same type of information when we trade? Traders have an even greater ability to prevent possible loss via use of available controls. An insurance company insuring a property right on a California fault line may look at a worst-case scenario on a particular property, but how would they assess worst-case scenarios on their entire insured California real estate book of business? How about their Florida hurricane or flood exposures?

I hope you can see these similarities to managing risk in trading. In summary, we do not know when the "big one" will hit our capital account. What we do know is the tools and controls we have as traders to limit our exposure on each trade and with our capital account. As traders we have many control options available to us to protect our assets. A homeowner on a fault line can't move the house once an earthquake strikes. Traders can simply hit the off button during a Federal Reserve announcement (in which the market often reacts in tremor-like fashion) on their platform and eliminate any risks to capital.

You might ask, "If there are all of these controls available and I use them effectively, how come most traders suffer earthquake-type disasters to their trading accounts and never recover?" What is all too common is to focus on the biggest potential loss or maximum possible loss. While worst-case scenario planning and monitoring are crucial, it is the more realistic probable losses that are not managed with the same level of concern. The difference between a natural disaster such as an earthquake and in trading is that earthquakes generally occur without relative warning or at least the inability to control the event. Taking precautionary methods such as protecting windows and getting family members to safe ground can minimize loss. One thing people know (or at least the actuaries do) is the possibility of total loss occurring during such an event. As long as we are willing to build real estate on fault lines and in hurricane belts, there is always the possibility of a total loss. Insurers, like traders, can diversify their risk by insuring a maximum amount of properties in high-peril exposure areas. This was a great lesson learned from many insurance companies during the Hurricane Andrew disaster in 1992. Diversification of assets is one of the first forms of risk management learned by investors and traders. As we know, many 401(k)s went bust during the 2008 financial crisis regardless of investors' awareness of not putting too many eggs in one basket.

Traders need to place equal if not more focus and importance on probable loss vs. possible loss. The potential exists for traders to have their earthquake trade that wipes their capital clean, and this should not be ignored. Homeowners use risk transfer methods to protect themselves against such low-occurrence/high-frequency risks. Traders have the ability to manage these risks and can do so rather easily in today's world of electronic platform controls.

Mitigating Worst-Case Scenarios

What controls can we use to protect ourselves from worst-case scenarios? We discussed many of them earlier in the text in the risk control section. The use of stops, hedging, and confluence of support and resistance all play a positive role. Separation is a control whose the primary role is to prevent catastrophic loss. For example, if you have a $50,000 capital account and only keep $7,500 in your trading account at any given time to trade, you have in all practicality eliminated nearly all potential worst-case scenarios or total loss of capital on a trade. How many realistically put in practice this simple risk control technique? I hope you do. Nothing short of an entire wipeout of our financial and banking system, including account records, would prevent you from ever losing your entire capital account on a trade if you followed this one form of risk control. As you can now tell, the next black swan event is always on the mind of a risk manager.

Here is a simple yet effective technique to effectively manage both maximum possible loss vs. the probable loss. When managing your trading business, always be considerate of ultimate possible loss and use separation of funds, daily loss limits, graduation plan management, and business plan compliance to reduce the worst-case scenario loss from occurring. When managing a specific trade, focus on knowing the probable loss on each entry using stop-losses, average point loss for any given setup, trade avoidance on high-risk trades, and trade management compliance. When implemented effectively, even the struggling trader has the ability to develop during the challenging times that all traders go through.

KNOWING YOUR RISK APPETITE

No two traders are truly alike. Your past experiences, upbringing, and ability to handle adversity are all brought to the trading desk and often greatly affect the ultimate outcome. One of those traits is not only our ability to accept risk but thrive on our desire for risk taking. Sadly, some who seek this business as a vehicle to express their desire to take risk often fall into the

90 percent failure statistic. When managed properly, this business contains relatively low risk when compared to other business ventures that include a risk of capital component. Startup costs are reasonably low compared to those of any brick-and-mortar establishment. Ever see the costs in opening a restaurant? Wow, and those dollars are shelled out even before the first customer complaint! Nevertheless, a desire for or at least a minimum acceptance of risk is one of the core competencies for the profession.

How we measure that can be challenging and subjective and is best left to the various risk profiler professional advisors who analyze the psychometrics of hedge fund resumes just as job recruiters validate educational backgrounds.

Risk tolerance is the level of risk that one is willing to accept. "One" can be an individual trader, a prop or hedge fund, or even an institutional financial firm. Having a trading plan that is specifically designed to support each trader's willingness is critical. Any examples of trading plans used in this text are reflective of a trader with full acceptance of trading risk but who is not willing to blow an account so he or she can attempt to try trading. Having a professional coach or advisor can really assist in developing or even discovering one's risk tolerance levels. Although one can search online for risk tolerance tests, the one-on-one assessment to determine appetite for risk is most effective.

There is an abstractness that is often better discovered in meetings with traders rather than on paper. Similarly, I have often recommended psychological consultations with traders who have communicated their seriousness on becoming successful and are willing to invest these startup consultative dollars into their business. When those options aren't feasible, I have found that speaking with the trader's support groups and centers of influence not only brings to light the trader's individual risk tolerance levels but also that of their family's needs. Only then can a true trading plan be designed to incorporate such appetite. I encourage all to explore written risk questionnaires as a baseline-only approach to learning more about your true risk acceptance level.

As a risk manager, I am more concerned about the gap between a trader's psychological needs and financial trading goals. That gap represents risk; particularly the ability to minimize the emotional element that can have virus-like effects in trading. I followed a prominent professional trader who was very successful in trading his own accounts. This led others to demand he use a hedge fund structure to trade other investors' money. After an internal assessment of his trading documents, there was indication that profits were being taken too early and dollar risk being reduced, resulting in an actual increase in trade risk. The result was disastrous and the fund eventually closed. The manager clearly had an appetite for risk and was successful in managing and accepting that risk. Only when the dollar amounts changed and the fiduciary role became present did he notice his tolerance for risk diminishing.

Risk Tolerance Guidelines

When taking the initial steps into assessing your risk tolerance, consider the following guidelines:

- Take a series of online risk assessment or psychological profile questionnaires. If at minimum it opens your awareness to the importance of risk tolerance, then it will have been beneficial.

- Monitor your emotions when trades are not working or when stopped out. Were you nervous during the trade? Were you mad? The differentiating gap between your appetite for risk and your willingness to accept risk needs to be a core part of your development plan until both are equally evident in your trading.

- Let your graduation plan determine risk tolerance. How does it feel when you have reached your goal at a particular share or contract level and are ready to move up to the next higher level? Excited? Nervous? Scared? Any trader who has the results to move higher and decides to stay at the same level needs to build that tolerance up. For some it is one of the most difficult walls to break when en route to reaching one's trading goals.

- If you are trading other capital, what is the risk-taking nature of those investors? Your trading plan or the bylaws of the relationship should address the risk culture and expectations of the capital owners.

- What are the risk-taking abilities within the trading account or products that you trade? For example, foreign exchange and futures products are much more highly leveraged than stock and equity trading. A clear red flag goes up when I see ultraconservative traders with little risk appetite inquire about the opportunities in the spot oil futures markets.

- Consider the probable variance in expected gains and losses using your historical trade data. Generally speaking—with all other issues constant—the more reliable the results and the ability to produce them consistently, the greater allowance for risk appetite.

- The ability to hedge can greatly increase your ability to take on more core position exposures. While hedging may be initially seen as a technique used by conservative traders seeking to minimize risk, it actually may allow the trader to be more flexible with his or her outlook on appetite.

SUMMARY

Chapter 7 acts as a reality check for today's trader. Building your risk tolerance is a process that will evolve over your trading career. Follow the tolerance guidelines and the steps to overcome fear as outlined for you in this chapter. You are ultimately faced with the challenge of complying with a trading plan. Overcoming such obstacles will reduce your exposure to many of the business risks that thrive in the trading community.

 REVIEW QUESTIONS

1. The hunger for winning should be replaced with the hunger to _____.
2. Give an example of how a trader can overcome fear of capital loss.
3. List three examples each of what we can and cannot control in trading.
4. Explain the concepts of maximum adverse excursion and maximum favorable excursion.
5. Explain the concept of possible loss vs. probable loss and its relevance to trade risk.

Business Risk Management for Traders

I n the previous chapter, we discussed how insurance companies assess not only individual policy risk such as an individual home that is insured but also the portfolio of exposures in a particular product line, geographical area, or specific peril. Most of the discussion in this book so far has been devoted to trade risk, or the amount or chance of loss on any given trade. Various risk identification, assessment, control, measuring, and monitoring techniques were discussed so the trader can execute each trade with the historical hopes of yielding the most risk-to-reward value.

In Chapter 8 we take our trading magnifying glass and focus on the business of trading and related exposures. This could be the most important chapter you read in this book or any other book on trading survivability. The reason is that most traders do not fail in trading due to one trade. It is often a series or a large stretch of trades that were not successful, and the trader did not take risk-based actions after identifying that these events were unfolding. In other cases, it was not a trade but one unforeseen event that forced the trader to close his or her business. Traders often focus so much on each trade and lose perspective toward the goal at hand. We are constantly measuring ourselves in dollars when we should be keeping score through a KPI compliance dashboard. This chapter is geared toward identifying the quadrant-two risks that each trader or group should not only be aware of but should be continuously assessing, controlling, measuring, and monitoring through the rest of the five-step risk management process.

Closure prevention is a planning process, one that many traders neglect to do. However, when asked why a trader quit the business or lost all their trading capital, the answer is almost never, "I had a bad trade." I will walk you through the process of preparing for such events. Many of them require an investment in time and preparation. Do not bypass these processes so you can get to actual trading quicker. Most of the traders who were unprepared for such scenarios look back with regret.

THE FIVE STEPS OF CRISIS MANAGEMENT

Crisis Management   The act of preventing or reducing the impact of a catastrophic loss on an organization.

As traders, we need to view our activities of trading within a trading business. Crisis management is the act of preventing and/or reducing the impact of a catastrophic loss to an organization. This includes the planning, preparation, funding, measuring, and of course the button pushing. The loss, as noted in the definition, is threefold for a trader. One is the potential loss of capital or drawdown as a result of trading. Loss of income is also a common possibility as traders. While loss of the business itself is also a risk, it does not necessarily have to come from the first two events. Going forward, be sure not to look at business risk solely as loss of capital which is all too often a common barometer in the "How is your trading going?" response. A trader can temporarily or even permanently be put out of work for a loss of any asset, not just capital. Let us use the following real-life example of an event that resulted in the need for future preparation:

Event: During a severe and dangerous rainstorm, lightning hit a trader's house, blowing out the entire computer system.

Result: The trader had a minor shock to his arm and felt numbness in his upper extremity. He went to the hospital and was cleared with little injury. There were no open trades on at the time, thus no individual trade risk. While the computer monitor and ancillary equipment were functional, the hard drive and server used to trade were completely destroyed. Trade data and other business information was backed up every other Friday. Three business days of trade data were not saved. All software applications such as the trading platform and spreadsheet (for the trade journal) were lost. After

spending the day getting checked out at the emergency room, the
trader rested the remainder of the day. On day two he started the
damage assessment and equipment needs. The trader was back up
and running on the following Monday with a total of three trading
days lost.

A scary yet true scenario, the overall event could have had a more ter-
rible ending. In the end, only 2.5 trading days were lost and the trader was
up and running with a new system that following Monday. The weekend
was tirelessly spent reloading software and reviewing electronic brokerage
statements to repopulate the trade journal entries that were not backed up.
Not your typical trading risk, but this example was used to illustrate that
the unexpected will happen if you trade over a long period of time. Can you
name the exposures in this event?

Clearly the loss of income or at minimum the opportunity cost of those
days was lost. The cost of the equipment repair and replacement was quite
unexpected but reasonable. While one could argue about other issues such
as the hospital bill, from a business scope, these two items stand out as the
obvious exposures.

Let's look at the five crisis management steps and what could have
been done:

1. **Planning**—The trader could have considered such an event (lightning storm) or at least considered what would happen if his computer
   stopped functioning for a period of several days.
2. **Preparedness**—The trader kept all receipts and warranties for his
   equipment at his father's house. This allowed him easy access to the
   computer manufacturer's warranty information.
3. **Prevention**—Although the trader did have a surge protection jack in
   his wall, it obviously did not prevent the event from occurring. One
   could argue he should have had more frequent backup of his trade data
   as well as taking a small trading break until such a severe and unusual
   lightning storm had passed.
4. **Response**—His immediate response was for him (and his frantic wife)
   to go to the emergency room to address his shock.
5. **Recovery**—Other than a little pain overnight from the bolts of electric-
   ity in his arm, he was out and about the next day. Clearly his objective
   was to restore his operations and start trading again.

Hindsight is always 20/20, but what other issues could have been considered in the business plan? The restoration gap of 2.5 days was clearly
the greatest loss to the trader. The availability to trade is often the biggest

risk, that being of opportunity. Would the risks have increased if there were an open trade on at the time? What if the voltage had severely injured the trader? Did the fact that his wife was home potentially minimize the potential exposure? Was the cost of waiting for the new computer replacement cheaper than the trading income lost? Where was the backup laptop? The risk manager must make certain assumptions about these potential exposures. When preparing for these events, seek to focus on the result rather than the peril. In other words, do not focus as much attention on preparing to minimize risk during a lightning storm but rather on what to do if your computer system and data are lost. A proper risk management plan will include both and specifically encourage these angles to be addressed in a partnership, proprietary, hedge fund structure, or even for individual traders who are managing capital.

SCENARIO PLANNING AND TESTING

Each trading business has its unique set of continuity risks. Individual traders may have a small setup in their home while managed funds can have multiple offices and cloud computing data server structures. Regardless of the entity shape, size, and number of employees, testing your risk mitigation exposures using scenario planning techniques in some form or another should be completed.

Some perform scenario tests with consideration of what can happen. In the example discussed earlier, a lightning bolt struck a house. This form of scenario planning is effective; however, it can be quite cumbersome and omit some events that are currently considered unrealistic and outside the box. Of course, when they occur, they become inside the box, and the lessons-learned process can be quite a costly one. Rather than assess the event, consider the asset, tool, data, resources, or time value and its importance and impact to your business. You might think your computer or system platform is the most essential part of your business. If so, it probably should be up there at the top of the list of critical assets. Of course, if your data connection has failed, it does not matter how advanced your computer or platform is because there will not be any trading being conducted when the Internet or other cable connection is lost, barring a backup plan.

Brainstorm uncommon scenarios such as your physical ability to perform your trading. I never realized how important my index finger was until I injured it one day. In another example, one might name one's coach as a critical team member in one's success. It makes sense to recognize these assets and their importance to your business. One trader noted the most critical exposure is his spouse's job security, noting that if his spouse loses her job, he would have to delay his trading business indefinitely and go back to a "real job." These are real scenarios that require real assessment through the risk management process.

Sample Risk Identification Checklist

Consider using a risk identification checklist when performing your initial scenario test.

- Data feed speed and reliability
- Internet connection continuity
- Trade execution latency
- Partner's other business activities
- Ability to continuously generate capital funding
- Personal/family expenses
- Trading room or other vendor reliability
- Brokerage service levels
- Commission or other fee structures
- Peril-related exposures in trading office (i.e., flood, electrical power stability)
- Tax changes to specific trading products
- Family and other personal needs during trading hours
- Ability to incorporate knowledge/development plan into your week
- Disciplinary compliance and trade execution risks
- Regulatory, risk reporting, and accounting exposures
- Loss of key partner or trader in firm
- Slippage
- Fear of increasing share or contract size
- Data storage–related exposures
- Tax planning exposures

Each applicable risk identified in the checklist should proceed to the risk assessment step in the risk management process. What are the potential exposures to your trading? Revenue? Capital preservation? Asset or data risk as in the case of the computer crash? Business closure risk in the case of the unemployed wife? Be creative and explore many avenues with this exercise, but take it very seriously. This preparation can prevent you from severe business loss when such a scenario occurs. Murphy's law historically looms over many trading desks.

RESTORATION REQUIREMENTS

During your scenario testing review, I hope your transition of thinking about the business of trading rather than actually trading is working effectively. In the end, our business is about entering and exiting trades with the goal of taking advantage of edge in the markets. To perform this function effectively and consistently, traders have to assess their business goals and ask themselves what is an acceptable period of time that trading operations can be temporarily halted within the confines of the business plan. In essence, how quickly do you need to be back in operation? More precisely, what aspects of your business do you need to have back in operation and in which order of priority?

One might think that the ability to trade is the most important element of trading. No argument from most traders. For managed firms, there may be other resources or technologies that are critical during the monthly reporting cycle. Hedge funds may be required to meet regulatory requirements or face severe penalties. While the revenue engine is always a top priority, do not discount other critical operational needs and how quickly they need to be restored.

The restoration time frame may also be affected by other seasonal factors. Some traders have business continuity plans that normally require 15-minute restoration time frames for their trading platform while during the holiday weeks of December, they can have a two-week outage and not be too concerned. A loss of a critical resource, such as a coach, can be devastating to a small operation; however, the company that referred the coach can have one replaced within three business days should that person decide to exit the coaching business. The same is true for auditors, accountants, financial professionals such as bankers, and the like. Those who rely on trading rooms have extreme exposure to business risk should the vendor close the shop or decide to make an administrative change that affects your ability to trade. I've seen traders wiped out from an essential reliance on a particular trading room moderator who one day decided to call it quits. Some resources are so valuable to one's trading operation that "key person" insurance is purchased on their life should they die unexpectedly.

BUSINESS IMPACT ANALYSIS

So how does one go about assessing one's restoration time objective (RTO) needs? Trading firms, funds, and props generally obtain the use of a professional risk manager or consulting firm specializing in business continuity risk management. Individual traders or small groups can attempt to determine their personal RTO requirements. Let us walk through the process together. The first step in determining your RTO is to assess your current needs and dependencies.

Functions—List the current functions of your trading business. Your continuous ability to trade is a good start. Trade journal data entry and KPI analysis are a critical part of the risk-based approach if you decide to pursue such a method. Other functions may include coaching, accounting/tax management, monthly reporting, and so on. Trading partnerships or other entities can also include Web hosting, marketing, disclosure, legal, regulatory functions, staffing, compensation and benefits, and benchmarking, to name just a few.

Assets—List all of your assets required in order to perform your role as a trader in your trading business. Technical hardware such as your computer is an obvious priority for many. Others may include your workspace, trade journal software, licenses, and so on.

Resources—Including but not limited to market data feed, broker, coach, other human resources, capital sources, educational vendors, and trading "network" of individuals.

As you create your list of needs and dependencies, start to ask yourself how long you can go without them and have a level of impact to your business that is unacceptable to you or your firm. For example, a hospital may be required to have critical resources such as oxygen and lighting up and running within 30 seconds. If their legal staff were unable to come in the day of a disaster, the hospital would probably survive. Many corporate operations can go one or two days without major long-term disruption. Companies often instill "pizza Saturday" events that allow a company to catch up on operational needs so as to reach business as usual status the following Monday. During the entire two-day stoppage, their business continuity plans were never implemented with the exception of update status calls to customers and critical vendors.

Take your list of functions, assets, and resources and estimate a reasonable restoration time for each. Consider that a temporary backup solution would at least get you back to trading and generating revenue. In the case of the poor trader struck by lightning, actual trading restoration could have been resumed as quickly as booting up a preloaded laptop with a copy of the trading platform. Be honest in regard to your or your company's acceptable needs. Risk tolerance, culture, and personal needs should be considered as well as any personal priorities that may come up during restoration. For example, it would not have mattered what the lightning trader had as his RTO since he was going to the hospital immediately after the incident. Figure 8.1 provides a sample restoration time objective timeline

Restoration Time Frame Activities

1–2 HOURS	TRADING DAY	DAYS 2–4	WEEK-MONTH
■ Wait for exposure to end. ■ Have backup plan in place for readiness in 30 min. ■ Work on operational duties (i.e., trade journal, development plan).	■ Budget days in trading year to expect such outages. ■ Review trading plan and related compliance. ■ Network with other traders.	■ Project financial impact of loss. ■ Communicate strategy to stakeholders. ■ Lessons learned to improve future restorations. ■ KPI YTD statistics and impact.	■ Legal implications or recovery matters. ■ Business continuity assessment. ■ Set up temporary alternative shop ■ Vendor implications.

FIGURE 8.1   Restoration Time Objective (RTO) Chart for Three-Person Proprietary Firm

chart and the business resumption options that could be used in a similar operation. How would you change it to reflect your financial and operational trading needs?

An important element in the restoration process is the financial component. The general rule is that the quicker your demands for restoration, the more costly it would be to get back to a full or partial operation. Your firm may require no longer than a one-day RTO, thus requiring a same-day server replacement with IT support and reprogramming throughout the overnight hours. Backup data centers customarily have a pecking order when it comes to restoration of backup data. Getting high on that priority list usually requires a premium fee structure for the user. Again, individual traders may have a one-day restoration period to start trading again. Of course, one assumes that the broker has at least the same RTO, right? If your broker has a two-day restoration objective and you want to be back up within one day, could that create an RTO gap? Is it prudent to have a backup broker to diversify your RTO risk as well as the separation of funds risk reduction? Do you know what your data feed vendor's RTO is?

Business continuity is an important facet in the risk management process. It devotes its efforts to generally unpredictable low-frequency/high-severity exposures. The information you obtain will not only help reduce business risk but will also bring to the surface operational concerns and improvement opportunities that you may never have otherwise considered.

VENDOR RISKS

Many of you ready to venture out into the world of trading want to be a part of the excitement and glamour that the trading world allegedly provides.

For those who make a career out of trading, most see it as a profession with valuable benefits like flexibility, being your own boss, and making money in one of the most fascinating of industries. If you haven't already found out, those who wish to venture out in a solo attempt at trading quickly notice that it is difficult to do it alone. You eventually will require the tools, technology, and the professional assistance needed to get your business running. One thing that is certain is if there is a product that can possibly make your job easier and allow you to improve your game, there probably is a vendor who is willing to offer their services to you. The trading world is no different from any other business where vendors are happy to assist in your journey to success. Like any vendors, there are good and bad ones. No exception here for the trader to exercise his or her caveat emptor principles.

The debate as to what should you outsource often results in conjecture. What necessary services are needed often has few options in trading. One will not be able to execute any trade unless one has access to price data provided by an exchange. If you wish to trade a futures contract, for example, you will be required to sign up for a data feed from the Chicago Mercantile Exchange, or CME Group in Chicago. Other exchanges in New York such as the NYSE data or NASDAQ feeds are also a staple in many traders' fees. London and other financial centers around the world can accommodate a variety of other products for trading. Trading platforms are another must-have if you are trading independently. Speed, execution, platform features, and customer service are only a few of the considerations to determine which is best suited for your specific purpose. Other services you may consider are tax accounting assistance and software, trade journal software, trading room, auditing, risk management, Internet connection services, and coaching services.

Choosing a Vendor

What factors should be considered when deciding on the must-haves such as data feed, Internet, and the other outsource-based services? We often look at price, features, and service but often don't consider the risk of non-delivery of services. How many times did an Internet or server stop, which forced you to stop trading or shift to backup plans? It is ironic how often they happen just prior to the trade setup of the decade, too. Exchange data feeds are fairly reliable from the big houses, but even then there are occasions when disruptions in service will occur. The "flash crash" day in May 2010 resulted in limited ability to feed live data prices accurately, and the best of direct platforms showed prices "jumping" rather than the smooth delivery that we expect in real time. Identifying vendor or supplier risks should be considered prior to going live and you should continuously address these risks on a regular schedule.

TABLE 8.1 Vendor Risk Identification Chart

Trade Accessibility Risk	Quality Trade Risk	Business Risk
Trading platform	Trading room	Tax professional
Connectivity	Trading coach	Broker
Exchange feeds	Personal execution skills	Custodial funds
Computer hardware	Valid trade confirmation	Personal demands

A concern is that most traders only consider the risks that are controllable to a degree. The risk identification role is to identify any exposures that may impact your ability to conduct your business and reach your trading goals. One should address the determination of control during step three of the risk management process, appropriately named risk control. If a trading platform vendor is known for their continuous platform shutdowns during trading hours, one can move to a more reliable vendor. Other exposures such as data feed supplier risk may be more challenging since they often come from one source, the exchanges themselves. Part of your role as a risk-based trader is to identify these potential exposures in your business and assess the impact it may have on your ability to reach your trading goals. Table 8.1 shows a vendor risk identification table to help you get started. Also included is the potential impact each may have on your trading and a logical control methodology should you decide the assessment phase dictates the need for some controls. Many have a common theme: If you cannot trade, you lose your ability to generate revenue.

Other exposures are often not discovered until they actually happen. A solid risk-based business is designed to identify potential risks prior to their happening, but nonetheless traders and society as a whole tend to ultimately find out the stove is too hot by touching it. Make your risk identification process a part of your due diligence prior to starting your trading business. Do not expect to eliminate all exposures that may lead to a disruption in your trading. The objective of risk management is to proactively anticipate what could go wrong and take the necessary and reasonable precautions to either reduce the capability of that event happening or have a backup plan in place when it does occur.

PARTNERSHIP RISKS

Teaming up with another person or persons in your venture can be one of the most effective ways to manage your operation. The responsibility of an individual trader goes well beyond the skill of trading, and often one can benefit by having a partner with different skill sets to leverage the talent. A popular partnership combination used in trading is where one performs the trading and the other supplies the capital. Any marriage between investor and producer has its own inherent risks. Expectations of the money arm can often be exuberant and based on perfectly consistent markets that spoon-feed edge throughout the day. Traders often trade with greater scarcity when trading funds other than their own, thus creating the initial disconnect within these partnerships.

How do we go about determining if we should go the partnership route as a trader? The same way we determine any other risk in trading. We walk it through the risk management process. Table 8.2 is a sample of what one might consider before entering into a trading partnership.

The realities are that many partnerships end unsuccessfully. Other partnerships have a great business and personal relationship that supports the needs of the partners and works in harmony. The risk manager is required not only to use the proper contractual documentation but also to be in compliance with all state and tax regulatory rules. A thorough due diligence prior to starting a partnership is a must with high consideration of outsourcing to a legal professional to be sure it is structured to address all your identified risks that require some form of controls.

SUPPORT RISKS

There was much debate in the planning of this text as to whether support risk or the inability to maintain a supportive stakeholder network would fit in such a formalized textbook approach to trading risk management. During my research for the book, I watched one of my favorite documentaries related to trading. *Floored*, by James Allen Smith, walks you through the challenges of floor trading at the Chicago Mercantile Exchange in an electronic trading world. The film profiles floor traders and the inability of some to overcome their transition to platform-based electronic trading. One trader lost nearly everything including his personal life and family, with the exception of his son, who ironically got a job on the same floor where his dad once made the money to support him. After watching this brilliant compilation of trader stories, it was very evident that support risk must be included within the scope of identified risk, regardless of its disassociation with the other logical classifications of risk.

My experience with traders over two decades shows without any doubt that loss of a support network during challenging times as a trader is one of the most frequent causes of traders giving up the business. The topic surfaces in nearly every risk profile assessment ever conducted on my behalf. Like all other potential exposures, let us place it through the risk management process.

TABLE 8.2 Risk Management Process for a Trading Partnership

Identification	Assessment	Control	KPI Measure	Monitoring
Past individual performance may not replicate in partnership format.	YTD differential is 52% partnership vs. 61% individual trading edge.	Reduce expectation language or utilize fixed share size graduation plan.	Trade performance.	Monthly KPI.
Expectations are high to perform.	Verbal and contractual notes asking for returns on high end of current results.	Include "if" or "subject to" clauses in agreement.	Contractual due diligence rating.	Monthly KPI.
Partner talks about average return per day but markets do not provide average returns per day.	Verbally references such in daily discussions. Was not happy on first day when results were below annual average.	Restructure partner involvement in daily trade activity. Also change result reporting to monthly.	Average return per day.	Monthly KPI.
Contractual risks.	High-water mark language in agreement.	Modify pay structure to fixed at a lower rate with "out" clause.	Contractual due diligence rating.	Semiannual partnership review.
Regulatory and licensing risks.	Agreement language drafted using state laws of partner's residence.	Perform comparison due diligence to assure your protection.	Contractual due diligence rating.	Semiannual partnership review.
Compensation structure and ability to get paid.	Do not have any history of partner paying another trader to perform.	Incorporate performance fees for payment delays or incentives for earlier payment of services.	Invoice/ payment compliance.	Quarterly compliance review.
Other options come along when investor leaves.	Prior partnership had such event.	Include a trial partnership with 6-month assessment to continue.	Contractual due diligence rating.	Semiannual partnership review.
Partnership fees.	Clause that says each partner equally will absorb fee increases. These increases are unknown.	Agree to have required vendor assessment upon fee increase notifications.	Contractual due diligence rating.	Semiannual partnership review.
Death of partner.	Entire trading capital account is funded by partner.	Set up buy-sell or key-man policy or alternative funding.	Contractual due diligence rating.	Annual policy updates.

Support risk is critical for the beginning traders seeking a new career or the lure of easy profits. Convincing a spouse that you want to quit the day job and become a trading junkie may not be that hard. Convincing the same spouse that you are building a successful business isn't so easy, especially when the dreaded question gets asked over and over again, "How did everything go today?" The question is innocently asked and is answered almost routinely without any thought. For traders, it could mean almost anything. Did I trade today? Did I follow my plan? How did the market do? Probably the ultimate question, whether directly or subliminally inferred, is, "Did you make any money today, honey, and how much?"

Having a trader support network is almost as necessary as a data feed. An effective support team needs to understand the randomness of the markets and that averages are just that . . . averages. Results are based on opportunities that are never consistently provided by the markets. Those opportunities are sometimes missed by the trader, thus resulting in even more variability in results, especially if those results were simulated. There's nothing like raking in profits to convince your spouse or other support person that the decision to trade was the right one. Of course, if that happened, there would never be an identified risk that requires us to walk it through the risk management process. Let us attempt to do so at this time. Any form of support can be used in the process such as a coach, peer trader, or friend. Table 8.3 walks you through the risk management process using a spouse as the example.

PERSONAL RISKS

There are many facets to the business of trading, and technology allows a choice of several options on how to participate in the markets. Work as an independent trader from home, work for a proprietary firm or hedge fund, or join forces with a partner or partners. You have available the latest in resources to help you and the information delivered to you faster than light. You have proven setups that detect edge and the ability to assess data to determine its predictability in a trading model and the ability to execute your plan in a controlled risk environment. There is only one other element to consider: yourself

The human element is a required but dangerous component in the success model of a trader. All the psychological challenges come into play when trading live. We are prone to making mistakes or allowing fear and other emotions to act as immobilizers separating us from our financial and personal goals. Working for a firm allows certain risks to be contained within an employee relationship framework. Big city commuting hassles, corporate limitations, and teamwork struggles can test your personal

TABLE 8.3 Risk Management Process for Determining Support Risk

Identification	Assessment	Control	KPI Measure	Monitoring
I do not have a trading support team.	There are no persons who are on the distribution list of my monthly reports.	Trading business plan to include policy statement to recognize the importance of a support team and to have the team in place within three months.	Support team in place: three persons (coach, spouse, and professional trader).	Setting objective of attending next trading exposition to introduce myself to other traders and speakers.
My spouse is supportive but eventually wants to see consistent results.	Noticed greater frequency in spouse asking about results rather than generic trading questions.	Include spouse on monthly summary report list as well as discussion at dinner on Friday about the week's trading and results.	Communication/ compliance metric: Timely distribution of monthly summary reports to all support team members and stakeholders.	Continuously observe the commitment from spouse and keep open communications regarding development plan items.
Spousal support is waning.	Discussion about why results aren't meeting goals that were set and when that will start happening.	Development plan to include specific trade signal development.	Monthly development plan completion KPI.	Listen to spouse about his or her concerns and your plans in place for development.

ability for success. Individual traders need to overcome their own demons that can prohibit any chance of victory. There are obvious exposures such as the inability to trade your plan through a series of losses or other types of pressures. Inability to detect edge, manage your business, or maintain focus all are risks that need to be identified and assessed. As you consider your personal exposures that may be or already are in play, run them through the risk management process. Those identified as critical competencies or limitations need to be addressed.

Determining Your Personal Immobilizers

Here are some personal identified risks that more often than not have had devastating results for some traders, resulting in a quick exit from the business. Which ones can you relate to?

- I do not have sufficient capital to trade.
- I need to make a minimum number of dollars per week.
- I cannot hold a trade until target.
- I do not have the discipline after losing trades.
- I often chase trades.
- I review my plan every morning but still cannot execute it properly.
- I do not keep a trade journal.
- I'm out of shape and often get tired during the day.
- I'm a good trader but do have distractions in my life.
- I am reluctant to change my methods because I know they work.
- I sometimes have family obligations such as picking up the kids from school.

Think of other personal aspects in your life that influence your work. They may have nothing to do with trading. One of the most popular preparation items on poker players' checklists before the month-long World Series of Poker is related to fitness and nutrition. Many will admit they actually cut down on their playing the month prior and focus on mental preparation. Remember that these exercises are not just conducted in the beginning of a trader's career. The professionals are constantly identifying new risks that will affect their ability to reach their performance goals. As your personal life and the people in it change, so does your portfolio of potential immobilizers. The risk management process is a series of steps where all potential risks are within the five different steps at different times. As old concerns are controlled or accepted, new exposures are identified. The beauty of the risk management process is that it is continuously at work.

The outcome of many personal risks that require an element of control or management should fall into the developmental category. These are the areas of your business or personal situations that require attention in order to minimize their negative impact on your trading. Your development plan is designed to attack all areas of your business that requires improvement. They can be categorically listed in terms of education, personal fitness, psychological, trading technique, business structure, and many others. No aspect of trading, for anyone, is perfect, and having a repository within the structure to create action plans for these deficiencies will allow you to progress as a trader. For many, it is often the missing link in their success formula.

CREATING A DEVELOPMENT PLAN

Your development plan consists of all the skills that you need to learn or improve in to enable you to reach your trading goals. As your knowledge and skill base improves, so should your results. At least, that is what the objective of the plan is. Many can argue that your development plan is equally as important as your trading plan, since a trading plan is meaningless if it cannot be implemented effectively. Both plans go hand-in-hand with the development plan activities aligned with a trading plan objective. Successful development simply reduces risk in the ability to implement your plan.

How do we find the areas worthy of the need for further personal development? There are several. The most common source of potential development is derived from your trade journal. In addition to allowing you to make better trading decisions, your valuable time spent assessing trade data also shines a light on areas that need improvement. Consider an example where you had an easy time detecting a particular setup when backtesting but find it hard to do during the live session. One might consider an action plan to investigate the nature of the setup and the possible charting alert tools that can help warn you that a setup is looming. A Fibonacci entry at the 0.618 retracement level might warrant an audio alert set at the 0.50 level. Perhaps you need additional training with your trade journal software or the advanced features that it offers. Placing these items in your plan on a regular basis allows you to take accountability in your development. It forces action or noncompliance. Other developmental opportunities are born not from a trading error but merely a plan for continuous improvement in your craft. Attending trading conferences, building a center of trading influence, or even brainstorming ideas with other traders online can be part of your overall developmental activities.

If you are struggling to come up with opportunities for development, you probably should be looking harder. If it is a challenge to find fault in your work, have your coach or other independent second party do it for you. Hire a risk manager, trading coach, or even a fellow trader to perform an assessment to determine areas of improvement. A spouse or family member can also add value in finding areas for development. They may not understand how to perform a trade journal audit, but they probably know if you need to work on maintaining a level of focus or another behavioral skill.

Performing a Self-Assessment

If you do not have any independent resources available, you can perform your own self-assessment called a SWOT analysis. This assessment documents what you believe to be your strengths, weaknesses, opportunities, and threats to your business.

Your strengths do not have to be limited to your trading skills. Your passion to learn and your ability to maintain focus are valuable skills that are found in professional-level traders. Weaknesses should also have that dual-dimensional characteristic. When conducted by an outside party, this information can be extremely valuable. Those truly honest with themselves can also create information from areas of weakness. Opportunities should include areas where you may wish to expand your knowledge, thus allowing you to develop. For example, you may be an excellent stock trader but do not realize your setup evaluation can be equally as profitable using forex or futures contracts. An opportunity for development may call for expanding your knowledge in these different product lines and understanding the nuances and risks of each. Many futures, options, and forex traders have started out making stock trades only to realize profits awaited them with less risk in other markets. Threats are behaviors or situations that are required to be overcome in order to be successful. These are the immobilizers we have discussed throughout the book. Perhaps it's a lack of discipline or the inability or lack of desire to follow a trading plan. Support risk is a potential source of threat that may require immediate attention. Most traders love the independence of trading and not having a boss to work under. While this is an attractive part of the job, can you work in an unsupervised environment? Many traders cannot, and this threat resulted in their ultimate demise as a trader.

Table 8.4 gives an example of a SWOT analysis, the development plan tasks produced from each, and the results of working on each task.

SUMMARY

As you identify your personal and professional risks, allow yourself to step back and assess the risk management program you have put into place. Perhaps there are a few developmental opportunities in the program itself.

TABLE 8.4 SWOT Analysis

Strengths	Task	Result
Execution/decision-making skills.	Continue to maintain these sharp and critical skills.	Slippage costs are insignificant in my trading results.
Desire to learn more about the business.	Attend two of the next four expos and attend breakout session topics outside of my comfort zone.	Learned more about gold and bonds and will start testing my strategies with these products in simulation.
Weaknesses	**Task**	**Result**
Not very skilled at data analysis techniques.	Adding this to my development plan.	Taking online course in data analytics and how to create effective KPIs.
Little work/life balance since becoming a trader.	Make agreement with spouse that I will shut computer down 30 min. after market close.	Still struggling in this regard. Need to continuously remind self about priorities in my life.
Opportunities	**Task**	**Result**
Learn other trading products such as commodities or options.	To read two books on these two products.	Do not believe commodities are for me but plan on incorporating SPY options when futures liquidity is low.
Take next step from individual trader toward working for or starting a proprietary firm.	Learn more about my options and set up interview with two proprietary firms. Also need to prepare package that includes my summary results and risk management approach.	Found that proprietary firm is a viable option given their capital support. Starting a firm would impede on my work/life balance at this time.
Threats	**Task**	**Result**
Recent layoffs at spouse's company.	Assist wife in supporting her in her career efforts and help her with discovering new options.	Will need to continue to do my part in being focused and optimizing my trading results.
Trading room where I get my trade signals is closing down.	Need to develop as an independent trader.	Recognized that I need to take serious developmental steps if I want to be a professional trader.

The system is not designed to be an exact science. How could it be, since we are working in a business that is supported and fueled by random activity and decisions by different participants? In any business activity, the risk management process is designed to focus on the potential exposures that prevent you from being successful. In its design, the assessment phase is designed to kick exposures out that haven't met a level of concern worthy of any additional investment. Those risks that have reached the control stage force action to prevent or at least minimize exposure. Measuring the impact of the controls and monitoring of the entire program round out the risk-based process until new risks are identified and the process starts all over again.

Understanding the dynamics of risk including the acceptance of it allows one to make the decisions using parameters that have little to do with money. It's strange, unimaginable, or at times ridiculous to think that we can apply such nonmonetary theories to a game that is all about money, profits, and wealth accumulation. The surface disconnect is why so many traders trade within a psychological state of scarcity and do not consider how being a risk manager allows for greater success than a typical trader's mind-set. It's all about edge discovered from historical patterns that provides an opportunity. It is up to you, the trader, to take advantage of these opportunities by doing one of the simplest tasks on earth: pushing a button when it tells you to. We know, of course, that mastering this profession is not easy at all, but if you identify the immobilizer, control it, remove it, avoid it, or minimize its impact, you are on your edge manipulation journey to realizing the vision written out in your trading plan. Allow your risk-based plan to overcome these obstacles and let your achievements give you all the prosperity that you have worked so hard to obtain.

 REVIEW QUESTIONS

1. Define and list the five steps in crisis management.
2. Give three examples of a risk identification checklist for a trader's operation.
3. How may restoration requirements differ from large hedge funds vs. the individual trader?
4. Give an example of how a trader can control a partnership risk.
5. Explain the benefits of a trader having a development plan.

Bibliography

Adams, Gary W. and Campbell, Mary. "Where Are You on Your Journey to ERM?" *Risk Management Magazine* (September 2005), 16–20.

Bahadur, Nigel. "The Manual Work in Mechanical Trading." *SFO Magazine* (July 2007), 73–76.

Beals, Rachel Koning. "Home Base? Is Yours a Good Fit for Trading?" *SFO Magazine* (October 2006), 55–58.

Bollinger, John. *Bollinger on Bollinger Bands*. New York: McGraw-Hill, 2002.

Broadie, Mark. "The Inspired Side of Modeling." *Capital Markets Guide 2011*, Sybase, 2011.

Bulkowski, Thomas N. "Developing a Trading Style." *SFO Magazine* (October 2006), 68–72.

Busby, Tom. "Tricks for Overnight Success." *Futures Magazine* (March 2008), 44–46.

Busby, Tom. "Risk Management Is the Key to Day-Trading." *Futures Magazine* (December 2007), 38–40.

Carr, Mike and Blackman, Matt. "Day Trading: Much to Do to Get Nothing?" *SFO Magazine* (October 2007), 48–52.

Carter, John F. "How My Worst Trade Turned Me into a Better Trader." *SFO Magazine* (October 2006), 28–34.

Champagne, David. "Analytics R Us." *Capital Markets Guide 2011*, Sybase, 2011.

Changler, Neil. "Key Performance Indicators for Corporate Performance Management." Gartner RAS Core Research (December 2009).

Covel, Michael. *The Complete Turtle Trader: How 23 Novice Investors Became Overnight Millionaires*. New York: HarperCollins, 2007.

DiPietro, Josh. "Learn from My Mistakes: 5 Day-Trading Truths to Work By." *SFO Magazine* (June 2009), 38–43.

Douglas, Mark. *Trading in the Zone*. New York: New York Institute of Finance, 2000.

Douglas, Mark: *The Disciplined Trader: Developing Winning Attitudes*. New York: New York Institute of Finance, 1990.

"Driving Business Performance with Enterprise Risk Management." OpenPages.com white paper (June 2009).

Dubner, Steven J. *Freakonomics*. New York: Harper Perennial, 2009.

Eckerson, Wayne. "Performance Management Strategies: How to Create and Deploy Effective Metrics." The Data Warehouse Institute, 2009.

Farnstrom, Amy. "Build Your Trading Brain. A Framework to Manage Thoughts, Emotions and Actions." *SFO Magazine* (July 2007), 19–24.

Galant, Mark and Dolan, Brian. "10 Habits of Successful Currency Traders." *SFO Magazine* (October 2007), 76–77.

Gordon, Jon. *The Energy Bus*. Hoboken, NJ: John Wiley and Sons, 2007.

Grant, Kenneth. *Trading Risk: Enhanced Profitability through Risk Control*. Hoboken, NJ: John Wiley and Sons, 2004.

Hansen, Toni. "The Market Never Sleeps." *SFO Magazine* (September 2008), 79–84.

Head, George L. and Horn, Steven II. *Essentials of Risk Management*, 3rd Edition, Volume 1. Malvern, PA: Insurance Institute of America, 1997.

Head, George L. and Horn, Steven II. *Essentials of Risk Management*, 3rd Edition, Volume 2. Malvern, PA: Insurance Institute of America, 1997.

Holm, Nicholas. "Harness the Power of In-Database Analytics." *Capital Markets Guide 2011*, Sybase, 2011.

Hope, Jeremy. "How KPIs Can Help Motivate and Reward the Right Behavior." White paper (March 2010).

IBM Corporation Software Group. "Unleashing GRC Intelligence." White paper (February 2011).

Jobman, Darrel. "So You Wanna Be a Trader?" *SFO Magazine* (September 2006), 27–30.

Jobman, Darrel. "Day Trading: Does It Fit You?" *SFO Magazine* (October 2007), 37–41.

Kaplan, Peter. "Finding the Value in Losses." *SFO Magazine* (September 2006), 33–36.

Kaplan, Peter. "Know the Enemy." *SFO Magazine* (January 2007), 63–65.

Lenth, Russel. "Some Practical Guidelines for Effective Sample-Size Determination." Department of Statistics, University of Iowa (March 2001).

Ma, Jeffrey. *The House Advantage, Playing the Odds to Win Big in Business*. New York: Palgrave Macmillan, 2010.

Mezrich, Ben. *Bringing Down the House*. New York: Free Press, 2003.

Pearson, Neil. *Risk Budgeting: Portfolio Problem Solving with Value-at-Risk*. Hoboken, NJ: John Wiley & Sons, 2002.

Pesavento, Larry and Shapiro, Steven. *Fibonacci Ratios with Pattern Recognition*. Greensville, SC: Traders Press, 1997.

Rosenbloom, Corey. *The Complete Trading Course*. Hoboken, NJ: John Wiley & Sons, 2011.

Shaw, Jack. "Managing All of Your Enterprise's Risks." *Risk Management Magazine* (September 2005), 23–28.

Shull, Denise. *Market Mind Games*. New York: McGraw-Hill, 2012.

Silverman, David. "Behavior Economics." *SFO Magazine* (July 2007), 50–55.

Singh, Raj. "Solvency II: Changing the Risk Management Landscape." *Risk Professional* (August 2010), 43–45.

Steenbarger, Brett. *The Psychology of Trading: Tools and Techniques for Minding the Markets*. Hoboken, NJ: John Wiley & Sons, 2003.

Steenbarger, Brett. *The Daily Trading Coach: 101 Lessons for Becoming Your Own Trading Psychologist*. Hoboken, NJ: John Wiley & Sons, 2007.

Vince, Ralph. *The Handbook of Mathematics: Formulas for Optimal Allocation and Leverage*. Hoboken, NJ: John Wiley & Sons, 2007.

Vozian, Ecaterina. "Value-at-Risk: Evolution, Deficiencies and Alternatives." *Risk Professional* (August 2010), 46–50.

Zwick, Steve. "Trader Profile." *Futures Magazine* (May 2009), 58.

Index

Printed and bound by CPI Group (UK) Ltd, Croydon, CR0 4YY

16/04/2025

14658501-0002